AF251136

The Province of
Jurisprudence Democratized

ALLAN C.
HUTCHINSON

The Province of Jurisprudence Democratized

OXFORD

UNIVERSITY PRESS

OXFORD
UNIVERSITY PRESS

*Oxford University Press, Inc., publishes works that further Oxford University's objective of excellence
in research, scholarship, and education.*

Oxford   New York
Auckland   Cape Town   Dar es Salaam   Hong Kong   Karachi   Kuala Lumpur   Madrid   Melbourne
Mexico City   Nairobi   New Delhi   Shanghai   Taipei   Toronto

With offices in
Argentina   Austria   Brazil   Chile   Czech Republic   France   Greece   Guatemala   Hungary   Italy
Japan   Poland   Portugal   Singapore   South Korea   Switzerland   Thailand   Turkey   Ukraine
Vietnam

Copyright © 2009 by Oxford University Press, Inc.

Published by Oxford University Press, Inc.
198 Madison Avenue, New York, New York 10016

Oxford is a registered trademark of Oxford University Press
Oxford University Press is a registered trademark of Oxford University Press, Inc.

All rights reserved. No part of this publication may be reproduced, stored in a retrieval system, or transmitted, in any
form or by any means, electronic, mechanical, photocopying, recording, or otherwise, without the prior permission of
Oxford University Press, Inc.

____

Library of Congress Cataloging-in-Publication Data

Hutchinson, Allan C., 1951-
  The province of jurisprudence democratized / Allan C. Hutchinson.
    p. cm.
  Includes bibliographical references and index.
  ISBN 978-0-19-534325-0 ((hardback) : alk. paper)
  1. Jurisprudence. I. Title.
  K230.H88A37 2008
  340--dc22

                                                2008030659

____

1 2 3 4 5 6 7 8 9

Printed in the United States of America on acid-free paper

Note to Readers
This publication is designed to provide accurate and authoritative information in regard to the subject matter covered.
It is based upon sources believed to be accurate and reliable and is intended to be current as of the time it was written.
It is sold with the understanding that the publisher is not engaged in rendering legal, accounting, or other professional
services. If legal advice or other expert assistance is required, the services of a competent professional person should be
sought. Also, to confirm that the information has not been affected or changed by recent developments, traditional
legal research techniques should be used, including checking primary sources where appropriate.

*(Based on the Declaration of Principles jointly adopted by a Committee of the
American Bar Association and a Committee of Publishers and Associations.)*

*This Book is Dedicated to
Richard Rorty (1931–2007)*

CONTENTS

PREFACE

As usual, many people have played important parts in helping me to complete this book. I have benefited from a host of critics and colleagues, mostly friendly, who have shared their time and insights—John Bartholomew, Paul Brady, Mary Condon, Marissa Curran, Greg Epstein, Noah Feldman, David Fraser, Leslie Green, Ran Hirschl, P. J. Javdan, Nicola Lacey, Frank Michelman, Derek Morgan, Richard Mullender, Matt Murray, Jessica Patton, Andrew Petter, Ron Podolny, Richard Posner, Joe Singer, Brian Tamanaha and Rachael Walsh. In particular, I am especially grateful to Paul Hughes, who pushed me hard on my pragmatic commitments, and Joel Colon-Rios, whose intellectual generosity and friendly support proved invaluable. I wrote this book while on sabbatical and am grateful to the law schools at Sydney, Harvard, British Columbia, Victoria, Osgoode, Monash, Newcastle, and London for opportunities to present my developing ideas. Also, I was the grateful beneficiary of generous research funding from Osgoode Hall Law School and Harvard Law School.

In writing this book, I took a trip down memory lane to when I first caught the jurisprudence bug: I was skeptical then of analytical jurisprudence's merit, but it has taken me too many decades to work out exactly why. Grey Denham deserves some credit for getting me started and old friends, Gerald Carter and Dave Bowen, insisted from the beginning that I at least spell *Austin* and *sovereignty* correctly. Duncan Kennedy remains a strong influence. Finally, Hans Mohr died as I completed this manuscript; I hope that he would have been pleased with my efforts, as I am one of the many beneficiaries of his warmth and wisdom. Thanks again to my family for their forbearance, love, and support.

Allan C. Hutchinson

July 2008

*Man's capacity for justice makes democracy possible,
but man's inclination to injustice makes
democracy necessary.*

—Reinhold Niebuhr

CHAPTER ONE

The Province of Jurisprudence Compromised

Hir y bydd y mud ym mhorth y byddar
The dumb will wait a long time at the door of the deaf.
—Welsh Proverb

Contemporary jurisprudence is based on a heist of spectacular proportions. Perpetrated over 175 years ago and carried on by subsequent generations of jurists, the general study of law has been hijacked by a strictly philosophical approach. Although there are many different ways—sociological, economic, anthropological, *etc.*—to explain the operation of law and legal systems in modern society, a certain brand of philosophical analysis has managed to delineate and claim the province of jurisprudence for its own. Although it is practiced in a number of styles and there is heated dispute among its ranks, analytical jurisprudence has adopted an agenda of inquiry in which the main goal is to make philosophical sense of the social facts of law and clarify what is peculiarly legal about them. Whereas other disciplines can illuminate important dimensions of law's workings, it is the self-proclaimed prerogative of these analytical jurists to be the final arbiters of law's nature.

Analytical jurists have made many contributions to the understanding of law as a privileged mode of social ordering. Nevertheless, their fundamental claim is offensive, namely, that a strictly philosophical and conceptual approach to law is the primary and best jurisprudential method by which to proceed. The assertion of disciplinary authority over rival approaches is the full measure of their wrongdoing. Their analytical focus has done much more harm than good: its presumptive refinement and clarity have been outweighed by its revealed narrowness and abstraction. Masquerading as a general and detached pursuit that can be relevant to all legal systems in all places at all times, analytical jurisprudence has a definite history and is part of a contested political tradition. Indeed, for all its claims to rigor and exactness, this philosophical tendency has much softer and more contingent foundations than is supposed or claimed: It is not the hard and detached discipline that its proponents believe it to be. Accordingly, as a partial and particularized practice, analytical jurisprudence deserves a much less prominent and influential part in the jurisprudential enterprise than it presently commands. To be blunt, jurisprudence—which Karl Llewellyn strikingly insisted was "as big as law—and bigger"[1]—would be much better if the analytical project was abandoned.

The burden of this book is to expose the failings and frailties of analytical jurisprudence and suggest an alternative approach to legal theory. Although the work of leading analytical jurists is examined critically and in depth, the main challenge will be to the overall project of analytical jurisprudence. Treating it as part of a larger philosophical tendency, I will demonstrate that analytical jurisprudence is a political intervention in legal practice that is passed off as a theoretical reflection; it is no different than any other jurisprudential endeavor, including this one—like law itself, legal theory is politics. Stripped of its philosophical paraphernalia, analytical jurisprudence can be evaluated in terms of its social affiliations and political ambitions, which reveal it to be far from politically innocent or neutral; it is largely a defense and justification of the *status quo* in modern industrial states. In particular, it fails to take seriously the demands and possibilities of a democratic politics and, on occasion, works to stifle and defeat them. As such, this book contributes to a developing tendency to expose the dirty little secret that contemporary jurisprudence is at odds with the unsettling demands of an uncompromising democratic project.[2] Consequently, it strives to wrest contemporary jurisprudence from the stifling grip of traditional philosophy and open it up to a more thoroughly democratic approach to law and legal theory.

The Crime of The Centuries

Efforts to understand law's general workings and character have been legion. The attempt to appreciate the role of law in society has been a standard feature of academic texts and popular commentary since before Plato.[3] However, until the beginning of the nineteenth century, these inquiries were very much part of a larger literature on justice and government; scant attention was paid

---

[1]   KARL LLEWELLYN, JURISPRUDENCE 372 (1962).

[2]   *See* ROBERTO MANGABEIRA UNGER, WHAT SHOULD LEGAL ANALYSIS BECOME? 72–73 (1996) and JEREMY WALDRON, LAW AND DISAGREEMENT 8–9 (2001).

[3]   *See, for example*, EDWIN PATTERSON, JURISPRUDENCE: MEN AND IDEAS OF THE LAW (1953).

to the more rarified task of understanding law in and on its own terms. However, in 1832, John Austin set about changing that state of affairs. Championed by the self-interested efforts of his future partners-in-crime, Austin stole the agenda of legal theory and assured that *The Province of Jurisprudence Determined* (*The Province*) would attain canonical status. In short, Austin's dubious achievement is that, though it is possible to be for or against him, it is almost impossible to do jurisprudence without him. In establishing the provenance and province of jurisprudence, he also managed to compromise its usefulness and worth.

With his *The Province* and its central ambition to develop "the *science of jurisprudence* (or, simply and briefly, *jurisprudence*),"[4] he pulled off a double maneuver that amounted to the jurisprudential crime of the centuries. At bottom, John Austin's misdeed was first to decree that, What is law? was *the* question to be answered by legal theorists and second that philosophical analysis was *the* way to go about answering it. Although Austin's own exertions to provide a convincing answer were unsuccessful and of no lasting significance, his pioneering efforts to delineate the intellectual territory in which these endeavors take place and suggest legitimate ways to perform them has become the official *modus operandi* of jurists. The basic thrust of analytical jurisprudence is the sustained effort to provide an understanding of law which is both universal (*i.e.*, it transcends any particular or local practices) and general (*i.e.*, it encompasses and informs all other inquiries into law). By committing themselves to maintaining an uncluttered, clear-sighted, hard-headed approach, analytical jurists have occupied a pole position in delivering defensible and convincing accounts of law's basic nature and structure as a universal phenomenon. Periodically, other disciplinary approaches come into favor in legal academe, but they are treated as supplementary and secondary. Analytical jurisprudence has become jurisprudence *tout court*.

For over a century after Austin's *The Province* launched the central project of analytical jurisprudence, his ideas remained dominant and were uncritically followed by several generations of jurists. However, by the 1940s, it seemed to be generally conceded that, whatever its former significance and intellectual preeminence, analytical jurisprudence was on the ropes, if not actually down for the count. For instance, in 1941, John Dewey had opined that positivism "already wears a certain antiquarian air, so that it is hard even

---

4 JOHN AUSTIN, THE PROVINCE OF JURISPRUDENCE DETERMINED 126 (1832: H.L.A. Hart ed. 1955).

in the imagination to see why once it had such vogue."[5] By 1944, when Julius Stone published his famous essay, "The Province of Jurisprudence Redetermined," he had reasonable cause for genuine optimism in committing "an act of revolt" against the Austinian tradition.[6] Fresh from an invigorating stretch in the United States during the 1930s, where he was inspired by the Realists writings and especially the work of his Harvard mentor, Roscoe Pound, Stone was imbued with a broader sense of jurisprudence's possibilities for understanding law as a social phenomenon. Consequently, after a reign of over a century, it seemed that the long-standing dominion of analytical jurisprudence was finally reaching the end of its influential life.

Yet, only a few years later, a revival of an Austin-based analytical jurisprudence had begun in earnest. This was largely down to the singular efforts of Herbert Hart, who had been appointed to the Oxford Chair of Jurisprudence in 1952. Almost single-handedly, he undertook a bracing and critical revitalization of the analytical tradition; it was Hart's dubious destiny to dispel the musty fug around *The Province* and to bring analytical jurisprudence, especially in its positivist incarnation, squarely and decidedly back in vogue. Although he completely rejected Austin's command theory of law, Hart did so in order to fulfill better Austin's broader analytical ambitions and locate "the key to the science of jurisprudence."[7] The effect of this was not simply to give Austin's *The Province* a new lease on life, but to elevate it to an importance and prominence that had hitherto seemed unimaginable as jurisprudence's foundational text.

Nevertheless, despite its undoubted dominance in the second half of the twentieth century, analytical jurisprudence is now considered to have had its day. Indeed, there is much to be said for the standard and increasing chorus of contemporary disapproval—"flat and repetitive;" "socially unaware but philosophically obsessed;" "repetitions, trivial, and almost entirely pointless;" and "almost scholastic"[8]—about analytical jurisprudence. However, any

---

[5] John Dewey, *My Philosophy of Law* in MY PHILOSOPHY OF LAW 81 (1941). For similar assessments, *see* Ivor Jennings, *A Plea for Utilitarianism*, 2 MOD. L. REV. 22 (1938).

[6] Julius Stone, *The Province of Jurisprudence Redetermined*, 7 MOD. L. REV. 97 (1944).

[7] H.L.A. HART, THE CONCEPT OF LAW 81 (2nd ed. 1994). It has always struck me as odd that, although *The Concept of Law* is feted as a monumental contribution to legal philosophy, it was, as Hart reminded his readers in the Postscript, originally written "with English undergraduate readers in mind." *Id.* at 238.

[8] Jeremy Waldron, *Legal and Political Philosophy* in THE OXFORD HANDBOOK OF JURISPRUDENCE AND PHILOSOPHY OF LAW 381 (2002); Frederick Schauer, *Positivism Through Thick and Thin* in ANALYZING LAW; NEW ESSAYS IN LEGAL THEORY 69 (Brian Bix ed. 1998); William Twining, *Imagining Bentham: A Celebration* in CURRENT LEGAL

assessment that an Austin-inspired analytical jurisprudence is on its last legs is hasty and merely wishful thinking. If the amount of material published in and about analytical jurisprudence is any indicator, it is very much alive and kicking. Also, the quantity of output is reasonably matched by its high quality. Some of the leading academics of their generation are part of the analytical tradition; Joseph Raz, Ronald Dworkin, and Jules Coleman stand in the first rank of legal scholarship, by any lights. Although the United Kingdom remains its traditional seat, many analytical jurists reside and write in the United States: Fred Schauer, Stephen Perry, Jeremy Waldron, and others cannot be dismissed as mere bit players.[9] Although the leading figures of analytical jurisprudence are predominantly male, there are a few important female contributors, such as Nicola Lacey and Julie Dickson, to this tradition. Notwithstanding its continuing publishing presence, critics still contend that analytical jurisprudence has lost any genuine relevance and influence for the performance of modern legal scholarship and study at large. Though this is a tempting assessment, it is mistaken.

Analytical jurisprudence is still very much an intellectual force to be reckoned with not only in legal academe, but also for the bench and bar. In direct opposition to the claims of its would-be undertakers, analytical jurisprudence can be treated as the default theory of the legal world; its influence is so common and so ingrained that it has become almost pervasive and unappreciated. Although there is no deep and monolithic causal link between analytical jurisprudence and all contemporary law jobs, there is a strong connection and, at least, a plausible complementarity between analytical jurisprudence and the doctrinal tradition of legal scholarship. Indeed, the available data strongly suggest that, though there has been a definite increase in the amount

---

PROBLEMS 1998: LEGAL THEORY AT THE END OF THE MILLENNIUM 21 (M.D.A. Freeman ed. 1998); and James Allen, *A Modest Proposal*, 23 OXF. J. OF LEG. STUD. 197 at 209 (2003). *See also* David Dyzenhaus, *Positivism's Stagnant Research Programme*, 20 OXF. J. OF LEG. STUD. 703 at 719 (2000); Dennis Patterson, *Notes on the Methodology Debate in Contemporary Jurisprudence: Why Sociologists Might be Interested*, 8 LAW & SOCIOLOGY 254 at 258 (Michael Freeman ed. 2005); and Brian Tamanaha, *The Contemporary Relevance of Legal Positivism*, 32 AUST. J. OF LEGAL PHIL. 1 (2007).

9 The empirical literature is weak and offers little serious help. Available data tends to be jurisdiction-specific and subject-specific. *See* Fred R. Shapiro, *The Most-Cited Legal Books Published Since 1978*, 29 J. LEGAL STUD. 397 (2000) and Brian Leiter's *Law School Reports* at http://leiterlawschool.typepad.com/. Ironically, analytical jurisprudence fares best and tends to dominate in the category 'British Legal Books Most Cited in Social Sciences Citation Index' with five (H.L.A. Hart, John Finnis, Neil MacCormick and Joseph Raz, twice) in the top Ten. Shapiro, *id.*

and range of law and scholarship, there is no convincing sense that "law journal articles became significantly less doctrinal in the period between 1982 and 1996." The resort to a variety of instrumental and empirical approaches has tended to operate "as methods to enrich the analysis of doctrine, not as substitutes for it."[10] Insofar as analytical jurisprudence gives priority to theoretical argumentation, sound evidence, avoidance of ambiguity, conceptual clarity, systemic coherence, and ahistorical orientation, doctrinal scholarship aspires to adopt similar tools and techniques: it takes a set of accepted legal materials and sources, extracts from them their underlying patterns and essential structures, and reorganizes those materials in line with a more coherent and compelling account of the issue to be analyzed. Of course, though such conceptual work is often supplemented and reinforced by reference to some favored set of instrumental, empirical, or teleological criteria, such reference is selective: it is the non-analytical exception that proves the analytical rule. Moreover, this style and approach remains the stock-in-trade of most law reviews and periodicals.

A similar claim can also be made about legal education generally. Apart from legal theory courses (which still orient themselves around analytical debates), the analytical/conceptual approach dominates in the classroom. Teachers, often indifferent to subject matter, present the basic resources and materials of the law in their most coherent and organized manner: Criticism is largely reserved for pointing out inconsistencies, discrepancies, incongruities, etc. For instance, an examination of standard and popular casebooks reveals that the core mission is to select the basic legal sources and doctrinal materials, to pose a series of questions about how one case or principle relates to another, and to thereby illuminate the formal categories and structures which underpin the law. Again, of course, many teachers bring to their classes a variety of different perspectives (economic, historical, social, moral, *etc.*), but they are used to counterbalance and, only occasionally, subvert this predominantly analytical exercise. The often unstated premise, which law students soon seize upon, is that it is their ability to learn the formal tools of legal analysis (rather the extant details of legal doctrine) and then apply them to extant legal materials that will be most prized.[11]

---

[10]   Robert Ellickson, *Trends in Legal Scholarship: A Statistical Study*, 29 J. LEGAL STUD. 517 at 523 and 524 (2000).

[11]   *See, for example*, W. FARNSWORTH, THE LEGAL ANALYSTS: A TOOLKIT FOR THINKING ABOUT THE LAW (2007). Of course, similar arguments can be made about approaches to adjudication and professional responsibility. *See* ALLAN C. HUTCHINSON, IT'S ALL IN THE GAME: A NON-FOUNDATIONALIST ACCOUNT OF LAW AND ADJUDICATION (2000) and LEGAL ETHICS AND PROFESSIONAL RESPONSIBILITY (2nd ed. 2006).

Consequently, although the influence of Austin and *The Province* is more indirect than direct, analytical jurisprudence remains highly significant to the worlds of legal theory, legal scholarship, and even legal education. Lawyers remain in relative thrall to its intimations and admonitions. However, while this might offer some reassurance to analytical jurists, it ought not to suggest that its pervasive, if unappreciated influence is testament to its validity or merit. Its ubiquitous and long-standing presence cannot underwrite its contested theoretical status. Although the jurisprudential rejection of analytical jurisprudence will not necessarily end its influence on legal scholarship and legal education, it will demand that there be a different and better defence of its customary dominance or, at least, that the political basis of its enduring appeal will be more widely appreciated. In this book, I intend to push through on an unconditional critique of analytical jurisprudence and to recommend an alternative approach that derives its rationale and motivation from a robust commitment to what I term *strong democracy*.

For Democratic Politics

Nothing has come easy to the democrat. The history of democracy is a tale of resistance and courage. And it is no different today. Democracy is under pressure everywhere. It is not only struggling to win new national recruits around the world, but it is having grave difficulty in those nations where it is already considered to be established and enabling. This is particularly true of those Old World states who are intent on promoting its benefits to more skeptical New World countries: Domestic threats to democratic practices and ideals threaten to undermine the whole appeal and exemplar of democratic government. Moreover, this seeming crisis is mirrored by the state of democratic theorizing. Commentators and scholars lock horns over what is and is not demanded by a genuine commitment to democratic governance. In particular, the fundamental tensions between security and freedom, stability and change, and representative and popular participation have become more evident and acute. From all sides of the political spectrum, there is considered to be a crisis of confidence in the capacity of democracy alone to meet the challenges of the modern age. Indeed, there seems to be a deep anxiety that, though democracy has a role to play in contemporary governance, there are definite limits to its provenance and authority.[12] In short, debate rages over

---

[12] For a critique of how democracy is used to justify authoritarianism, *see* SHELDON WOLIN, DEMOCRACY INCORPORATED: MANAGED DEMOCRACY AND THE SPECTER OF INVERTED TOTALITARIANISM (2008).

the extent to which democracy has to be confined and circumscribed in the name of some larger and more encompassing political ideal.

Democracy, of course, is one of the most frequently mentioned, yet least specified ideas in the political lexicon. It can and has been utilized by many different people in many different situations to defend or promote many different states of affairs. Indeed, its malleable and contested nature is a large part of its enduring political appeal. By the 1950s, it was already reported that over 2000 years of political speculation had generated over 300 definitions of *democracy*.[13] Against such a theoretical backdrop, it is not surprising that democracy's ideals have often been belied and occasionally betrayed by their practical realization. Beginning in sixth-century BC Greece, there was less a democracy and more a *timocracy* in which wealth and land ownership (not to mention, being male and unenslaved) were a condition of the voting franchise. Indeed, a skeptical review of democracy's history provides the disturbing suggestion that there is almost an inverse correlation between the extension of the franchise and a reduction in the amount of power in which the enfranchised can participate: The more that people are allowed to participate as an electorate, the less is left to their decision-making authority.

Accordingly, despite the constant invocation of democracy as a rallying cry and source of legitimation for governmental decisions, there has been a distinct distrust of ordinary citizens' capacity to participate fully, freely, frequently, and actively in their own governance. In the twentieth century, democracy came to be associated almost exclusively with the institutional and competitive struggle for people's votes by those leaders who sought political power. Accommodating prescriptive ideals to descriptive realities, commentators and politicians reduced popular participation to little more than the demand for free and fair elections among multiple political parties in a context of relatively open information: "Democracy is government by officials who are accountable and removable by the majority of people in a jurisdiction."[14] Along with the judicially enforced protection of basic civil

---

[13] *See* DEMOCRACY, IDEOLOGY AND OBJECTIVITY (A. Naess *et al.* eds. 1956).

[14] JOSEPH NYE, THE PARADOX OF AMERICAN POWER: WHY THE WORLD'S ONLY SUPERPOWER CAN'T GO IT ALONE 109 (2002). This exemplifies the dominant tradition in political theory. *See* J.A. SCHUMPETER, CAPITALISM, SOCIALISM AND DEMOCRACY (1947); ROBERT A. DAHL, A PREFACE TO DEMOCRATIC THEORY: HOW DOES POPULAR SOVEREIGNTY FUNCTION IN AMERICA? (1956); ANTHONY DOWNS, AN ECONOMIC THEORY OF DEMOCRACY (1957); and HARRY ECKSTEIN, A THEORY OF STABLE DEMOCRACY (1961). There is a subfield of scholarly endeavor which attempts to measure democracy by establishing objective indicators that measure Dahl's contestative and participatory dimensions of democracy. *See, for example,* DEMOCRACY AND

rights, this constrained idea of democracy as *elective aristocracy* has come to dominate and is the accepted gold standard of democratic legitimacy for almost all contemporary regimes; the goal of a more extensive popular participation seems to have fallen by the wayside. Yet this radical separation between the rulers and ruled is a very far cry from what democracy meant just a few centuries ago, even to its opponents. By and large, democrats have been thwarted in their efforts to institutionalize the belief that the governed are not only competent to elect their governors, but also entitled to make political judgments for themselves about all, not only some substantive issues.

Suffice it to say, by way of introduction, that the core of the democratic ideal is the preference for ordering power and authority in line with the views and requirements of the citizenry. The *cri de coeur* of democrats has been the need to involve people as fully as possible in all those institutions and agencies that influence and affect their daily lives. Weak and strong forms of democracy can be distinguished by the extent of the gap between the rulers and the ruled, and between the powerful and the powerless: the smaller the gap, the more strongly democratic the society. Indeed, a strong form of democracy recommends that there is no governing elite and no governed majority; there will be an almost flat structure of government in that the state will be more disaggregated and indistinct. Instead, people will play a role as fully and as frequently as possible in the governance of their society. Whereas weak democracy contents itself with claiming that it is a government *for* the people, strong democracy aims to approximate as closely as practicable to governance for and *by* the people. At its strongest, democracy is seen to be not only a formal device for tallying people's preferences, but also an extensive process for popular participation in governance and a substantive vision of what the 'good life' should or could be.[15]

Viewed this way, democracy is the commitment *par excellence* to the idea that almost all choices and actions have political roots and political consequences: People can tackle those politics within a framework within which their active participation is more important than (or, at least, as important as) that of elected representatives, political sages, or judicial officials. In contrast

---

DEVELOPMENT: POLITICAL INSTITUTIONS AND WELL-BEING IN THE WORLD, 1950–1990 (A. Przeworski *et al.* eds. 2000) and David Beetham, *Towards a Universal Framework for Democracy Assessment*, 11(2) DEMOCRATIZATION 1 (2004).

[15] *See, for example,* John Dewey, *Creative Democracy: The Task Before Us* (1939) in JOHN DEWEY: THE LATER WORKS,1925–53 vol. 13, 155 (Jo Ann Boydston ed. 1981–1990) and BENJAMIN BARBER, STRONG DEMOCRACY: PARTICIPATORY POLITICS FOR A NEW AGE (1994).

to its present weak and anemic practice, therefore, strong democracy has a broad mandate (*i.e.*, including social and economic as well as political matters) and deep mandate (*i.e.*, requiring regular and sustained acts of participation), which combine to ensure that people become full and active citizens. Members of society are neither subjects nor subservients, but *citizens* in the fullest sense of the term. In such a strong democracy, questions about whether the legal system generally, or its substantive laws in particular, are just or legitimate cannot be separated from questions about the formal pedigree and source of that legal system or its substantive laws. Strong democracy recommends a vital connection between the important questions of formal validity and substantive legitimacy. Though it does not collapse the questions into each other entirely, it does insist that they relate to each other in crucial ways and cannot be treated separately. For the strong democrat, therefore, insofar as the state exists in the traditional sense, a paraphrasing of Louis XIV's old saw might be appropriate—*L'Etat, c'est nous.*[16]

Analytical jurisprudence has had little to say about democracy generally and even less to say about democracy in its strong form. Of course, this relative silence in itself is very telling. Because the major ambition of analytical jurisprudence has been to develop accounts of law and legal systems that have universal relevance and applicability, it has prided itself on maintaining an indifferent or neutral stance on the political schemes of governance within which law functions. Its emphasis has been on addressing conceptual issues— the nature of legal rules, legal authority, legal obligation, law and morality's relation, etc.—that are claimed to transcend the contingent particulars of any specific legal system. Consequently, though jurisprudential work has been done on how democracy fits into the general theories of law and the implications of a particular theory of law for democracy, it is treated as a secondary concern or an interesting diversion. When analytical jurists have turned their attention to democracy, they have restricted themselves to the present treatment of democracy as being constituted and fulfilled by elective aristocracy. When it comes to addressing a stronger set of democratic arrangements, analytical jurists have been less than even-handed and, therefore, have not even

---

[16] Much of my basic critique of analytical jurisprudence does not depend on a defence of strong democracy as the best means for governing social and political life: it applies with similar effect whether or not strong democracy is considered to be a desirable mode of political governance. However, it will come as no surprise that I do not adopt an agnostic stance towards democracy's appeal, but go on to defend it as a desirable political ambition. *See* ALLAN C. HUTCHINSON, THE COMPANIES WE KEEP: CORPORATE GOVERNANCE FOR A DEMOCRATIC SOCIETY (2006).

lived up to their own philosophical ambitions; their theories are more capable of incorporating the governance schemes of authoritarian states than those of strong democracy. Indeed, on occasion, analytical jurisprudence is decidedly dismissive of democratic considerations and its approach can be described as non-democratic and, on occasion, anti-democratic.

Accordingly, in this book, I want to turn the tables on analytical jurists. Instead of asking whether analytical jurisprudence can accommodate the interests and concerns of democrats, I want to inquire into what a jurisprudence would look like if it were viewed and assembled from an unconditional democratic standpoint. Rather than reflect philosophically on the universal nature of legal rules, legal authority, legal obligation, law and morality's relation, *etc.* (insofar as that is at all possible), I recommend that jurists would be much better off concentrating on the institutions, structure, practices, values, purposes, and commitments of democratic societies and cultures as they actually arise and present themselves in social history. As well as exploring practical processes and institutions for actualizing the emancipatory potential of democracy, legal theorists might direct their considerable intellectual resources to grappling with pressing topical issues of political and moral significance—the relevance of national security concerns to citizen's entitlements; the social impact of biotechnological advances; the consequences of increasing economic inequality; etc. If legal theory continues to be dominated by the present analytical mind-set, it will miss a wonderful opportunity to become useful and instrumental in advancing the democratic project. Jurisprudence will remain an increasingly precious activity in which its select analytical participants will pretend that "chewing historic cud long since reduced to woody fibre"[17] has deeper and more sustaining substance than it actually has.

Against Analytical Philosophy

In developing a democratic jurisprudence, it will be important to ensure that jurists do not become part of another ruling elite. Democracy is opposed to all efforts to accumulate and exercise power by the few over the many. Indeed, history shows that the main contemporary challenge for democracy remains less whether the majority will ride roughshod over the minority, but whether

---

17   John Dewey, *The Need for a Recovery of Philosophy* in JOHN DEWEY: THE MIDDLE WORKS: 1899–1924, vol. 10, 47 (Jo Ann Boydston ed. 1976–83).

a minority—be it a monied few, a judicial aristocracy, a political elite, a bureaucratic oligarchy, a workers group, or a corporate organization—will ride roughshod over the majority. The democratic initiative recommends against all such divisions; it seeks to exert a centrifugal rather than centripetal influence on power. As such, power is not the problem in itself, but its aggregation in unaccountable cliques and privileged circles. Too often, democracy and its institutions are hijacked by an elite, even if claiming to speak and act for the interests of all society. No matter how well intentioned or benign, the claims of elite factions that they know better than an informed citizenry are to be resisted. Understood as a social as well as political way of life, democracy aims to empower people so that they can tackle all matters that affect their lives within an organizational framework in which their active participation and control are its most important and distinguishing features.

This democratic admonition against elite control is particularly pertinent with regard to analytical jurisprudence. Claiming to speak in the name of universal truths and under the authority of abstract authority, analytical jurists represent a subtle, yet substantial threat to the democratic project. As a philosophical enterprise, analytical jurisprudence commits itself to the idea that a successful theory of law must locate those essential properties of law which are both necessarily true and adequate to distinguish it from other modes of social control: It must "tell us truths which illuminate that which is most important about and characteristic of law."[18] Indeed, much of contemporary jurisprudence has become largely epistemological in that a central concern is with determining the truth conditions for knowledge about law. Although there are indications of less hubris of late, a certain confidence remains that the traditional analytical tools—theoretical argumentation, objective evidence, conceptual clarity, systemic coherence, ahistorical orientation, *etc.*—are up to the task of laying solid epistemological foundations for the essentialist project of analytical jurisprudence. This is an elitist enterprise of the first order. By holding out the alluring prospect of objective knowledge about law's practices, analytical jurists exhibit a lack of confidence about their fellow citizens and set themselves up as philosophical experts who not only know something better about law, but know something better about knowing.

In contrast, the strong democrat insists that there is no philosophical authority that can claim priority over a democratic community of good-willed

---

[18]   Julie Dickson, Evaluation and Legal Theory 25 (2001).

participants coming together and deciding what is the most useful thing to do in difficult circumstances: "There's no God, no reality, no nothing that takes precedence over the consensus of a free people—there's no court of appeal higher than a democratic consensus."[19] In allowing for the epistemological possibility that there is an analytical method for 'illuminating truths' which is separate from a democratic society's own efforts to act justly and fairly and which can underwrite those efforts, analytical jurists betray the democratic spirit of inquiry, debate, and action. To differing degrees, analytical jurists set themselves up as comprising an illegitimate court of appeal and claim expert status in determining knowledge about the reality of law's truth.

Strong democrats resist such analytical claims. Locating knowledge and truth within a communal set of practices and engagements, they evince an implacable opposition to epistemological methodology generally. They want to engineer a shift from philosophical reflection to political engagement. This involves a relentless insistence that there are no bright-line boundaries or essential methodological differences between theory and practice, natural and social science, facts and values, philosophy and conversation, and, of course, law and politics. It is not that these categorical distinctions are thought to collapse in on each other and have no relevant differences at all, but that such differences are contingent and social because they always arise from and within, directly or indirectly, their sustaining historical and political context. Like law itself, legal theory is seen to be thoroughly political in scope and substance.

As such, a thoroughgoing democratic approach maintains that there is no possibility of a purely descriptive jurisprudence insofar as that entails resort to any kind of epistemological device that strives to ascend to a higher ahistorical ground from which to deliver truths about law's identity or the essential

---

¹⁹ *A Conversation with Richard Rorty*, ATLANTIC UNBOUND, April 23rd 1998. RICHARD RORTY, PHILOSOPHY AND THE MIRROR OF NATURE 181 (1979). *See also* RICHARD RORTY, CONSEQUENCES OF PRAGMATISM (1982) and RICHARD RORTY, CONTINGENCY, IRONY, SOLIDARITY (1989). While my debt to the writings of Richard Rorty is large, I do not embrace his ideas uncritically or entirely. *See infra*, chs. 7 and especially ch.9. He was committed to revitalizing a Deweyan pragmatism not as a faithful act of historical remembrance, but as a committed exercise in engaged advocacy; he challenged and reworked it as he rescued and reinvigorated it. TAKE CARE OF FREEDOM AND TRUTH WILL TAKE CARE OF ITSELF: INTERVIEWS WITH RICHARD RORTY (Eduardo Mendieta ed. 2006) and RICHARD RORTY AND PASCAL ENGEL, WHAT'S THE USE OF TRUTH? (2007). I challenge and rework Rorty's pragmatism in line with a stronger commitment to democratic politics.

qualities of other social practices. Although experience has taught that given techniques or resources are better suited to produce reliable results in some fields than others, there is no detached or definitive vantage point from which to determine which technique or resource is objectively best suited to one task or another. There is no Method of methods and no Context of contexts. The only arguments and reasons needed are those that have passed social muster in an open and intelligent exchange. Moreover, because these social conversations and philosophical conventions are themselves open to the changing and dynamic forces of historical challenge, they are at least vulnerable to and often affected by political and social values. Such an appreciation casts the analytical project in a very different light. Once the connection between philosophy and politics is conceded, the whole epistemological tradition of analytical jurisprudence is vulnerable and suspect.

Rather than being appreciated as a self-contained philosophical pursuit, analytical jurisprudence can be more usefully apprehended as part of a continuing political tradition that privileges certain values and interests over others.[20] Once understood as an engaged political intervention, analytical jurisprudence can be evaluated in terms of its compatibility with the demands and standards of a democratic approach. As with almost all other social practices, the disciplinary strictures of analytical jurisprudence will be shown not to be immune from the push-and-pull of various social, economic, institutional, ideological, and cultural currents. Because objectivity is about compliance with those accepted and agreed-upon standards for justifying knowledge, it will be crucial to ascertain and examine the terms and conditions under which such social agreements are reached and enforced. Of course, it ought to come as no surprise that such understandings and arrangements are themselves subject to the contingent play of various practical forces and professional interests. Consequently, what has managed to get itself accepted in the relevant community of scholarly study will be attributable to more than (or, perhaps, less than) the raw force of a good idea. A close examination of the descriptive/evaluative distinction draws attention to the extent to which epistemology (*i.e.*, What is it to have true knowledge of law?) and political theory (*i.e.*, What political interests and values are promoted by law and legal theory?) are as related and dependent as much as they are separate and apart. In regard to analytical jurisprudence, this strongly suggests that the virtues of factual or epistemic values are not as apparent or insulated from

---

20   *See* David Dyzenhaus, *The Genealogy of Legal Positivism*, 24 OXF J. OF LEG STUD 39 at 40 (2004).

political values as their proponents suggest: They are similarly, if not equally connected to the social matrix of forces that gestate and perpetuate them.

A more suitable characterization of the jurist's function can be found in the exhortation to worry less about flying higher or digging deeper to ascertain truth and knowledge about law, which has enduring validity beyond society's own situation and challenges. Instead, jurists who are prepared to follow through unconditionally on the democratic imperative look to explore and broaden the ways in which a society's conversations about law can be made more useful to its members. This involves the acceptance that there are no conversation-ending or truth-fixing arguments other than those that gain acceptance in engaged debate and open inquiry in particular historical circumstances. Consequently, democratic jurists will eschew the analytical tendency to take such matters entirely out of the hands of citizens and reserve them as only for those with philosophical or jurisprudential competence. The more modest role of jurists is to use their technical skill and institutional experience to facilitate and contribute to democratic debate, not usurp it in the name of philosophical authority. In meeting such a task, the effort to determine and defend insights about law in terms of their universal merit or enduring appeal is simply a distraction. Rather than take an almost perverse pride in the unworldliness of their views, democratic jurists will recognize that treating their work as local enthusiasms is a useful compliment, not a dismissive criticism.

Some Cautionary Notes

In making these introductory observations in defence of a democratic approach to jurisprudential study, I have sought to offer the beginnings of a more thoroughly democratic approach to law and legal theory. In particular, I have suggested that it is important to avoid assuming the familiar role of an analytical jurist, including a disappointed or frustrated one. Nevertheless, my dissatisfaction with the analytical project of jurisprudence is not new or unusual. There are a number of juristic contributions, past and present, which claim to be anti-analytical in posture and performance, but there are crucial differences between those positions and my own. Accordingly, it is necessary to offer some cautionary notes about the precise basis and thrust of my democratic stance. The main three anti-analytical positions are those that I will term the realist, naturalist, and non-ideological.

First, though I build on the realist project in denouncing the philosophical ambitions of analytical jurisprudence, I am not simply rehashing their critical approach and behavioralist assumptions. The realists did much to expose the foundationalist and formalist pretensions of much juristic commentary. For instance, Felix Cohen was unstinting in his efforts to demonstrate that it was mistaken and misleading to suggest that it was possible to separate the descriptive and critical tasks of legal analysis: "Legal description is blind without the guiding light of a theory of values." However, for all his insistence on the wrongheadedness of the fact/value distinction as a device for explaining legal reasoning and legal concepts, Cohen, like many of his realist colleagues, still remained committed to the belief that, "we never shall thoroughly understand the facts as they are, and we are not likely to make much progress towards such understanding . . . [except] through the union of objective legal science and a critical theory of social values."[21] Consequently, although the realists had lost faith in any defence of law's formal and uncritical performance, they continued to maintain that an *objective science* was possible and attainable, and that it might ensure the redemptive promise of law and legal theory. In contrast, although I fully acknowledge the continuing need to understand law's facts and its operation as a social practice, I insist that this cannot be achieved by reliance upon the charms and claims of pseudoscientific methods for obtaining knowledge about law and/or society at large. A pragmatic approach neither needs nor craves such empty reassurances.

Second, I am not simply passing off under more obscure garb the familiar naturalist rejoinder to positivists that any factual inquiry will demand "a judgment of significance and importance" and thereby implicate moral values.[22] I fully accept that (positivist) theorists are not engaged in a covert campaign to instill their own moral preferences into law by some furtive scheme. Although the occasional analytical jurist might engage in such a disingenuous effort, I fully accept that this is not generally the case. My claim is more political than moral. A democratic stance insists that all efforts at theorizing are affected by and colored by the political interests at play in the larger social context within which the theoretical enterprise takes place. Although the practice of legal theory cannot only be reduced to such interests and values, it is also never entirely free of them. Law and legal theory are

---

[21] Felix Cohen, *Transcendental Nonsense and the Functional Approach* (1935) 35 COLUM. L. REV. 809 at 849 (1935). Stone, *supra,* note 6. In a similar vein, it was Justice Brandeis' prediction that little progress in society would be made until the lawyers' obsession with "the logic of words" has been healed by their attachment to the "logic of realities." *See DiSanto v. Pennsylvania,* 273 US 34 at 43 per Brandeis J. dissenting (1927).

[22] JOHN FINNIS, NATURAL LAW AND NATURAL RIGHTS 17 (1980).

never only about political interests or power: they are also about the justification and masking of those interests and power. The precise nature and extent of the relationship between theory and its informing context is not itself fixed or formulaic, but varies from one context to another. Like law, therefore, legal theory is politics by other means. Consequently, the claim that legal theory is thoroughly value-laden is not the same as the contention that it is always morally motivated; the absence of moral judgments or designs does not mean that legal theory is free or politically innocent of value commitments.

Third, there are a number of contemporary legal theorists who are prepared to concede that the analytical attachment to a fact/value distinction is itself based on some set of substantive evaluative commitments. However, they also maintain that those commitments are themselves non-political and can be defended in general and non-ideological terms. For instance, while Leslie Green recommends that "legal theory is value-laden" in that any account of law "can have no deeper ground than the complex set of interests and purposes to which legal theory responds," he insists that this does not render legal theory "purely ideological" or completely reducible to those interests and purposes. Resisting the idea that law and its connections to such interests and purposes are "essentially contested" in the way that democracy or justice might be, he simply maintains that legal theory cannot be any purer than the political theory of which it is part.[23] In contrast, my pragmatic approach does not shy away from the claim that both law and legal theory are *ideological* in the sense of resting on deeply controversial and contested premises. Legal theory arises in political circumstances, is motivated by political concerns, and has political consequences. In a manner of speaking, it is politics and values all the way up and down: there are no stable or secure footings on which the jurisprudential debate can be based which are not themselves part of that very debate. Consequently, any and all jurisprudential claims to political innocence and ideological neutrality are unsustainable.

In contrast to each of these positions, I maintain that the best way to challenge analytical jurisprudence is to forego any lingering attachment to such traditional shibboleths as truth, objectivity, and universality in offering conceptual certainties or sociological insights. I offer a broadly democratic account that measures the worth of legal theory less by the lights of abstract philosophical speculation and more by the demands of useful political knowledge. In an important sense, therefore, though I agree with a leading contemporary

---

[23]   Leslie Green, *The Political Content of Legal Theory*, 17 PHIL. OF SOC. SCIS. 1 at 15 and 16 (1987). The reference to 'essentially contested' is obviously from W.B. GALLIE, PHILOSOPHY AND THE HISTORICAL UNDERSTANDING 157–91 (1964).

jurist that, "we have no choice but to ask [judges and lawyers] to confront issues that, from time to time, are philosophical,"[24] I reject the analytical understanding of what it means to be 'philosophical'. Instead, I insist that the whole philosophical enterprise must be reworked in line with a more democratic and less analytical sensibility in which the abstract emphasis on truth and objectivity is replaced with a more practical concern for usefulness and substantive values. Rather than persist in pretending that the best way to engage with and understand law's facts is by assuming that they represent some independent set of historicallygiven data that can be analyzed from some a historical vantage point, it is more beneficial and convincing to recognize the inevitable connection between philosophy and politics and, therefore, between truths and values. In so doing, it might be possible to turn legal theory to more democratic effect.

The analytical effort to say something profound about all law and legal systems is a recipe for saying almost nothing about any particular system; there are no theory-independent facts about law that can offer a reliable or uncontroversial grounding for further jurisprudential analysis. If "the first call of a theory of law is that it should fit the facts,"[25] then knowledge of and about law must be local and particular, not universal and general, in its origins and outcomes. As a social and professional practice, the creation and maintenance of legal knowledge is not characterized by compliance with a universally valid set of formulaic procedures. Because legal knowledge is determined by the conventional norms of social practice rather than the logical criteria of objective validity, there are no privileged descriptions or contexts of law that give ultimate grounding to all others. Legal theory is itself conditioned and framed by a contingent set of working commitments that delineate those prevailing techniques and methods which are considered adequate to underwrite certain contingent insights about law and its operation. Situated in an inevitable historical context of political interests and ideological commitments, legal theory is affected by and accountable to those interests and commitments. Again, like law, legal theory is politics by other means.

---

[24] RONALD DWORKIN, JUSTICE IN ROBES 73 (2006).

[25] O.W. HOLMES, THE COMMON LAW 167 (1881). *See also* HART, *supra*, note 7 at 80 AND RONALD DWORKIN, LAW'S EMPIRE 255 (1986).

The Path Ahead

Both jurisprudence and democracy have seen better days. Despite their enormous promise, each seems to have been taken hostage by those who are more intent on perpetuating their own prestige and authority than improving society. Yet, unless there is a concerted effort to arrest this unfortunate development, the distinctly cloudy present will only usher in an even gloomier future. In short, jurisprudence and democracy have become much less than what they could or should be. And society is much the worse for it. As I will suggest throughout this book, the best response to this state of affairs in both politics and jurisprudence is the same—a redoubling of efforts to fulfil the emancipatory and ennobling potential of democracy; it is more, not less democracy that is required. Accordingly, in the next four chapters, I will detail the many and different ways in which the Austinian-inspired theoretical project of analytical jurisprudence fails by both its own and democracy's lights; contemporary efforts to salvage the analytical project have made matters worse. After that, I will utilize Ronald Dworkin's liberal legalism as an important, but limited bridge between the older analytical tradition and the newer democratic approach; he distances himself from the dominant positivist rendition of the analytical tradition, but defends a moralist approach that remains too beholden to the same analytical tradition. In the last three chapters, I will explore the shape and substance that a more uncompromising democratic approach to legal theory might take. Throughout, the emphasis will be on the extent to which democracy can serve as both means and ends for an improvement in legal theory and legal practice.

CHAPTER TWO

The Province of Jurisprudence Revisited

Austin . . . was sometimes clearly wrong; but . . . when this was so he
was always wrong clearly.

—Herbert Hart

2007 marked the terquasquicentennial anniversary of the publication of John Austin's *The Province of Jurisprudence Determined* (*The Province*). This classic work is universally acknowledged as one of law's undisputed canonical texts: Its formative role in the history of Anglo-American jurisprudence is undisputed. The fact that *The Province* is no longer referenced as frequently is less an indication of its dated quality and more a testament to its foundational status. Although the details and substance of his work are now only of historical value, including his infamous command theory of law, Austin's ideas about the task and ambition of general jurisprudence remain enormously and actively influential. Indeed, it would be no exaggeration to report that, as confirmation of its enormous stature, *The Province* continues to provide the general intellectual framework—to develop "the *science of jurisprudence* (or, simply and briefly, *jurisprudence*)"[1]—within which most traditional thinking about law and legal theory occurs. Whether they appreciate or acknowledge that fact, this is as true for its moralist detractors as well as for its positivist defenders. As such, it is clear that any serious effort to appreciate, let alone transform, the theory and practice of contemporary jurisprudence must pay close and critical attention to John Austin's *The Province*.

Although there is little dispute about the historical influence of *The Province* in inaugurating the project of *analytical jurisprudence*, there is plenty of heated disagreement about what that influence should be and whether it has been good or bad. Accordingly, in this chapter, my intention is to review

---

[1] JOHN AUSTIN, THE PROVINCE OF JURISPRUDENCE DETERMINED 126 (1832: H.L.A. Hart ed. 1955).

the broad outlines of Austin's approach to jurisprudence and trace its continuing influence upon the performance of jurisprudence today. Rather than offer a flat chronological narrative, I will present a more schematic survey and capture the important themes that make better sense of the contemporary jurisprudential project—conceptual analysis, the law/morality relationship, its methodological orientation, and power's role. As well, Austin's *The Province* will be situated within a more general intellectual and social context in order to emphasize the extent to which his own legal theory and jurisprudence more generally are part of a contested political tradition. In particular, I will assess the (un)democratic thrust of his legal theory and lay out the challenge to be met by later jurists in improving or making good on that democratic deficit. Throughout the chapter, therefore, I will utilize Austin's pioneering work to set the terms for the continuing struggle over the philosophical and political soul of contemporary jurisprudence.

A Commanding Presence

Although it is customary to treat John Austin as being more closely associated with legal positivism, his overall approach to the general task and mandate of jurisprudence is more general in sweep and ambition. He made a pioneering effort to focus jurisprudential inquiry on elaborating a philosophically defensible account of law's essential nature. Although most lawyers and citizens can offer countless examples of laws, they have grave difficulty in offering a plausible account of *what law is* more generally. For Austin, this is the point at which legal theorists can play a useful and important role. Inaugurating the project of *analytical jurisprudence*, Austin maintained that the only way to develop a legitimate and reliable mode of theoretical inquiry into law was to "imitate the method so successfully pursued by geometers" and, aspiring to the certainty of Euclidean geometry, to produce "the *science of jurisprudence* (or, simply and briefly, *jurisprudence*)." Although there are various theoretical approaches—sociological, economic, anthropological, *etc.*—that could claim to be able to fulfill that task, Austin insisted that a proper science of jurisprudence must take law seriously on its own terms and elucidate its essential features from within. As such, "the proper subject of General or Universal Jurisprudence . . . is a description of such subjects and ends of Law as are common to all systems."[2]

---

[2] Austin, *id.* at 77–78, 126 and 373.

So guided, Austin sought to formulate a strict discipline that could cut through the contingent clutter of different examples of law and come up with a broad definition of law which will make sense of law's myriad instances. By putting the *science of jurisprudence* on a firmer and more intellectually rigorous footing, lawyers would be able to carve out that area of study that was uniquely legal by distinguishing it from other related modes of social regulation, like ethics and religion. This project entailed developing an understanding of law as both universal (*i.e.*, transcending any particular or local practices) and general (*i.e.*, encompassing and informing all other inquiries into law). In this way, Austin introduced the basic analytical move of taking a set of legal phenomena as sociohistorical givens and extracting from them those underlying patterns and essential structures that best provide an adequate and true explanation of their identity and existence as law. It is this philosophical (and, more precisely, epistemological) effort to identify the core commitments and distinctive components of law as a social practice that has been the hallmark of analytical jurisprudence. Indeed, for the past 175 years or so, jurists have joined issue over the method and means by which such an inquiry can be successfully achieved and defended. Although this debate has deepened and broadened over the years, as well as taking a number of different detours and deviations, its basic Austinian orientation has been largely consistent and continual.

Nevertheless, although Austin set the general task and tone of jurisprudential study, he also put forward his own imperative account of what those distinguishing features and essential characteristics of law comprised. His imperative theory of law was intended to clear away some of the "mistiness and intricacy" around legal study and locate the essential nature of law's formal character. Although he conceded that "divine law is the measure or test of positive law and morality," he also insisted that "to say that human laws which conflict with the Divine law are not binding, that is to say, are not law, is to talk stark nonsense." For him, it is those particular laws that are "purely or simply of human invention and position" that are the appropriate and proper concern of jurists. By way of an elaborate typology, *The Province* is an extended, if rather strained meditation on how it is possible to distinguish positive law, properly so-called, from those analogous rules; these include, as those set by men in a state of nature, those set by a sovereign (but not as a political sovereign), and those set by subjects as private persons. After ranging broadly over the legal terrain, he came to the (in)famous conclusion that "the *science of jurisprudence* (or, simply and briefly, *jurisprudence*) is concerned with positive laws, or with laws strictly so called, as considered without regard to their goodness or badness." In so doing, he laid the modern foundations for legal positivism with its defining insistence that "the existence of law is one thing; its merit or demerit is another."[3]

Developing this positivistic approach, Austin settled upon the idea of command as "the *key* to the science of jurisprudence." He noted that "every positive law (or every law strictly and properly so called) is set, directly or circuitously, by a sovereign individual or body, to a member or members of the independent political society to . . . a persons or persons in a state of subjection to its author;" these laws are backed by the sovereign's power "to inflict an evil or pain" as a sanction. In this Austinian account, the sovereign's power is sustained by the fact that "the *bulk* of the given society are in a *habit* of obedience or submission" to it: "command, duty, and sanction are inseparably connected terms." However, as law's character is to be found in facts and not morals, Austin was unconcerned with the actual causes of obedience because they "belong to the province of statistics or the province of particular history." There was no need or expectation of any moral allegiance by those civic subjects, even though Austin accepted that law and morality were related and combined as a matter of empirical happenstance.[4] Consequently, Austin's imperative theory of law claimed to go beyond the historical peculiarities of contemporary law and to analyze the nature of law as a universal phenomenon to be distinguished from other forms of social control, like morality and religion.

Although this only gives the barest outline of Austin's account in *The Province*, it will hopefully salvage enough of his most important themes and arguments. It is less the details of Austin's account and more its general thrust that are of present significance. Indeed, there are no jurists that accept his imperative account of law. Even in his own lifetime, Austin's *The Province* was received with huge indifference. Yet, over the years, this disinterest begun to give way to more active criticism. However, it is only by appreciating the broader intellectual and political context in which Austin formulated and published *The Province* that its deeper shortcomings and, therefore, those of the analytical tradition of jurisprudence that it spawned can be grasped. As with all scholarship, *The Province* did not simply flow from the pen of its author in a social vacuum and as an act of intellectual ingenuity alone: it arose, was created, and had consequences within a particular matrix of historical circumstances.

---

[3] Austin, *id.* at 10, 6, 185, 5, 126 and 184.

[4] Austin, *id.* at 13, 350, 14, 17–18, 93–94 and 301. *See generally* W. CONKLIN, THE INVISIBLE ORIGINS OF LEGAL POSITIVISM: A RE-READING OF A TRADITION 137–70 (2001).

The Provinciality of Jurisprudence Determined

John Austin's appointment as the first Professor of Jurisprudence and the Law of Nations at the University of London in 1826 was very much a signal event. In the creation of University College, he was specifically enlisted to be part of the wider academic struggle to have law, particularly its jurisprudential study, accepted as a suitable staple of the university curriculum and given its disciplinary stripes as a genuine scholarly pursuit. As a close neighbor and full-fledged disciple of Jeremy Bentham (who was actively involved in and approved of his appointment), Austin was also a reformist. He sought to wrest law's development from the naturalist mind-set in which the Blackstonian notion of law as customary, inchoate, rational, and inherently fair was still regnant. The informing naturalist assumption was that what the courts are doing is largely right and that the jurist's task was to elucidate the accumulated wisdom of common law precedents. In contrast, Austin argued that "all judge-made law is the creature of the sovereign or state" by the circuitous process of transmuting, adopting or acquiescing in customary law under the delegated authority of the sovereign or state.[5] Such arguments, along with many others and especially the emphasis on the need to separate law's validity from its moral worth, were devoted to breaking the stranglehold that a Blackstonian vision of individual liberty had upon the law and its future direction.

Accordingly, building on the philosophical work of Thomas Hobbes and John Locke, Austin sought to develop a science of general jurisprudence which would clarify the proper focus of legal theory and set it on a very different intellectual trajectory than the traditional English seat-of-the-pants, casuistic approach to law. He sought to incorporate a more continental European sensibility through the reliance on positivistic methods with the overt ambition of delivering a legal theory that was less centered on the common law and more attuned to legislative and utilitarian intervention. Accordingly, although Austin explicitly stated that "the teacher of jurisprudence . . . ought not to attempt to insinuate his opinion of merit and demerit under pretence of assigning causes," it should come as no surprise that his

---

5. Austin, *id.* at 31 and 163. See BLACKSTONE'S COMMENTARIES I, 2 and II, 425 and IV, 435. *See also Fisher v. Prince* (1762), 3 Burr. 1363 per Lord Mansfield ("the reason and spirit of cases make law, not the letter of particular precedents"); *Jones v. Randall* (1774), Cowp. 37 per Lord Mansfield ("precedents serve to illustrate principles and to give them fixed certainty"); and MATTHEW HALE, HISTORY OF THE COMMON LAW 67 (4th ed. 1739).

positivist project was highly compatible with, if not entirely attributable to, his own and Bentham's campaign to recast law's content in line with utilitarian teachings. Austin's commitment to a separation of law and morality was as much strategic and political as theoretical and analytic in scope and ambition. In the same way that the immediate popularity and lasting appeal of Blackstone's *Commentaries* owed as much to the ideological leanings of its author as to its intellectual excellence, so Austin's *The Province* (and its role as the midwife of analytical jurisprudence) was less an exercise in abstract theorizing and more part of a very definite ideological campaign. The origins and political slant of *The Province* are to be found in Austin's commitment to the political goal of ensuring that "the final cause or purpose for which government ought to exist, is the furtherance of the common weal to the *greatest* possible extent."[6]

Of course, such a scholarly intervention did not recommend Austin's ambition and approach in *The Province* to all readers. In particular, *The Province* was roundly criticized for its partial and contingent quality. Although Austin claimed a certain scientific and universal validity for his jurisprudential inquiry, he restricted his scholarly attention to the legal systems of only a limited number of nations (*i.e.*, "the writings of Roman jurists; the decisions of English judges in modern times; and the provisions of French and Prussian codes as to arrangement"). He defended this imperialist focus on the basis that, apart from only being able realistically "to become acquainted, even imperfectly" with a few jurisdictions, "from these, however, the rest may be presumed."[7] Furthermore, almost all critics commented upon how Austin's command theory not only failed to offer a convincing conceptual portrait of law generally, but also did not even do a sound job of explaining the actualities of the nineteenth-century English legal system. So intent was Austin in his reliance on an exclusively sanction-based account of law that he backed himself into some very tight and unconvincing corners. For instance, he was obliged to conclude that neither international law nor constitutional law was

---

[6] Austin, *id.* at 374 and 269. His contemporary critics were mistaken to condemn Austin's writings as "mere amusements of the closet, and of trivial practical utility." *See Review*, 18 WESTMINISTER REVIEW 244 (1832). *See* W. TWINING, BLACKSTONE'S TOWER: THE ENGLISH LAW SCHOOL 123–52 (1994) and Duncan Kennedy, THE STRUCTURE OF BLACKSTONE'S COMMENTARIES, 28 BUFF. L. REV. 205 (1979). For an account of Austin's continental influences, *see* Andreas Schwarz, *John Austin and the German Jurisprudence of His Time*, 2 Politica 178 (1934).

[7] Austin, *id.* at 373.

law properly so-called.[8] Such counterintuitive arguments gave the lie to his vaunted scientific claims to be offering an empirical and detached accounting of law's historical manifestations.

However, the most pertinent and pressing criticisms of the Austinian model came from a political and emerging democratic perspective. The central claim was that Austin's account was more an encomium for authoritarian government than anything else. Dismissive of democracy and the "lovers of democracy," Austin thought "the distinction between free and despotic governments . . . [to be] extremely inappropriate and absurd;" the only relevant consideration was whether the government advanced the interests of "the common or general weal."[9] In offering a theory of law whose hallmark was the top-down, threat-backed, and end-measured power of an omnipotent ruler, he left little or no room for the possibility of an even minimally democratic organization of society in which ordinary people might have a genuine claim to, let alone a share of power; people were only grateful subjects, not citizens in waiting. Indeed, Austin's efforts at designating the abiding conceptual identity of *law properly so called* worked as something of a barrier to or check on the development of a democratic understanding of law and politics. As H. L. A. Hart later noted, Austin's model only applied to "the simplest form of society in which [there] was an absolute monarch;" his efforts to explain how his notion of sovereign power applied in a democracy had "no plausibility" because this would be tantamount to saying that "the 'bulk' of society habitually obeys itself."[10]

Austin's antipathy to democracy ought not to come as a surprise. It should be remembered that, although 1832 was a signal year in the nascent movement for greater democratic governance with the enactment of the Reform Act, England was far from being a democratic state; large batches of the population remained disenfranchised and power was securely in the hands of the propertied elite. For Austin, this was not a bad thing because he was no supporter of perceived French-imitating revolutionary changes in English society.

---

[8]   Austin, *id.* at 187–216 and 259–64.

[9]   Austin, *id.* at 273–74. There are some unexpected parallels between Austin's and Ronald Dworkin's general constitutional view of democracy's limited role in constitutional governance. *See infra*, ch.6.

[10]   H.L.A. HART, THE CONCEPT OF LAW 75 (1963: 2nd ed. 1994). For early critiques of Austin's failure to accommodate or account for even minimal democratic societies, *see* W.J. BROWN, AUSTINIAN THEORY OF LAW (1906) and C.A.W. MANNING, *Austin Today; or 'The Province of Jurisprudence' Re-examined* in MODERN THEORIES OF LAW 180 (W. Ivor Jennings ed. 1933).

He had been a commissioned army officer for five years before becoming a lawyer and, as one chronicler noted, "his jurisprudence always smacked of the drill-sergeant."[11] Indeed, his final publication was *A Plea for the Constitution* in 1859. Intended as a paean to the old aristocratic order and a defiant stand against further democratisation of the English political system, it gave normative and moral weight to the positivist image of a commanding sovereign. As such, therefore, his political and intellectual interests made fine allies in their combined effect of allowing Austin to inculcate a paternalistic posture by maintaining the existence of a largely authoritarian state, by conferring jurisprudential legitimacy upon it, and by working to reform the substantive merits of the laws enacted.[12] In short, Austin was a liberal reformer, but a democratic antagonist. Although his efforts were far from successful, Austin contrived to have his jurisprudential cake and to eat it politically, too.

This assessment of Austin's stance towards democracy is hardly controversial or new. However, it would be a simple matter of historical record only if not for the continuing significance of *The Province* and its agenda for analytical jurisprudence. The decidedly undemocratic slant of Austin's ideas remains pertinent for any assessment of analytical jurisprudence's present relevance and contemporary appeal. For instance, although modern analytical jurists have offered a thorough reworking of Austin, they still build on Austinian foundations and work within the Austinian account of the analytical project. Whereas Austin offered a top-down, sovereign-obeyed, and threat-backed theory of law, his analytical heirs have undoubtedly offered a more nuanced account in which law rests on a more general form of social consensus. Notwithstanding that however, the central issue remains—Have modern analytical legal scholars, both positivists and moralists, done enough to meet the undemocratic and even antidemocratic criticisms so reasonably directed at Austin's *The Province*? Though they have improved on the theoretical foundations of the analytical project in their reworking of Austin's ideas, it is far from clear that they have made or even tried to make any real progress in giving these democratic concerns a more central role in his theory of law. Indeed, consideration of the legal aspects of a social commitment to democratic governance remain very low on the agenda of contemporary jurisprudence.

---

[11] F.J.C. HEARNSHAW, as quoted in W. RUMBLE, THE THOUGHT OF JOHN AUSTIN: JURISPRUDENCE, COLONIAL REFORM, AND THE BRITISH CONSTITUTION 12 (1985).

[12] *See* J. AUSTIN, A PLEA FOR THE CONSTITUTION (1859). *See also* EIRA RUBEN, *Austin's Political Pamphlets 1824–1859* in PERSPECTIVES IN JURISPRUDENCE ch.2 (Elspeth Attwooll ed. 1977).

Nevertheless, despite the frequency and strength of particular criticisms of Austin's law-as-command theory in *The Province*, they belie the deeper and more lasting contribution of his seminal book. Although Austin's own theory has been almost universally dismissed, the project and agenda of analytical jurisprudence that he laid out took hold and set the standards for jurisprudential study for decades to come. Although *The Province*'s influence did not begin to exert itself until after Austin's death in 1859, he became the belated parent of an English jurisprudential lineage which runs from Sheldon Amos and E.C. Clark through Thomas Holland and John Salmond to Herbert Hart and Joseph Raz, today, and perhaps on to John Gardner and Leslie Green tomorrow.[13] As well, some American jurists, like Oliver Wendell Holmes, Jr., took a positivist leaf out of Austin's book and ensured its insights were taken seriously. Despite various intellectual assaults and much critical anxiety, the analytical tradition continues to be the implicit default theory of much legal inquiry and academic scholarship.

An Austinian Revival

Over the past half century, the revival of an Austinian-established analytical jurisprudence has proceeded apace and gone through a number of different phases. Although there is widespread disagreement among the contributors to this unfolding drama, there remains a shared analytical ambition—*to provide a compelling and cogent account of law's essential nature and structure.* Rather than offer a flat chronological narrative of this revival, I will present a more thematic survey of the present jurisprudential state of play; this better captures the important issues that thread together the Austinian-influenced agenda of contemporary analytical jurisprudence. There are four phases to this neo-Austinian renaissance—conceptual; moral; methodological; and power-oriented. These will operate as a structural introduction to the first half of the book and provide the platform from which to develop a more democratically attuned account of jurisprudence's possibilities

---

[13] *See* NEIL DUXBURY, *English Jurisprudence Between Austin and Hart*, 91 VA. L. REV. 1 (2005). Austin's ideas met with widespread indifference during his lifetime. *See* Wilfrid E. Rumble, *Austin in the Classroom: Why Were his Courses on Jurisprudence Unpopular?*, 17 J. LEGAL HIST. 17, 17 (1996). For a general survey, *see* G. POSTEMA, BENTHAM AND THE COMMON LAW TRADITION (1986) and WILFRED E. RUMBLE, DOING AUSTIN JUSTICE: THE RECEPTION OF JOHN AUSTIN'S PHILOSOPHY OF LAW IN NINETEENTH CENTURY ENGLAND (2005).

(1) A Conceptual Turn

The main thrust of Hart's *The Concept of Law* is to make a better fist of explicating law's essential nature than Austin himself did. Demonstrating that Austin's "model of orders backed by threats obscures more than it reveals,"[14] Hart offered his own account of law as 'a union of obligation-imposing primary and authority-conferring secondary rules' as the best way to fulfill the analytical mandate. Insisting that law must be understood positivistically as something separate from its substantive moral merits, Hart also introduced a more rigorous philosophical mode of inquiry that was intended to revise and strengthen the analytical canon.

Hart sought to move away from Austin's empirical focus and offer a more thoroughly conceptual approach. Hart's analytical approach is resolutely philosophical in reaching for a systematic and, therefore, objectively authoritative account of law's character as a separate disciplinary and practical category. Offering "an improved analysis of the distinctive structure of a municipal legal system and a better understanding of the resemblances and differences between law, coercion, and morality, as types of social phenomena,"[15] Hart gave the analytical function a more critical edge by striving to unpack and disaggregate a complex jumble of social facts. So armed, he was purportedly better able to isolate and understand those salient and important features that fix those phenomena as peculiarly 'legal' in nature and identity.

Hart's *The Concept of Law* is a revival of Austin by way of a transformation. He abandoned Austin's imperative theory in order to redeem Austin's broader jurisprudential project. As such, Hart's ambitions remained as lofty and as broad as Austin's—he presented an account of law that was intended to be universally valid for all mature legal systems. He did not claim to be simply offering a conceptual unpacking of any one legal system (*e.g.*, the British model), but a "clarification of the general framework of legal thought."[16] This is analytical jurisprudence on a grand scale and demands an equally grand defence. The burden upon Hart and other analytical jurists, therefore, is to demonstrate that such a conceptual account of law can be justified as being compatible with a vast range of

---

[14]   Hart, *supra*, note 10 at 49.

[15]   Hart, *id.* at 17.

[16]   Hart, *id.* at v.

legal systems and as being neutral between different political systems of governance. If it can be shown that these analytical accounts represent and apply more readily to some legal and governmental regimes than others, then they will be exposed as not having lived up to their universalist requirements. Moreover, insofar as a society committed to strong democracy fails to mesh sufficiently with such accounts, then the partiality and contested nature of such conceptual work will be further displayed. Shorn of its universalistic claims, analytical jurisprudence would become exactly the kind of politicized theorizing which its proponents claim to reject and from whose work they distinguish themselves. In short, if the universalistic credentials of conceptual inquiry are undermined, the provinciality of analytical jurisprudence will be on display.

(2) A Moral Challenge

Hart's reworking of Austin's *The Province* not only revived the flagging fortunes of analytical jurisprudence, but also gave a shot in the arm to legal positivism. Although Hart accepted that there were profound and various connections between law and morality, he presented "a concept of law which allows the invalidity of law to be distinguished from its immorality" and insisted that "it is in no sense a necessary truth that laws reproduce or satisfy certain demands of morality, though in fact they have often done so."[17] His was a commitment to both analytical jurisprudence and its positivistic rendition. Indeed, many began to treat analytical jurisprudence and legal positivism as one and the same thing.

However, this rousing affirmation of legal positivism in a revived, if modified Austinian form provoked heated and partisan debate. The most sustained and anticipated response was by those, like Lon Fuller and Ronald Dworkin, who rejected Hart's positivistic leanings and insisted that there was a necessary moral component to law's nature. They took the view that it was not possible to talk about law without also talking about morality. However, their work remained largely conceptual and analytical in scope and ambition in that they still sought to identify those elements and characteristics of law that were essential to law's nature as a separate and authoritative mode of social regulation. For such moralists, a full account of law's social facts demanded close attention to its moral content and normative purposes. For instance, Dworkin's basic analytical move was to take "the brute facts of legal history" or "the raw

---

[17] Hart, *id.* at 211 and 185–86.

behavioral data of [legal] practice" and offer "the best justification of legal practice as a whole" so as to be able to identify the "circumstances in which particular propositions of law should be taken to be sound or true."[18]

Nevertheless, many analytical jurists stood firm and defended the positivist cause. Although most were content to shore up Hart's arguments against the moralist assault, others introduced important adaptations to Hart's ideas. The ensuing debate among soft/inclusive and hard/exclusive positivists was over the precise extent to which law had to be identifiable without reference to contested moral reasoning. The soft positivists, staying closer to Hart, were content to state that law's identity is not necessarily defined by morality and, therefore, can incorporate reference to moral standards. On the other hand, the hard positivists insisted that law must necessarily be defined without reference to morality and therefore by resort to social sources alone.[19] Over the years, the hard positivists have begun to gain the upper hand and to stake out a more authentically positivist position in contrast to the moralists.

The whole debate around the *separation thesis* (or, as Austin termed it, between law's existence and its merit or demerit) has become highly stylized and abstruse. Although the debate has illuminated much about law's identity as a distinctive mode of social regulation, it has also obscured and hindered a better understanding of the role and nature of law in modern political systems. Whereas the critical claims of legal positivism are either revealed to be one more partial and value-based normative account of law or so trivial and qualified as to be of no theoretical weight, the moralists' claims introduce an evaluative moral dimension to jurisprudential debate, but only to contain the subversive implications of that powerful insight, especially from a democratic standpoint. As such, both analytical interventions run into severe trouble in trying to map a

---

[18] R. DWORKIN, LAW'S EMPIRE 255, 52, 152 and 110 (1986). *See also* L. FULLER, THE MORALITY OF LAW (1969); J. FINNIS, NATURAL LAW AND NATURAL RIGHTS (1980); and N.E. SIMMONDS, LAW AS A MORAL IDEA (2007). I term this group *moralists* as it better captures the main thrust of their analytical stance and in order to distinguish them from the 'naturalist' purveyors of a more scientific brand of positivism. *See infra* ch.5.

[19] Compare J. COLEMAN, THE PRACTICE OF PRINCIPLE: IN DEFENCE OF A PRAGMATIST APPROACH TO LEGAL THEORY 179–98 (2001) with J. RAZ, AUTHORITY OF LAW 105 (1979). For a sound survey and distinction, see MARK MURPHY, PHILOSOPHY OF LAW: THE FUNDAMENTALS 14–45 (2007).

convincing and universal theoretical relation between law's validity and its moral legitimacy. Again, the connecting thread of my critique will be that there is no escape in jurisprudential analysis, whether from a positivist or moralist position, from the contested world of ideological disputation.

(3) A Methodological Shift

Although debate around the *conceptual approach* and the *separation thesis* remains heated, the focus of much critical attention has shifted to a different and more theoretical level. With the posthumous publication of Hart's *Postscript* in the second edition of his *Concept of Law* in 1993, the debate began to take a distinctly methodological turn. The scene of engagement moved from a first-order skirmish about whether law could be said to exist without the need to engage in difficult moral evaluations to the second-order issue of whether that first-order question can be answered in a way that does not itself necessitate resort to some moral standpoint. Hart affirmed his soft position that it was possible to detach questions about law's validity from its immorality and, at the same time, to insist that "a criterion of validity may be in part a moral test." Yet, it was Hart's pithy summation of his position that triggered off a change in the line of critical engagement: He concluded that his account of law's nature was meant to be "*descriptive* in that it is morally neutral and has no justificatory aims; it does not seek to justify or commend on moral or other grounds the forms and structures which appear in my account of law."[20] If anything, the intensity of debate heightened as the theoretical stakes became more fundamental.

The ensuing methodological or metatheoretical encounter shook up the whole jurisprudential debate and jurists began to align themselves along very different axes. Some jurists took the relatively radical step of staying with a strictly positivist account of law, but did so on openly normative grounds. Although they conceded that the separation thesis rests on some substantive commitments, they also maintained that those commitments are themselves non-political and can be defended in general and non-ideological terms. For instance, Leslie Green conceded that "legal theory is value-laden" in that any account of law "can have no

---

[20] Hart, *supra*, note 10 at 253 and 240. For a more complete account of this methodological turn, *see* JOHN OBERDIEK and DENNIS PATTERSON, *Moral Evaluation and Conceptual Analysis in Jurisprudential Methodology* in CURRENT LEGAL ISSUES: LAW AND PHILOSOPHY (Ross Harrison ed. 2007).

deeper ground than the complex set of interests and purposes to which legal theory responds," but he was equally insistent that this does not render legal theory "purely ideological" or completely reducible to those interests and purposes.[21] Still others have gone so far as to offer a defense of legal positivism as a full-blown ethical theory.[22] This whole methodological confrontation has set the pragmatic cat among the epistemological pigeons.

In light of this methodological turn, jurists are required to defend not only their theoretical claims about *what law is*, but also the deeper epistemological status of those theoretical claims. Indeed, once relatively isolated from broader philosophical currents, analytical jurisprudence has now had to move out into the open and account for itself in more fundamental terms. It is not simply a particular take on the analytical project that must be justified, but the whole enterprise of analytical jurisprudence. This entails addressing and refuting the pragmatic challenge of whether it is ever possible, let alone useful, to participate or intervene in the jurisprudential debate about explanatory theories of law without being implicated in or taking a stand on contested values of a social, moral, or political character. At its sharpest, the issue is whether the whole enterprise of analytical jurisprudence is built on the insecure footings of evaluative sand rather than on the solid foundations of descriptive rock. If the former, then the project is in genuine theoretical peril as any analytical contribution has no greater validity or cogency than the extent to which those values are shared or uncontested among the jurisprudential community. In other words, legal theorizing becomes less an exercise in detached reflection and more an episode in purposive advocacy.

---

[21]   Green, *The Political Content of Legal Theory*, 17 PHIL. OF SOC. SCIS. 1 at 15 and 16 (1987). The reference to 'essentially contested' is from W.B. GALLIE, PHILOSOPHY AND THE HISTORICAL UNDERSTANDING 157–91 (1964). *See also, for example*, John Gardner, *Legal Positivism: 5½ Myths*, 46 AM. J. OF JURIS. 222 (2000); Stephen Perry, *Hart's Methodological Positivism* in HART'S POSTSCRIPT 311 (J. Coleman ed. 2001) and Jeremy Waldron, *Normative (or Ethical) Positivism* in HART'S POSTSCRIPT 420 (J. Coleman ed. 2001). For a rejection of these claims, see Andrei Marmor, *Legal Positivism: Still Descriptive and Morally Neutral*, 26 OXF. J. OF LEGAL STUDIES 683 (2006).

[22]   *See, for example*, T. CAMPBELL, THE LEGAL THEORY OF ETHICAL POSITIVISM 84 (1996). For a characteristically early intervention along these lines, see Neil MacCormick, *A Moralistic Case for A-moralistic Law*, 20 VALPARAISO L. REV. 1 (1985). *See also* David Dyzenhaus, *The Genealogy of Legal Positivism*, 24 OXF J. OF LEGAL STUDIES 39 (2004).

(4) A Powerful Omission

Although enormous attention remains focused on the jurisprudential project outlined in *The Province*, there is an important aspect of Austin's work that remains relatively overlooked and even ignored. Whatever the shortcomings of his law-as-command theory, it did point up and give a central role to the insight that law is about the exercise of power and authority. He saw that "laws and other commands are said to proceed from *superiors* and to bind or oblige *inferiors*" and that "the term *superiority* implies *might*: the power of affecting others with evil or pain, and of forcing them, through fear of that evil, to fashion their conduct."[23] Although Austin's explanation of sovereign force was much too crude and one-dimensional, it did grasp the extent to which coercion and violence are insistent parts of law's regular operation and claim to authority. In short, he recognized that law was fundamentally about the allocation and legitimization of power in the state's effort's to control and discipline people in accordance with a particular vision of right conduct. Later generations of analytical jurists have tended to downplay this feature to their own and analytical jurisprudence's detriment.

For instance, although Hart clearly appreciated the more nuanced and diverse ways in which systems of rules functioned as channels and frameworks for directing social life, he evinced a distinct tendency to elide some difficult issues about how power functions and legitimates itself through law. He was content to observe rather cursorily that "so long as human beings can gain sufficient cooperation from some to enable them to dominate others, they will use the forms of law as one of their instruments."[24] Consequently, although Hart's union of primary and secondary rules has a definite edge over Austin's law-as-command in offering a better explanation of law's essential nature (at least in modern twentieth-century industrial states), he might well have achieved this success at the considerable cost of marginalizing and understating law's role as a coercive implement of state policy. Moreover, in depoliticizing law in this way, Hart and other analytical jurists have managed to ignore the extent and manner to which law contributes to maintaining

---

[23] Austin, *supra*, note 1 at 24.

[24] Hart, *supra*, note 10 at 210. One contemporary theorist who has recognized the central role of public coercion in any account of law is Ronald Dworkin, who acknowledges that law's purpose is to constrain state coercion. *See* DWORKIN, *supra*, note 18 at 96. For a more general discussion, see *infra* ch.6.

hierarchical, patriarchal, racist, or other disciplinary and discriminatory regimes.

This neglect of law's role in establishing and sustaining society's relations of power represents a major failing in the analytical canon. If Austin placed too much emphasis on the part that coercion and force play in law's performance and gave insufficient weight to law's more subtle wiles, modern legal theorists have significantly understated the extent to which law functions as an official medium for ordering society and its power relations and, where demanded, utilizing violence to enforce its designs. However, this should come as no surprise as analytical jurists claim to be dealing in abstract and ahistorical matters: the analytical method is prized because of, not in spite of its capacity to keep its hands clean. Instead, a non-analytical approach will ensure that it incorporates inquiries into not only how law works as a coercive (*i.e.*, power over) and enabling (*i.e.*, power to) force in actual historical and social circumstances, but also how law functions as a constitutive network in which social relations and political values are nurtured and legitimated. In any democratic transformation of legal theory, there will need to be an appreciation of the role that both positivist and moralist accounts of law fulfill in helping to preserve the established and elite values of legal politics and to thwart its emancipatory possibilities.

Conclusion

Over 175 years after Austin's *The Province* was first published and received a distinctly cool reception, its influence on contemporary jurisprudence has grown to become warm and strong. However, when understood as part of a political tradition as much as a mode of philosophical inquiry, the democratic credentials of analytical jurisprudence remain highly suspect. Consequently, it is the burden of this book to examine whether not only Austin's imperative theory of law, but also analytical jurisprudence more generally, can address various democratic concerns and still remain true to its analytical commitments. My blunt response, of course, is *no*. Although modern jurists have improved considerably on Austin's efforts, their analytical efforts are fatally flawed: The philosophical wrapping may now be more sophisticated, but the substantial contents of the analytical package remain thoroughly defective. The project of analytical jurisprudence falls foul of the democratic critique and fails to deliver on the analytical jurists' own promise to offer a politically neutral account of law and legal systems. In short, analytical jurists have simply shifted the jurisprudential pivot from sovereign rulers to bureaucratic officials. In doing so, both positivists and moralists have continued to give theoretical reinforcement to the historical barriers to the establishment and operation of a strong democratic polity.

CHAPTER THREE

The Provinciality of Jurisprudence Determined

Whatever the uses certain features of {international} law . . . may or may not sometimes have in ordering relations between states, they are, those features, neither lowest common denominators of the world's catalogue of legal outlooks nor universal premises underlying all of them, but projections of aspects of our own onto the world stage. This as such is no bad thing (better, by my local lights, Jeffersonian notions of rights than Leninist ones), except perhaps as it leads us to imagine there is more commonality of mind in the world than there is or to mistake convergence of vocabularies for convergence of views.

—Clifford Geertz

By and large, most lawyers and citizens manage to negotiate their daily lives with little anxiety about what law is; They know what courts are, what the rules for driving are, and how to buy and sell goods. However, although they can offer countless examples of law, they experience grave difficulty in offering a plausible account of *what law is* more generally. This is the point at which legal theorists are supposed to have something to offer: They are thought to be able to explain the general nature of law and its distinguishing features as a special mode of social regulation. Although many legal theorists have abandoned this largely philosophical pursuit for more welcoming and promising interdisciplinary pastures, analytical jurists have simply redoubled their efforts to continue, if not complete, the apparently Sisyphean task of offering a theoretical sound and cogent account of law's essential nature and structure. As such, analytical jurisprudence considers itself to be a strict discipline that seeks to cut through the contingent clutter of different examples of law and come up with a broad account of law that makes sense of its myriad instances and practices across time and geography.[1]

---

[1] For a critical survey of efforts to offer a convincing definition of law, *see* IAIN STEWART, *The Uses of Law*, 8 CURR. LEGAL PROBS. 259 (2005) and THURMAN W. ARNOLD, THE SYMBOLS OF GOVERNMENT 367 (1935).

Yet, after much time and effort, there remains not only strong disagreement among analytical jurists about *what law is*, but also considerable controversy over the best or most appropriate technique by which to go about answering that central puzzle.

In this chapter, I want to examine the nature and performance of the most favored mode of philosophical inquiry, namely, *conceptual analysis*. My critique is quite straightforward and direct—that analytical jurisprudence's practice of conceptual analysis, despite its trumpeted claims to the contrary, is not neutral between different political systems of governance. Put bluntly, its account of law might easily capture the operation of authoritarian regimes and some industrialized modern states (*e.g.*, the United Kingdom and the United States), but it fails to accommodate some other kinds of governmental arrangements. In particular, it does not lend itself to be applied to strongly democratic modes of governance and, on occasion, places considerable obstacles in the way of their development. Consequently, contrary to their most cherished contentions, analytical jurists must defend the partial thrust of their analytical jurisprudence in directly and substantively normative terms. Divested of its universalistic claims, analytical jurisprudence becomes exactly the kind of politicized theory that it claims to reject and from which it strives to distinguish itself. So understood, it becomes one more normative effort at passing off political preferences as descriptive truths; it is a strategic mode of political engagement passed off as a philosophical insight of universal significance. In short, analytical jurisprudence's reliance on conceptual analysis is provincial, not universal.

Analyze This

Even Oliver Wendell Holmes, Jr. might have been surprised by how seriously modern legal theorists have taken his advice that "the first call of a theory of law is that it should fit the facts."[2] For analytical jurists, the primary task of jurisprudence is to provide an understanding of law's factual existence which is both universal (*i.e.*, it transcends any particular or local practices) and general (*i.e.*, it encompasses and informs all other inquiries into law). They have committed themselves to maintaining an uncluttered, clear-sighted and hard-headed approach to law in order to deliver a defensible and convincing account of its basic nature and structure as a universal phenomenon.

---

[2] O.W. HOLMES JR., THE COMMON LAW 167 (1881).

Indeed, for some legal theorists, this philosophical undertaking is the exclusive task of analytical jurisprudence.

As expected, John Austin set the analytical tone when he insisted that, because a proper science of jurisprudence must take law seriously on its own terms and elucidate its essential features from within, "the proper subject of General or Universal Jurisprudence . . . is a description of such subjects and ends of Law as are common to all systems." Although he conceded that "the determination of the province of jurisprudence . . . is not a perfectly complete and perfectly exact determination,"[3] he sought to offer a scientific account of law that would be able to claim more than parochial validity as an adequate account of English law or similar legal systems. His analytic ambition was to provide an empirical account of those institutions and regularities that were considered to comprise law throughout history and across societies. In his efforts to fit the facts, Austin's externalized and ethnographic view of the analytical task seemed to mesh relatively smoothly with his own ultimate understanding of law as a set of commands by omnipotent sovereigns to their obedient subjects. However, as the weaknesses of Austin's command theory became more apparent, his historical-empirical approach was also recognized to be inadequate to the analytical task. In particular, with a widespread recognition of Hart's insight that the incorporation of citizens and officials' internal attitudes towards law was essential to any improved and complete understanding of it, the need for a less empirical and more conceptual approach to the analytical project recommended itself.[4]

Accordingly, a more conceptual approach to the study of law and legal systems has become the favored *modus operandi* for those jurists of an analytical bent. This comprises a distinctly philosophical orientation that emphasizes the virtues of a clear and precise procedure with particular weight being placed upon theoretical argumentation, objective evidence, terminological clarity, logical consistency, systemic coherence, and ahistorical orientation; it does not engage in empirical research or ethnographic study. However, because law as a social practice is not like a physical object, it demands a different style of conceptual analysis that takes into account the social actors' self-understanding about what it is that they are doing. The basic analytical move is fairly standard—that of taking a set of legal commonplaces as social

---

[3] JOHN AUSTIN, THE PROVINCE OF JURISPRUDENCE DETERMINED 373 and 354 (1832: H.L.A. Hart ed. 1955).

[4] *See* H.L.A. HART, THE CONCEPT OF LAW 81 (1963: 2nd ed. 1994). The general Hartian approach to analytical jurisprudence is developed later in the chapter. *See infra* pp. 45–49 (this ms. Ch.)

givens and extracting from them those underlying patterns and essential structures which provide an adequate and true explanation of their identity and existence as law. A simple and comprehensive theory is considered preferable to a more complex and conditional account. At its most philosophically rigorous, it demands that, while other disciplines deal "with the contingent and with the particular, [legal philosophy deals] with the necessary and universal."[5]

This conceptual analysis is not exclusively semantic or empirical in orientation. It is intended to filter out unnecessary and peripheral features in order to offer a systematic and, therefore, objectively authoritative account of law's character as a separate disciplinary and practical category. As such, the analytical approach is resolutely philosophical in seeking to "retrieve, determine, or capture the content of a concept in the hope that by doing so, we will learn something interesting, important, or essential about the nature of the thing the concept denotes."[6] Interested in more than simply clarifying the use of the word *law* among its users or replicating the social actors' self-understanding, There is a critical dimension to the analytical function; conceptual analysis is not simply about drawing up a laundry list of law's characteristics. It aims to unpack and disaggregate a complex jumble of social facts so as to isolate and understand better those salient and important features that fix the phenomena as peculiarly legal in nature and identity. At its most uncompromising, therefore, the analytical method turns the most important issues of jurisprudence and law into epistemological puzzles—What is it to have true knowledge of law?—to be solved by resort to an unflinching application of the analytical technique of conceptual inquiry.[7]

The conceptual enterprise of analytical jurisprudence comes in many shapes and colors. Its main proponents remain the positivists who seek to draw a strong distinction between description and evaluation; the analytical study of law must eschew moral judgments and be relentlessly descriptive if it is to remain true to its analytical ambitions. Most famously, H. L. A. Hart

---

[5] J. RAZ, AUTHORITY OF LAW 105 (1979).

[6] J. COLEMAN, THE PRACTICE OF PRINCIPLE: IN DEFENCE OF A PRAGMATIST APPROACH TO LEGAL THEORY 197 (2001). *See also* F. JACKSON, FROM METAPHYSICS TO ETHICS: A DEFENSE OF CONCEPTUAL ANALYSIS (1998); B. BIX, JURISPRUDENCE: THEORY AND CONTEXT (3rd ed. 2004); and MARK MURPHY, PHILOSOPHY OF LAW: THE FUNDAMENTALS 3–4 (2007).

[7] *See* JULIE DICKSON, EVALUATION AND LEGAL THEORY 17–19 (2001). As she puts it, a successful theory of law "tell us truths which illuminate that which is most important about and characteristic of" law. *Id.* at 25.

offered "an essay in analytical jurisprudence . . . [and] descriptive sociology" which was intended to provide "an improved analysis of the distinctive structure of a municipal legal system and a better understanding of the resemblances and differences between law, coercion, and morality, as types of social phenomena." In so doing, he presented an account of law that was not simply intended to be a conceptual unpacking of any one legal system (*e.g.*, the British model), but a "clarification of the general framework of legal thought."[8] In short, Hart continued to subscribe to Austin's broader universalist ambitions, but employed a different set of analytical tools to achieve that.

Although analytical jurisprudence is often equated exclusively with legal positivism, there is also a moralist strain of analytical jurisprudence that builds on it as it transforms the positivist approach. It is analytical in focus and foundations, but non-positivist in operation and outcome. For positivists, it is vital to distinguish conceptual analysis from normative inquiry; theirs is purported to be a descriptive and general account of the concept of law that identifies those elements and characteristics of law that frame law's contingent historical and institutional manifestations. In contrast, moralists tend to offer a normative account of law which claims to explain how law's practices and institutional arrangements can be developed so as to offer an ethically defensible system of law. However, such moralists claim to work with the social, if morally imbued facts of law. Whereas positivists are content to be rigorous and exacting in their formal analysis, moralists insist that this preliminary quest must be supplemented by a much more expansive and substantive moral analysis. It is not that positivists deny that there is any role for a justificatory or prescriptive theory of law; it is simply that they insist that such an undertaking is not the appropriate domain for the jurist *as jurist*. As Austin notoriously stated, "the *science of jurisprudence* (or, simply and briefly, *jurisprudence*) is concerned with positive laws, or with laws strictly so called, as considered without regard to their goodness or badness."[9]

For instance, for all Ronald Dworkin's rejection of the positivist tradition and its controlling distinction between description and evaluation, he grounds his own interpretivist account of law and adjudication within a very definite analytical framework. Indeed, Dworkin is very much a part of the analytical

---

[8] Hart, *supra*, note 4 at v, 17, and v. *See also* H.L.A. HART, *Legal Positivism* in ENCYCLOPAEDIA OF PHILOSOPHY IV, 418 (1967). On different kinds of conceptual analysis, *see* John Oberdiek and Dennis Patterson, *Moral Evaluation and Conceptual Analysis in Jurisprudential Methodology* in CURRENT LEGAL PROBLEMS: LAW AND PHILOSOPHY 16–20 (Ross Harrison ed. 2007).

[9] Austin, *supra*, note 3 at 126.

tradition in his assumption that law is understandable in and on its own exclusive terms. Although he insists that law is suffused with an indispensable moral dimension, Dworkin makes the same basic analytical move by viewing his and other lawyers' responsibility to consist of taking "the brute facts of legal history" or "the raw behavioural data of [legal] practice" and offering "the best justification of legal practice as a whole" so as to be able to identify the "circumstances in which particular propositions of law should be taken to be sound or true." Moreover, although he concedes that such interpretive practices will implicate moral evaluations and, therefore, be controversial among lawyers, he maintains that "we have no difficulty in identifying collectively the practices that count as legal practices in our own culture" and that they are "treated as given in day-to-day reflection and argument." Indeed, he goes so far as to claim that "law cannot flourish as an interpretive enterprise in any community unless there is enough initial agreement about what practices are legal practices so that lawyers argue about the best interpretation of roughly the same data."[10] Accordingly, by insisting that his philosophical analysis is not "conceptual, neutral and disengaged, . . . [but] normative, engaged and conceptual,"[11] Dworkin is very much part of the same philosophical tradition in that, like his positivist cousins, he is working with the given practices and social facts of law in order to advance the epistemological project of analytical jurisprudence.

Of course, Austin's particular rendering of his own theory of law-as-command did not live up to the universalist ambitions of his more general analytical project. Indeed, Austin made a rather half-hearted job of his self-imposed analytical task. He restricted his scholarly attention to the legal systems of only a limited number of nations on the imperialistic basis that it was only realistic "to become acquainted, even imperfectly" with a few jurisdictions and that "from these, however, the rest may be presumed."[12] Nevertheless, the crucial question is less whether Austin's own account lives up the analytical agenda he set for it and more whether the analytical project is itself beyond

---

10   R. DWORKIN, LAW'S EMPIRE 255, 52, 152, 110 91, 66, and 90. Dworkin actually references J. RAZ, THE CONCEPT OF A LEGAL SYSTEM (2nd ed. 1980) on this point. However, although he does suggest that his approach would be applicable to all similar systems, he does not claim that his theory speaks to all legal systems; he is content with "defending an interpretation of our own political culture, not an abstract and timeless political morality." Dworkin, *id.* at 216. For a fuller discussion and clarification of Dworkin's analytical attachment, see *infra*, ch.6.

11   R. DWORKIN, JUSTICES IN ROBES 155 (2006).

12   Austin, *supra*, note 3 at 373. See *supra*, ch.2.

rescue or redemption. Before making that important assessment, it is necessary to look in more detail at the most fabled version of analytical jurisprudence—Hart's *The Concept of Law*. Although Hart does produce a more sophisticated and expansive analysis than Austin did, it still remains far too beholden to one particular and parochial version of law, namely, that of a modern Western liberal state. Its applicability to other political arrangements, especially more strongly democratic modes of law and governance, is problematic.

An Essay in Descriptive Sociology?

Almost exactly a century after Austin's death, Hart set about bringing English-speaking jurisprudence out of its intellectual doldrums. First published in 1961, *The Concept of Law* took direct aim at Austin's simplistic model of law as coercive orders and made a fresh stab at fulfilling the analytical mandate. Hart sought "to further the understanding of law, coercion, and morality as different but related social phenomena" and did so by offering a theory of "analytical jurisprudence . . . concerned with the clarification of the general framework of legal thought rather than with the criticism of law or legal policy." For Hart, law is not the hallmark of a more advanced or just society, and coercion is not its primary identifying feature; law is simply one institutional means through which a complex society copes with the need to supplement and augment the more direct forms of social order. Hart was adamant that the Austinian "model of orders backed by threats obscures more of law than it reveals." In particular, he considered that Austin's efforts to explain how his notion of sovereign power applied in a democracy had "no plausibility" because this would be tantamount to saying that "the 'bulk' of society habitually obeys its .f:" Austin's model only applied to "the simplest form of society in whic'. [there] was an absolute monarch."[13]

However, although Hart announced that there was "need for a fresh start," he uses this democratic deficiency in Austin's contribution as a springboard to developing his own "key to the science of jurisprudence"[14]—a sophisticated and unified system of rules in which there was a union of obligation-imposing

---

13   Hart, *supra*, note 4 at v, v, 49, 75, 75, and 75. It is far from clear why the idea of "society obeying itself" is so self-evidently implausible and why it differs significantly from the idea of *self-government*. See *infra*, ch.8.

14   *Id.* at 80 and 81. For an excellent account of how the older and newer versions of analytical jurisprudence differ, *see* ANTHONY SEBOK, ANALYTICAL JURISPRUDENCE IN AMERICAN JURISPRUDENCE 20–47 (1998).

primary rules that comprise the bulk of substantive legal doctrine, like criminal and contract law, and the authority-conferring *secondary* rules that distribute institutional power and jurisdiction, between legislatures and courts, for example, over the creation and enforcement of the primary rules.

What tied all this together was Hart's positivistic insistence that law and morality must be kept separate as a matter of conceptual necessity rather than empirical contingency. Although he accepts that there are profound and various connections between law and morality, Hart insists that there is no mandate for the notion that "the criteria of legal validity of particular laws used in a legal system must include, tacitly if not explicitly, a reference to morality or justice:" "it is in no sense a necessary truth that laws reproduce or satisfy certain demands of morality, though in fact they have often done so." Indeed, in the posthumously published *Postscript* to *The Concept of Law*, Hart confirmed that his account of law's nature was meant to be "*descriptive* in that it is morally neutral and has no justificatory aims; it does not seek to justify or commend on moral or other grounds the forms and structures which appear in my account of law." Consequently, abandoning Austin's imperative theory, but remaining squarely within its analytical guidelines, Hart offered his "essay in analytical jurisprudence . . . [and] descriptive sociology" as being adequate to explain the concept of law in "the modern state."[15] However, although Hart's celebrated work has obvious initial and widespread appeal, the devil is definitely in the details as far as any democratic evaluation is concerned.

There are two important and central dimensions of Hart's theory that are of particular concern to the democrat—the *internal attitude* and the *rule of recognition*. For Hart, law's authority is based on the convergence of behavior and attitude of both those subject to law and those who administer law; he supplements an exclusively empirical analysis with a hermeneutic dimension. In each case, validity depends upon the conventions of actual social practice rather than the quality of argument relied upon to justify that practice. Not surprisingly, Hart holds that, in line with the separation thesis, there is no requirement that people or officials feel any moral compulsion to obey the law. However, it will often be the case that such a moral imperative will exist in following particular rules or in regard to the system of laws generally. Determining that *obedience* is insufficient to explain why people follow rules, Hart supplements the existence of patterns of regular behavior with *a*

---

[15]   *Id.* at 185, 185–86, 240, v, and 60. For a more thorough critique of the law/morality separation thesis, see *infra* ch.4.

critical reflective attitude whereby rules are accepted as "common standards" which operate as the basis for "criticism (including self-criticism), demands for conformity, and in acknowledgments that such criticism and demands are justified." For participants in the system, therefore, primary rules operate "as the basis for claims, demands, admissions, criticism, or punishment" and "the violation of a rule is not merely a basis for the prediction that a hostile reaction will follow but as *reason* for hostility."[16] Hart insists that, without reference to this internal attitude that lawyers and citizens exhibit toward rules, a vital element of jurisprudential understanding would be lost. In the Hartian scheme of things, therefore, a cogent explanation of legal obligation is as much about attitude and acceptance as it is about fate and fiat.

Nevertheless, although primary rules might be enough for a primitive society, Hart insists that they need to be supplemented in more mature societies by a set of secondary rules; these will establish procedures and institutions through which to identify, apply, and change the primary rules. Indeed, Hart goes so far as to observe that the development of secondary rules was "a step forward as important to society as the invention of the wheel." Of these secondary rules, the rule of recognition is the most important as it allows for the "conclusive identification of the primary rules" and, as such, works as the ultimate source of legal validity. Hart accepts that the rule of recognition will not be entirely value- or moral-free. Although the rule of recognition's acceptance as "a matter of fact" is crucial to the existence and operation of the legal system, he concedes that it is likely to be hedged by a number of contingent moral and other considerations. For instance, the rule of recognition will rarely be explicitly stated, it "may be in part a moral test," and its meaning may be controversial, although not "in all or most cases." Accordingly, for Hart, "the union of primary and secondary rules is at the centre of the legal system" and their interactive existence is able to account for the necessary features of any functioning and mature system of governance.[17]

Hart's account and defense of his concept of law has become the gold standard by which other analytical efforts are to be assessed. Yet, whatever else it might be, Hart's jurisprudence is hardly "an essay in descriptive sociology." Like Austin, his efforts to survey the range of legal systems across history and societies are casual and impressionistic at best; he remains safe in his

---

[16]   *Id.* at 57 and 90.

[17]   *Id.* at 42, 95, 110, 253, 251, and 99. It is worth noting that Hart does state, if only later to forget, that the union of primary and secondary rules "may be justly regarded as the 'essence' of law, though they may not always be found together wherever the word *law* is correctly used." *Id.* at 155.

study and deep in thought, not out in the field and deep in data. Even if the jurisdictional focus of Hart's putative sociological inquiry was limited to modern Western societies, like the United Kingdom and the United States, there is much factual imprecision and obscurity to Hart's account—who counts as an *official*? How much acceptance of rules is enough? What of corrupt officials? Indeed, the union of primary and secondary rules can be applied quite easily to a variety of non-state institutions (*e.g.*, universities, corporations, clubs, trade associations) and social practices (*e.g.*, commercial customs, religious rituals, sporting norms); this tends to undermine any claim that the union of primary and secondary rules is *the* distinguishing feature of law. Accordingly, Hart's recommendation that he is offering "an essay in descriptive sociology" seems to be misplaced and inauthentic. As such, any serious assessment of *The Concept of Law* must be a decidedly philosophical affair.[18]

Nevertheless, for all its continuing celebrity and preeminent status, Hart's philosophical efforts to provide a universal account of law that "is not tied to any particular legal system or legal culture, but seeks to give an explanatory and clarifying account of law as a complex social and political institution" are equally unconvincing.[19] Like Hart himself, *The Concept of Law* is very much a product of an industrialized mid twentieth-century society. His preferred concept of law is parochial and provincial in scope and application; it offers an analysis of one relatively contingent mode of legal ordering (*i.e.*, a modern industrial state) and then claims that it is capable of capturing the essential qualities of law in all societies at almost all times (*i.e.*, aboriginal, theological, commercial, customary). In particular, there are two major philosophical objections that I wish to raise against Hart. First, despite his claim to offer a neutral account of a legal system which is applicable across a range of political systems and moral commitments, the union of primary and secondary rules contains certain built-in partialities and favors some political schemes of governance over others. And, second, the Hartian concept of law continues

---

[18] For a comprehensive and compelling survey of these sociological challenges, *see* B. Tamanaha, A General Jurisprudence of Law and Society (2001). Despite his misleading reference to *descriptive sociology*, Hart remained resolutely philosophical and increasingly conceptual in his work. Although he conceded that other disciplines could make an important contribution to understanding law, he did not think that they were engaged in legal theory. *See* H.L.A. Hart, *Analytical Jurisprudence in Mid-Twentieth Century: A Reply to Professor Bodenheimer*, 105 U. Penn. L. Rev. 953 (1957); Leonie Starr, Julius Stone: An Intellectual Life 162 (1992); and Nicola Lacey, *Analytical Jurisprudence versus Descriptive Sociology Revisited*, 84 Texas L. Rev. 945 (2006).

[19] Hart, *supra*, note 4 at 239.

Austin's undemocratic legacy by conferring power and legitimacy on a particular elite and placing institutional impediments in the path of any shift towards stronger democratic governance.

A Preference for Order

Although Hart is far from thorough or detailed in explicating his account of law's essential nature, it is clear that the idea of *ruledness* or *regularity* is at its analytical heart. Hart offers his union of primary and secondary rules as an important institutional device to facilitate the establishment and maintenance of an ordered and stable society. It is the express role of the system's secondary rules to supplement the primary rules by introducing institutional elements of certainty (*i.e.*, what the rules are), predictability (*i.e.*, how rules change) and efficiency (*i.e.*, what the rules mean); this will ensure and enhance the orderliness and stability of the legal system. In this way, Hart envisages the legal system as a (or perhaps *the*) major "method of social control" whereby "general standards of conduct [are] communicated to classes of persons, who are then expected to understand and conform to the rules without further official direction." In order for the law to function effectively, he also stipulates that the rules "must be intelligible and within the capacity of most to obey, and in general they must not be retrospective, though exceptionally they may be."[20] Understood collectively, therefore, an essential feature of Hart's concept of law and legal systems is that it will work to steady the ship of state as it sails through the stormy seas of political history.

Of course, Hart's is not the only conceptual account of law on offer in the analytical fold. For instance, Joseph Raz has garnered considerable support for his own different account of law which also emphasizes that people should be able to obey law and be guided by its directions. The primary feature of Raz's theory of law is that the law claims legitimate and efficacious authority over people who treat it as possessing some degree of priority over other competing authorities. Although this authority must be efficacious in that it actually guides people's actions, it need only manifest itself in the society's

---

[20] *Id*. at 207. As the good positivist, Hart goes on to say that compliance with these criteria remains "unfortunately compatible with very great iniquity." *Id*. However, he is unclear about what precise extent of people's knowledge about the extant rules is required: "the reality of the situation is that a great proportion of ordinary citizens—perhaps a majority—have no general conception of the legal structure or of its criteria of validity." *Id*. at 114.

institutions that purport to claim authority. For Raz, therefore, law comprises a set of standards that guide action and a series of institutional mechanisms, like openness and independent judiciary, which safeguard the efficacy of these action-guiding standards. So presented, the rationale for this analytical notion of law as authoritative guidance is to facilitate "a culture created over time, and evolving very slowly" and to mitigate against the "violent swings and panic measures" of legislatures.[21] Like Hart, therefore, the themes of orderliness and stability are front and center: Tradition and dependability are the universal hallmarks of law and legal systems.

Mindful that Hart and Raz are offering an analytical account of law which is intended to be morally neutral and politically impartial, there is much here that smacks of a certain normative bias. Although there may be widespread agreement that one function of a legal system is to provide a dependable and solid context within which people can go about their lives, it is mistaken to maintain that such stability is a politically neutral commitment. This partiality is most clearly glimpsed and reinforced in Hart's *The Concept of Law* in his discussion of the historical shift from primitive to mature societies. Although Hart recognizes that there are many societies that manage with only primary rules, he insists that they are "primitive" in legal terms and only "mature" when they develop a series of secondary rules to supplement the primary rules; a society is primitive because of its "lack of a legislature, courts with compulsory jurisdiction, and centrally organized sanctions."

There is much here that hints strongly about law as a civilizing force and that exhibits a preference for structured formality and ordered change over informal arrangements and organic variation.[22] Behind the analytical jurists' familiar model of institutional reliability and systemic maturity, there stands a definite and partial vision of social life—that there is one desirable set of social arrangements, that such arrangements require institutional entrenchment,

---

[21] JOSEPH RAZ, ETHICS IN THE PUBLIC DOMAIN: ESSAYS IN THE MORALITY OF LAW AND POLITICS 359–60 (1994). The most comprehensive account of Raz's analytical contribution is still to be found in Raz, AUTHORITY, *supra*, note 5. For further and more detailed critiques of Raz along democratic lines, see *infra*, ch.4 and SCOTT HERSHOVITZ, *Legitimacy, Democracy, and Razian Authority*, 9 LEGAL THEORY 201 (2003).

[22] Hart, *supra*, note 4 at 156. This whole distinction between immature and mature legal systems is fraught with normative significance and smacks of a lingering colonial mentality. *See* H. MAINE, ANCIENT LAW: ITS CONNECTION WITH THE EARLY HISTORY OF SOCIETY AND ITS RELATION TO MODERN IDEAS (1861); P. FITZPATRICK, THE MYTHOLOGY OF MODERN LAW 192–97 (1992); and R. COTTERRELL, THE POLITICS OF JURISPRUDENCE (1989).

that people fear significant and unchecked change, and that people crave predictability in their social relations above all other values. However, there is nothing neutral about such a constrained projection of institutional format or the deep structure of social life. By privileging such supposed virtues of regularity and orderliness, Hart's conceptual analysis introduces a distinctly controversial component to his account of law. There is a built-in bias about what is the most preferable form of social organization, about what kind of changes are permissible, and about the kind of lives people desire; it entirely favours establishment and a first-order skirmish about whether law could be said to exist without the need to engage in difficult moral evaluations. The second-order issue is whether that first-order question can be answered in a way that does not itself necessitate resort to some moral standpoint *status quo*.[23] As such, Hart's definitive concept of law as the union of primary and secondary rules is as much a political intervention in jurisprudential study as a technical exercise in conceptual analysis. *The Concept of Law* takes a partial and contested stand on what a good legal system is and, by favoring one particular vision of social life, helps to foreclose the realization of other competing possibilities. In short, Hart passes off one set of particular preferences as universal insight.

This intrinsic political partiality can be illustrated by contrasting these analytical recommendations with Roberto Unger's proposals for a *radicalized pragmatism*. This is the very antithesis of Hart and Raz's account of the modern liberal state. Working to loosen the hold of entrenched interests and social hierarchies, Unger champions a mode of social engagement that allows for a closing of the gap between habitual moves within existing social routines and revolutionary moves that remake that world. This will require institutional arrangements to be designed to maximize the opportunities for transformative politics so that innovation, not repetition, becomes the preferred political practice. As such, Unger challenges and highlights the problem of the very idea of stability and predictability, with its entrenched preference for slow and limited change, as the most prized and privileged features of legal systems. Indeed, emphasizing the merit and appeal of destabilizing and experimental interventions, he goes so far as to recommend that it might be desirable for specific institutions or segments of society to be able to "opt out of some part of the established rules of law, and to try other rules out."[24]

---

[23] For further development of this conservative bias, see *infra*, ch.7.

[24] ROBERTO MANGABEIRA UNGER, THE SELF AWAKENED: PRAGMATISM UNBOUND 188 (2007). *See also* ROBERTO MANGABEIRA UNGER, DEMOCRACY REALIZED: THE PROGRESSIVE ALTERNATIVE (1998). For the purposes of my present argument, the appeal

Although this form of politics may be considered unattractive and dystopian to some, the salient fact is that it offers a sharp contrast to Hart and Raz's supposedly neutral account of law's role in modern society. It subverts any claim that analytical jurists might have that they are simply describing law's essential and universal features as opposed to inscribing a set of partial attributes and contested qualities on law's theoretical tablet. Any choice between these competing accounts of law will be based on a starkly political defense of one underlying vision of institutional arrangements over another.

Finally, it is worth noting that, in order for Hart or Raz's rule-based account to maintain its vaunted conceptual rigor and neutrality, it will need to be demonstrated that a legal system's rule of recognition or *grundnorm* can be identified and fixed in a way that is sufficiently impartial and apolitical. For instance, Hart accepts that, while the rule of recognition will not be entirely value- or moral-free, its meaning cannot be controversial "in all or most cases;" there will be an inevitable and debatable "penumbra of uncertainty."[25] If that were not the case, as Hart concedes, the stability and regularity of the legal system will fall victim to political in-fighting and ideological appropriation: The rule of recognition will no longer be ascertainable as a matter of fact. However, leaving aside obvious revolutionary situations, almost all legal systems experience occasions of constitutional crisis (*i.e.,* where the basis of legal authority is challenged) more frequently than analytical jurists acknowledge or allow; there are reasonably regular institutional hiatuses in which matters can take a number of different turns.[26] It is exactly in these circumstances of controversy that the rule of recognition's guidance is most needed and yet becomes most elusive. Indeed, in those moments of constitutional wrangling and potential regime-shift, Hart's account is entirely silent and has nothing to tell us about vital questions of legal validity and their resolution. Consequently, insofar as analytical accounts of law rest on social facts, they can be no more helpful or reliable than the

---

of Unger's account is less important than its existence. For a friendly critique of Unger's general approach, *see* A. HUTCHINSON, IT'S ALL IN THE GAME: A NON-FOUNDATIONALIST ACCOUNT OF LAW AND ADJUDICATION 255–70 (2000) and *infra*, ch.8.

25   Hart, *supra*, note 4 at 251 and 123.

26   A number of prominent examples of when the *grundnorm*'s identity came under popular and political scrutiny can be easily brought to mind—Roosevelt's New Deal in 1930s United States; the declaration of independence by Rhodesia in 1960s; the entry of the United Kingdom into the European Union in the 1970s; the Quebec separatist challenge in Canada in the 1990s; and the Bush-Gore election fiasco in the 2000 in the United States. For an interesting take on the role of courts at such times, *see* ROBERT LIPKIN, CONSTITUTIONAL REVOLUTIONS (2000).

controversial stability of such social facts about institutional norms. And that sense of instability (as well as its perceived resolution) is a heated matter of continuing political engagement.

This rule indeterminacy is also debilitating in regard to the operation of primary rules as well as secondary rules. For instance, although Hart claimed that a degree of textual ambiguity "should be tolerated and indeed welcomed in the case of many legal rules," he recognized that there must be an operational degree of certainty or else "there is no central element of actual law to be seen in the core of settled meaning which rules have."[27] However, a strong case can be made that no such operational degree of certainty is available. Because convention and context are never historically stable and always socially contestable, the meaning and application of legal rules cannot be put beyond the possibility of disputation. Understanding that there is not so much textual ambiguity as structural indeterminacy, the practice of adjudication becomes an incorrigibly indeterminate and political exercise. Of course, although meaning is always parenthetical and can never be grounded, the possibility of meaningful dialogue is always available: It is the theoretical status of such practical meaning that is debatable. Consequently, although Hart is correct to observe that "for the most part decisions . . . are reached . . . by genuine effort to conform to rules consciously taken as guiding standards of decision," he is mistaken in believing that anything particular or reliable follows from that engagement.[28] The legal rules' hermeneutic stability is undermined by the social instability of their interpretive contexts.

Sovereigns and Citizens

The fact that Hart's concept of law is politically partial does not speak to whether it is more open or closed to a democratic system of governance. However, upon further inquiry, it soon becomes clear that his union of

---

[27] Hart, *id.* at 251–52. Similarly, Jules Coleman states that, although "some disagreement about a rule's requirements is not incompatible with the rule's conventionality," he also concedes that judges "could not disagree in every case or even in most cases, since such broad and widespread disagreement would render unintelligible their claim to be applying or following the same rule." Coleman, *supra*, note 6 at 116.

[28] *Id.* at 141. Morever, those values which underpin the interpretation of rules cannot themselves be determined in any objective or impartial way as moralists like Dworkin suggest. See *infra*, ch.6. I have offered only a very cursory and conclusory treatment of this important issue because I have addressed it at considerable length elsewhere. *See* HUTCHINSON, GAME, *supra*, note 24 at 54–85.

primary and secondary rules does not lend itself well to the major thrust of a strongly democratic mode of governance. There is no need to go as far as Unger's democratic experimentalism to demonstrate that Hart's system is ill suited to the institutional demands of strong democracy. Although Hart is critical of Austin for offering a vertical or top-to-bottom structure of authority and rejects his reliance on a sovereign authority to explain the operation of law in a broadly democratic society, he himself falls foul of those telling admonitions in his own account of law and legal systems. In a strongly democratic society, the Austinian authoritarian tendency is always anathema to the democrat. The authoritarian state and its commanding laws are inimical to a democratic vision of social justice and legal legitimacy. By insisting upon a sharp separation between state and society, Hart dislodges Austinian-like sovereigns from the apex of authority, but only to replace them with cadres of bureaucratic officials. If Austin did little more than provide an account of law that was the "gunman situation writ large,",[29] then Hart offers little more than an account of law that is the 'officialdom situation writ large'.

One of the crucial advances made by Hart over Austin's command-backed theory was his insistence that the concept of *obedience* was insufficient to explain and distinguish law's normative authority. Instead, he posited the need for a critical reflective attitude on the part of those who administer the rules and those subject to them. He also recognized that, although the law could and should be understood as a system of rules, there needed to be a central distinction, drawn and relied upon, between primary and secondary rules (even though it seems a tad hyperbolic to compare this to the "invention of the wheel"[30]). Nevertheless, in offering and justifying both these important supplements, Hart reveals his partial political colors and demonstrates the incompatibility between his account of law in the modern state and the operation of a strongly democratic system of law and governance. The Hartian model pre-supposes a centralized state in which officials and judges are separate and strongly differentiated from subjects. The fact that such officials could be the (s)elected representatives of the citizens and that adjudication might then be a fulfilment of civic responsibility is not taken seriously at all. At best, these possibilities are a marginal and contingent feature of Hart's analytical account. In Hart's script, subjects and officials have very fixed and definite roles to perform. However, in a strong democracy,

---

[29] *Id.* at 42 and 7.

[30] *Id.* at 42.

a major commitment will be to reducing and, ideally, abandoning the gap between the state and society, and between its officials and citizens.

For Hart, although people's allegiance to the legal system was essential, it need not be derived from any sense of moral obligation. Though it could be based on a perceived duty of moral force, it need not be: It might be grounded in a host of considerations, such as "calculations of long-term interest, disinterested interest in others, an unreflecting inherited or traditional attitude, . . . the mere wish to do as others do," "or the belief that society knows best what is to the advantage of individuals."[31] In short, Hart was indifferent to the source of people's willingness to treat the legal system or its rules as authoritative. However, this stands in sharp contrast to the strong democrat. In a strong democracy, the reasons why people consent and follow rules is vitally important; it is not a matter of political indifference. Indeed, the whole point of democracy is to challenge the idea that any state or set of governance arrangements can be legitimate if they fail to heed the distinction between societies in which its members follow the law out of fear or respect. Because the whole theory and practice of strong democracy is anchored in people's extensive and continual participation, that people participate willingly and freely (or chose not to) will go a long way to establishing the legitimacy of the society's governance structure and, therefore, its laws and their administration. It is not simply a matter of contingent interest whether people follow rules or accept the legal system generally out of a commitment to the system or because they are afraid to do otherwise. The existence of fear among its citizens will count as a strike against the legitimacy of the society's democratic arrangements. Unlike Hart, the strong democrat will be more concerned about the positive reasons for why people follow the law than the negative reasons for why they do not. A strong democracy depends upon its citizen's willing acceptance of the system's overall legitimacy through their own participation rather than a begrudging resignation to rules developed and administered by official others.

This incompatibility becomes even more disturbing when Hart's conditions for the existence and validity of the system's ultimate rule of validity are considered. If it is important to the strong democrat why people accept and follow the systems' legal rules, it is even more important why the officials do. Whereas the authority of citizens to govern their own lives is axiomatic for a strong democrat, the authority of officials is much more suspect and precarious. Indeed, in a strong democracy, the exercise of official power will only be

---

[31]   *Id.* at 203 and 257.

legitimate if it is done *by* the people as much as *for* the people: Citizens will be active participants in the day-to-day business of governance and not merely recipients of an elite's preferences, no matter how benign or beneficial. At its most basic, legitimacy requires popular participation and not merely official acceptance in a thoroughly democratic society. For democrats, the institutional source of law is essential not only to its formal validity as law, but to its substantive legitimacy. Indeed, validity and legitimacy begin to combine in that the law's operation and content is just, only insofar as it flows from appropriate and functioning sources of democratic participation.[32]

In Hart's account of law, there is no necessity for "ordinary citizens" to grasp the exact content and import of the secondary rules; it is enough that "officials," "courts," and "lawyers" have such knowledge and that those secondary rules are "effectively accepted as public standards of official behavior by its officials." Accordingly, officials and ordinary citizens accept "the existence of a legal system in different ways." Whereas "the ordinary citizen manifests his acceptance largely by acquiescence in the results of these official operations," the officials must accept the secondary rules in much the same critical way that ordinary citizens accept the primary rules. This acceptance is not mere obedience, but involves judges and officials internalizing the view that there is a standard of behavior by which they can and should "appraise critically their own and each other's deviations as lapses." Although there will usually be general acquiescence by society at large in the general import of these secondary rules, there need not be: A legal system can exist if there is only official acceptance of such rules. However, as Hart rather chillingly concludes, "the society in which this was so might be deplorably sheep-like; the sheep might end in the slaughter-house."[33]

It should be clear by now that this distinction between official acceptance and popular acquiescence is anathema to the strong democrat. Contrary to what Hart concludes, "what is crucial" is not "that there should be a unified or shared *popular* acceptance of the rule of recognition containing the system's criteria of validity," but that such acceptance must itself arise in and be expressed through acts and forums of popular participation. It is simply

---

[32] The integration of law's form and substantive content will be addressed at length later in the discussion of law and morality. See *infra*, ch.4.

[33] Hart, *supra*, note 4 at 60, 116, 61, 61, 117, and 117. This emphasis on adjudicative institutions as "the linchpin of all legal systems" is common to most analytical jurists, including positivists and moralists. *See* JOHN GARDNER, *The Virtue of Justice and the Character of Law*, CURR. LEGAL PROBS. 1 at 23 (2000) and Hanoch Sheinman, *The Priority of Courts in the General Theory of Law*, 52 AM. J. JURIS. 229 (2007).

unacceptable in a strong democracy that "a great proportion of ordinary citizens—perhaps a majority—have no general conception of the legal structure or of its criteria of validity."[34] Participation presupposes that all citizens, not simply a majority, have at least a working knowledge of the legal system. Without such knowledge, participation, insofar as it exists, will be rendered hollow and inauthentic. If the rule of recognition is a social rule whose identity and authority is almost wholly dependent on its acceptance from an internal point of view by the system's officials (*i.e.*, judges), then the law's validity is down to what the judges declare it to be; it hands law's identity and, therefore, its legitimacy as a means of social ordering, over to the political power and normative preferences of unelected bureaucrats. The strong democrat will reject such a possibility because such a state of affairs offends even the broad idea of what it means for a strong democracy to exist. It will be fundamental, not simply historically interesting, to clarify exactly how the prevailing mode of governance came into being.[35] From a democratic perspective, it is not sufficient to empower any system of governance with normative authority simply by virtue of its acceptance by officials who, after all, are themselves of little or no democratic pedigree and inclination.

At this point, a practical illustration might help to put some flesh on these bare critical bones. For example, imagine a society in which there exists a formal constitutional order and a typical range of governmental institutions (*e.g.*, a popular assembly, bureaucracy, and court system), but power is largely concentrated in a president who is a former head of the military and who retains its martial allegiance. In short, there is a loosely authoritarian regime with some modest trappings of democracy. There is an increasing amount of social unrest and demands for more genuinely democratic governance. As a result, after firing various senior officials, including judges, and replacing them with presidential loyalists, the government agrees to extend the franchise to almost all adults and to hold elections. After a fractious and often violent period of elections, there are widespread allegations of electoral irregularities, ranging from small discrepancies to large transgressions in official behavior in regard to voting and counting practices. Despite the predictions of neutral observers, almost all government candidates successfully return to office.

---

[34]   *Id.* at 114.

[35]   In general, it seems apparent that assessments of a legal system's legitimacy cannot be indifferent to the circumstances of its founding, whether by way of political coup, democratic revolution, military conquest, colonization, *etc. See* ANDREAS KALYVAS, *The Basic Norm and Democracy in Hans Kelsen's Legal and Political Theory*, 32 PHIL. AND SOC. CRIT. 573 (2006).

Severe measures are taken by the government to contain further and widespread civil protests and to arrest most opposition activists. After the country's chief electoral officer (and recent appointee of the president) declares the elections to be "fair and reliable," a series of legal actions are commenced that seek to have the polls invalidated and new elections called with special safeguards and enhanced oversight. These cases reach the country's highest supreme court.[36]

In such circumstances, it seems that the court is given enormous and unconditional power to determine both the society's rule of recognition and its application in the particular circumstances. It can be said with a vengeance that, to coin a phrase that Hart roundly decries, "the law (or the constitution) is what the courts say it is."[37] The fact that the political and popular conflict is itself over the society's governing framework and ethos (*i.e.*, its rule of recognition) serves to reinforce further the power and responsibility of these unelected and government loyal judges. From Hart's point of view, there is no legal vantage point from which to evaluate whatever the judges decide to do; they decide what is valid or not by their acceptance of the society's ultimate source of legal validity. Although they might want to keep an weather-eye on the limits of popular acquiescence in order to stave off wholesale revolution, there is no obligation, moral or otherwise, to do so; the populace's consent or approval is simply not relevant. What counts as society's ultimate standard of legal validity can, as in my hypothetical, be directly contrary to the people's wishes. Whether people only obey the laws out of abject fear or even terror seems of little or no consequence to the Hartian jurist. From a democratic standpoint, this is hardly neutral; it allows an elite to dominate and dictate terms to the mass of citizens who exist in a state of outright subjection. As such, democracy has no leverage or weight in Hart's governmental scheme of things. Understood in this way, Hart's account of law is antagonistic to the introduction and establishment of even a relatively weak, let alone strong democratic mode of governance.[38]

---

[36]   This hypothetical illustration is intended to resonate with several contemporary situations throughout the world and across ideological boundaries. Of course, North America is not immune to such difficulties, albeit of a slighter less revolutionary, but no less crucial kind. *See Bush v. Gore*, 531 US 98 (2000) and *Reference re Secession of Quebec*, [1998] 2 SCR 217.

[37]   Hart, *supra*, note 4 at 141–42.

[38]   Although Hart was far from undemocratic in his political affiliations, democratic considerations form no explicit or essential part of his moral or political efforts at change. At best, his support for a broader and deeper form of democratic governance was more implicit and modest: He did not work directly to enhance the participatory quality of

In conclusion, therefore, it can be reported that Hart and contemporary positivists are still haunted by the autocratic ghost of John Austin. For all its improvements, Hart's conceptual analysis still incorporates the top/down and us/them mentality that characterized and invalidated Austin's command theory of law; it helps to embed its authoritarian and non-democratic tendencies as it manages to soften them. In the one-way flow of authority, Hart deposes the unbounded authority of commanding sovereigns, but only to replace it with an elite cadre of compliant officials—from autocracy to bureaucracy. This separation of rulers and ruled not only undermines any claim to political neutrality generally, but fails to take seriously (and indeed inhibits the development of) a society that strives to institutionalize a vigorous mode of strong democracy. As Lawrence Sager notes more generally in the context of the United States, "once popular sovereignty is accepted as the proper account of democratic governance, the Constitution and our tradition of constitutional adjudication become conceptual embarrassments."[39] This is a damning indictment for Hart and other conceptualists.

Accordingly, *The Concept of Law* is a thinly disguised apologia for the *status quo* in industrialized late twentieth-century societies; democratic demands are only one secondary feature among others in constituting social and political arrangements. Although Hart, like Austin, concentrates on how to authorize the rule of an official elite over the rest of society, a strong democrat is more concerned about subverting that division and experimenting with ways to maximize the participation of people in a mode of governance that is not only *for* people, but *by* people. As such, Hart's positivist account of law's

---

the democratic process. Like Austin, Hart was a liberal reformer, but not a democratic protagonist. In lectures and broadcasts as well as pamphlets and books, he was a progressive proponent of more humane punishments in the criminal law. He campaigned for the legalization of abortion, the abolition of capital punishment, and, perhaps most famously, the decriminalization of homosexuality. *See, for example*, H.L.A. HART, LAW, LIBERTY, MORALITY (1963) and PUNISHMENT AND RESPONSIBILITY (1968). For a more general account of this aspect of his life and career, *see* NICOLA LACEY, A LIFE OF H.L.A. HART: THE NIGHTMARE AND THE NOBLE DREAM (2004). However, Hart remained relatively silent on the Nuremberg trials and international human rights generally. *See* JOHN MIKHAIL, *Plucking the Mask of Mystery from Its Face: Jurisprudence and H.L.A. Hart*, 95 GEO. L.J. 733 at 762–63 (2007). Consequently, although Hart sought to improve law's content in progressive ways, he still held on to the positivist credo of law as authority: He saw no contradiction or even conflict in maintaining a largely non-democratic practice of governance and law provided that individual laws were morally just and politically defensible.

[39] LAWRENCE SAGER, *The Incorrigible Constitution*, 65 N.Y.U. L. REV. 893 at 895 (1990).

nature fails to live up to its own demands and expectations of political neutrality; it facilitates tyrannical regimes by conferring legal legitimacy on them, but inhibits and occasionally prevents the development of strongly democratic governments. Although the union of primary and secondary rules might well be key to the science of jurisprudence, it fails to unlock and keeps firmly shut the door to the ideals and practices of a strongly democratic society.

A Useful Task

It is important to recognize analytical jurisprudence's very real political orientation and to appreciate its ideological implications; these are all the more insidious by virtue of analytical jurists' insistence that the conceptual analysis of law and legal systems is politically neutral. Any critic who dismisses analytical jurisprudence must be prepared to take it seriously as a political theory as much as an abstract philosophical indulgence: It is less that analytical positivism is practically pointless and more that it is politically perilous. However, once the conceptual project of analytical jurisprudence is revealed to be politically partial and, therefore, unable to live up to its own universalist and neutral lights, a number of pressing and pertinent questions come into play—Does this mean that analytical jurisprudence has no role to play? Is the disclosure that analytical accounts of law are politically partial and democratically antagonistic fatal to any rendition of the analytical project? Can they still make a contribution to efforts to understand how legal systems can be identified and analyzed? My answer is that there is still a role for analytical jurists and a valid contribution for them to make, but it must be of a much more modest and useful kind.

If the work of analytical jurists is to be useful, they must first shed their universalist ambitions and epistemological trappings. So unburdened, jurisprudence might be better able to concentrate on and illuminate the institutions, structure, practices, values, purposes, and commitments of a particular society and culture. Abandoning its pretension to discover universal truths about law, legal theory might begin to grapple with those pressing issues of political and moral significance—the relevance of national security concerns to citizen's entitlements; the social impact of biotechnological advances; the consequences of increasing economic inequality; *etc.*—that should rightly occupy the attention of the legal system and its participants. Of course, in grappling with such issues, jurists must eschew their traditional tendency to take them out of the hands of the citizens and to decide them as only matters for those with philosophical or jurisprudential competence. The more modest role of jurists is to use their technical skill and institutional experience to facilitate democratic debate, not usurp it. However, if legal theory continues to be dominated by the present analytical mind-set, it will miss a wonderful opportunity to become useful and instrumental in advancing the democratic project. Instead of facing the facts, it will remain an increasingly precious activity in which its select participants will pretend that "chewing historic cud long since reduced to woody fibre"[40] has some deeper and more sustaining importance than it actually has.

Of course, analytical jurists might retool entirely. They could shift their scholarly efforts to making a more serious go of developing a truly 'descriptive sociology' of law. If they believe that the first duty of a jurisprudential theory is to "fit the facts,"[41] then they must be prepared to handle some of law's muddier facts and get their hands dirty. Rather than be content to offer a disengaged exercise in armchair philosophy, they can engage in some genuine sociological reportage and begin to do the kind of empirical fieldwork that will give rise to rich and nuanced accounts of how law works in a variety of geographical, historical, and cultural settings. Of course, this would cease to be a purely philosophical undertaking. However, by abandoning the vain claim to be providing deep and enduring truths about law, they can begin to garner knowledge about legal systems that would be local and particular. This would be useful and illuminating in a way that analytical jurisprudence presently is not.[42]

In refocusing their analytical energies, jurists might come to realize that a more convincing response to the jurisprudential query *what is law* is context specific and politically engaged. The recognition (and non-recognition) of law and legal sources will come to be understood as a social practice in which lawyers, judges, commentators, and other legal actors gradually shift and change in what counts as law. Legitimate sources will be identified by way of diffuse and non-linear routes; the process will respond to a *range* of social stimuli and political exigencies.[43] Of course, the resulting knowledge about

---

[40]   JOHN DEWEY, *The Need for a Recovery of Philosophy* in JOHN DEWEY: THE MIDDLE WORKS: 1899–1924, vol. 10, 47 (Jo Ann Boydston ed. 1976–83).

[41]   Hart, *supra*, note 4 at 80 and Holmes, *supra*, note 2.

[42]   For good examples of efforts to do this, *see* TAMANAHA, *supra*, note 18; R. COTTERRELL, LAW, CULTURE, AND SOCIETY: LEGAL IDEAS IN THE MIRROR OF SOCIAL THEORY (2006); and ROGER COTTERRELL, *Transnational Communities and The Concept of Law*, 21 RATIO JURIS 1 (2008).

[43]   *See* A.W.B. SIMPSON, *The Common Law and Legal Theory* in LEGAL THEORY AND COMMON LAW 8 (William Twining ed., 1986).

the common features of certain legal systems will not be treated as if it gives access to those features which are essential in any supracontextual or universal sense to law's definitive nature. However, it will enable jurists to gain a fuller, if never final understanding of how law constitutes and reconstitutes itself in multiple and particular contextual settings. The parochiality of jurisprudence's ambition will be its strength; what it loses in universal pseudo-appeal it will gain in political pertinence.

Again, instead of asking open-ended questions about whether a certain norm is or is not law, it would be much more useful to ask what follows from such a determination at any particular situation and at any particular time. For instance, the general issue of whether the rulings of religious courts are or are not law has little meaning or purchase without some grasp of the *when*, *where*, and *why* of the inquiry being made: Its determination and the consequences of that determination will likely vary considerably depending on a host of contextual factors. What interests are in play? Who stands to gain and lose? What does or does not follow from a legal finding? Why has the issue become contestable? At some times and in some places, it will be treated as law and certain results will follow, but at other times and places different findings will be made and different effects will happen. Of course, the definition of law against which particular contested norms are measured will itself be contingent and shifting.[44]

Analytical jurisprudence's effort to say something profound about all law and legal systems at all times is a recipe for saying very little useful about any particular system or law. Moreover, the attempt to do so in a manner that claims universal legitimacy for its findings is as dangerous as it is disingenuous. Behind its serene and inscrutable facade, analytical jurisprudence is as unavoidably political as any other legal theory; it prioritizes some governmental schemes (*e.g.*, modern industrialized states) at the expense of others (*e.g.*, customary societies) and does so under the supposedly neutral cover of theoretical analysis. Hart's *The Concept of Law* is simply an exemplar of a more general tendency within the ranks of analytical jurists. By way of alternative, a democratic jurisprudence would favor a more parochial mode of theorizing which contents itself with local and temporal insights into particular manifestations of law; it seeks to maximize the emancipatory opportunities for direct and continuing participation by citizens in the governance of themselves. A more modest agenda for jurisprudential inquiry might make a more

---

44   *See* SALLY ENGLE MERRY, *Legal Pluralism*, 22 LAW & SOC'Y REV. 869 (1988) and AYELET SHACHAR, MULTICULTURAL JURISDICTIONS: CULTURAL DIFFERENCES AND WOMEN'S RIGHTS (2001).

telling contribution to that useful democratic task; it might show how law can have authority without being authoritarian. And, of course, such a legal theory would do so as a matter of political engagement, not philosophical detachment.

Conclusion

Whatever else democracy might imply, it challenges the exercise and basis of authority and power in law, legal theory, and politics. Indeed, a commitment to strong democracy entails "the recognition and the legitimation of conflict and the refusal to suppress it through the imposition of an authoritarian order."[45] This is especially so if authority comes packaged as expertise or truth and is claimed by an elite group whether they are autocrats, functionaries, or academics and no matter how enlightened or principled their interventions might be. Moreover, a jurisprudence which is informed by a strongly democratic approach is suspicious of any legal theory which claims to offer universalistic insights about law and legal systems. My claim is that analytical jurisprudence, as showcased by Hart's conceptual analysis of law and legal systems, is not only about authority as a conceptual puzzle, but is itself also susceptible to an authoritarian and distinctly non-democratic tendency. As such, a democratic jurisprudence is highly suspicious of the universalistic claims of analytical jurisprudence.

---

[45] CHANTAL MOUFFE, THE DEMOCRATIC PARADOX 113 (2000).

CHAPTER FOUR

The Morality of Jurisprudence Determined

Pure positivism comes close to pure emptiness.
—James Boyle

Few areas of legal theory are as strongly contested as that of law and morality. In fathoming the identity of each and the relationship between them, it has rightly been treated as "the Armageddon of jurisprudential controversy."[1] The stakes are high, the terrain is treacherous, and the casualties are heavy. Because there are so many dimensions and levels at which the issue can be addressed, there are almost as many views on the law/morality connection as there are jurists. Not surprisingly, misunderstanding is rife and the prospect of any definitive resolution is elusive. Although they do not exhaust the possibilities, the competing views of positivists and moralists (or natural lawyers) tend to dominate and set the terms of engagement—To what extent is it necessary to reference or incorporate moral considerations in identifying law? Since John Austin first launched the modern debate, the validity and usefulness of this so-called separation thesis has divided not only positivists and moralists, but also caused considerable divisions among the positivist ranks. As such, any intervention in jurisprudential study must take some stand on this perennial problem and put forward a convincing way to negotiate its pressing and punishing demands.

In this chapter, therefore, I want to offer a distinctly democratic approach which attempts to get beyond the disabling stand-off between positivists and moralists. Although the debate has illuminated much about law's identity as a distinctive mode of social regulation, it has also obscured and hindered a better and more useful understanding of the role and nature of law in modern political systems. I will argue that the best arguments put forward to defend the validity, relevance, and justification for a positivist account of jurisprudence

---

[1] EDWIN PATTERSON, JURISPRUDENCE: MEN AND IDEAS OF THE LAW 5 (1953).

are unconvincing. Apart from the trite assertion that it is possible for there to be a bad legal system (to which almost all jurists, moralist and positivist, can accede), legal positivism has little to offer. Its critical claims are revealed either to amount to, in direct contrast to its own *raison d'etre*, one more partial and value-based normative account of law or to become so trivial and qualified as to be of no theoretical weight. However, the moralist case is also of limited constructive worth when viewed from a democratic perspective; while it insists that there is an inescapable moral dimension to determining law's validity, it seeks to avoid and contain the subversive implications of that powerful insight. Accordingly, after introducing the separation thesis and its moralist critique, I will look at the three different responses—soft/inclusive, hard/exclusive, and ethical positivism—and assess their merits from a democratically leaning political alternative account of jurisprudence. Again, the connecting thread will be that there is no escape in jurisprudence or law from the contested world of ideological disputation.

Separation Anxiety

Although the dispute about the connection between law and morality is as old as law itself, it was John Austin's *The Province of Jurisprudence Determined* (*The Province*) which established the modern terms for the law/morality debate. Along with his insistence that the study of law must be put on a more rigorous and scientific methodological basis, Austin laid the foundations for a positivistic account of jurisprudence. He delineated positive law (*i.e.*, the law as it is) as something that could be analyzed as an entity entirely separate from both religion and morality: "the *science of jurisprudence* (or, simply and briefly, *jurisprudence*) is concerned with positive laws, or with laws strictly so called, as considered without regard to their goodness or badness." As a pioneering initiative to stake out a defined and specialized discipline for legal study, Austin's contribution cannot be underestimated. In resisting the more traditional claims of natural lawyers, his insistence that "the existence of law is one thing; its merit or demerit is another" has remained the central and unifying credo of legal positivists.[2]

However, the precise nature of this separation of positive laws and their merit or demerit leaves much to be desired. Indeed, it may have been the very

---

2   JOHN AUSTIN, THE PROVINCE OF JURISPRUDENCE DETERMINED 126 and 184 (1832: H.L.A. Hart ed. 1955).

vagueness and imprecision of Austin's distinction, as much as its illuminating and instructive potential, that has made it so significant and so enduring. Nevertheless, although there are many differences within the positivist canon, the basic understanding of Austin's claim is that it is important to separate questions of legal validity and moral legitimacy. For the most part, therefore, positivists fully accept and recognize that law and morality are inextricably connected as an historical matter of social fact and that morality features in a variety of ways in determining law's nature. However, they maintain that an analytical approach to law requires that, as a matter of philosophical clarity, the issue of law's validity conditions is best understood in terms of social sources, not moral merits: "legal positivism is normatively inert."[3] Accordingly, though all law has a moral content and can be evaluated in terms of its moral worth, its existence and identity as law not only can, but must be determined without taking any kind of stand on its moral substance. For positivists, there is no necessary connection between a legal system's validity as a legal system and its moral or political legitimacy. In the same way that rules or decisions which are considered to exemplify moral merit have no particular claim to be treated as valid law by that fact alone, so rules or decisions of an objectionable moral content are no less law as long as they satisfy the institutional and formal criteria for what counts as a valid rule or decision; there is no requirement for any consistency or connection between law's validity and its moral force.

Again, it is H. L. A. Hart's revival of the Austinian-inspired analytical tradition in the mid twentieth-century which still provides the basic framework for the contemporary law/morality debate. Although Hart rejected Austin's command theory of law and also reoriented his analytical focus towards a conceptual approach, Hart remained very committed to Austin's positivist ambitions and refurbished many of Austin's ideas so that he could make a better and more sophisticated case for why "it is in no sense a necessary truth that laws reproduce or satisfy certain demands of morality, though they have often done so." For Hart, law and morality must be kept separate

---

3 JOHN GARDNER, *Legal Positivism: 5½ Myths*, 46 AM. J. of JURIS. 199 at 213 (2000). *See also*, H.L.A. HART, *Legal Positivism* in ENCYCLOPAEDIA OF PHILOSOPHY Iv, 418 (1967); Jules Coleman and Brian Leiter, *Legal Positivism* in A COMPANION TO PHILOSOPHY OF LAW AND LEGAL THEORY (D. Patterson ed. 1996); LESLIE GREEN, *Legal Positivism* in STANFORD ENCYCLOPAEDIA OF PHILOSOPHY, http://plato.stanford.edu/entries/legal-positivism/; M. KRAMER, IN DEFENCE OF LEGAL POSITIVISM 1 (1999); and ANDREI MARMOR, *Legal Positivism: Still Descriptive and Morally Neutral*, 26 OXF. J. OF LEGAL STUDIES 683 (2006).

as a matter of conceptual necessity rather than empirical contingency. Although he accepted that there are profound and various connections between law and morality, Hart insisted that there is no mandate for the notion that "the criteria of legal validity of particular laws used in a legal system must include, tacitly if not explicitly, a reference to morality or justice." Indeed, Hart presents "a concept of law which allows the invalidity of law to be distinguished from its immorality." Consequently, in construing law as a union of primary and secondary rules, Hart stipulated that it was important that the rule of recognition which allowed for the "conclusive identification of the primary rules" and which was, therefore, the ultimate source of legal validity must itself be identifiable as "a matter of fact." Although it might be hedged by a number of contingent moral and other considerations, this master rule must be ascertainable without any necessary resort to moral referents.[4]

Although Hart put some healthy flesh on Austin's skeletal approach to the law/morality issue, he managed to galvanize a whole set of moralist objections to the positivist project. However, before canvassing those responses and Hart's rejoinder, it is important to note two important matters. First, despite the efforts of many critics and even some positivists to demonstrate otherwise, a basic commitment to the separation thesis has little to say about the role or performance of judges. At its strictest, the law/morality division carries no particular import for what judges should or should not do in resolving particular disputes that come before them. Indeed, Hart made a strategic error when he allowed himself to be forced on to the adjudicative terrain as a proving ground for assessing the strength and worth of his concept of law, at least in regard to the law/morality relationship. From his analytical standpoint, it would have been sufficient for him to note that, while adjudication might well involve resort to moral considerations in so-called hard cases, there was no necessary connection between law and morality in identifying valid legal rules and legal systems.

Second, Hart's revival of the analytical tradition had a very positivistic ambition. Like Austin, he did this in part as a way of facilitating his political efforts to challenge and change some of the English legal system's more unjust rules. For him, his academic reliance on the separation thesis was not an end in itself, but served (or, at least did not interfere with) his broader

---

4   H.L.A. HART, THE CONCEPT OF LAW 185–86, 185, 211, 95, and 110 (2nd ed. 1994). For a critical introduction to Hart's overall theory and its conceptual underpinnings, *see supra*, ch.3.

political ambitions.[5] However, this commitment makes him stand out from many of his contemporary positivist disciples and followers. They tend to pursue an analytical agenda in a very abstract and self-contained manner and do not engage in moral criticism of law's content; they are content to hide behind Austin's caution that, "by a careful analysis of leading terms, law is detached from morals and the attention of the student of jurisprudence is confined to the distinctions and divisions which relate to law exclusively."[6] Whatever their own motivations, Austin and Hart have combined to enable jurists to sidestep involvement and responsibility for law's moral content and thrust. Of course, in a world in which law comprises a special and important site for the exercise of power and in which there are not infrequent historical examples of its moral failings, the cultivation of a hands-off position is itself a certain political stand, if the quietist kind. As long as jurists contend that the law's moral quality is beyond the proper mandate of lawyers *as lawyers*, they will help to perpetuate those injustices. As such, some positivists might do well to remember that Dante reserved some of the worst tribulations of his Inferno for that "dismal company of wretched spirits" who had stood idly by and were unable or unwilling to commit to good or evil in their lives.[7]

Those two caveats having being stated, it becomes important to note that the development of legal positivism that followed *The Concept of Law* can only be appreciated in light of the moralist response to that seminal publication. As much by way of a compliment to its importance as anything, Hart's ideas came under considerable critical attack. Although he continued to remind jurists that he "originally wrote the book with English undergraduate readers in mind,"[8] it was treated as the authoritative manifesto of legal positivism. It was left to the moralist wing of the analytical tradition to spur Hartian positivists to further clarification and elucidation.

The Ronald Intervenes

The Concept of Law was itself part of a continuing dialogue with Harvard's Lon L. Fuller who had challenged Hart's revival of the positivist tradition. Fuller had taken the view that law possesses a certain inner morality which is an

---

5   *See supra*, ch.3.

6   *The Uses of the Study of Jurisprudence* in Austin, *supra*, note 2 at 371.

7   THE COMEDY OF DANTE ALIGHIERI, CANTICA 1 canto III, ll.31–51 (Dorothy L. Sayers trans. 1949).

8   Hart, *supra*, note 4 at 238.

inescapable feature to which law must comply to retain its status as valid law: Hart's positivism failed to acknowledge this important dimension of law. Although Fuller's criticisms did much to alert Hart to the important principles of legality and natural justice that inhere within law, they did not go to the core of Hart's positivist claim that moral merit was not to be confused with legal validity because, as Hart concluded, the observance of such legal norms was still "unfortunately compatible with very great iniquity."[9] It was left to the next generation of moralists to give positivists greater pause and to oblige Hart and others to rethink the precise meaning of the law/morality separation thesis.

The most prominent of those moralists was, of course, Ronald Dworkin. Beginning in the late 1960s, he managed in short order to establish himself as the major moralist critic of Hart's positivism. Although Dworkin was more interested in developing a full-blown theory of adjudication than anything else, he laid the foundations for that endeavor with a wide-ranging critique of Hart's characterization of the legal sytem as the union of primary and secondary rules. Arguing that it was not possible to talk about law without also talking about morality, Dworkin did not simply rehearse the standard natural law arguments against positivism. Instead, he situated himself within the broad analytical tradition by seeking to identify those elements and characteristics of law that were essential to its nature as a separate and authoritative mode of social regulation; law is understandable in and on its own terms. For Dworkin, therefore, a full conceptual account of legal validity demanded close interpretive attention to its moral content and normative purposes; it was less that positivism was entirely wrongheaded than seriously incomplete. In other words, he believed that it was only possible to satisfy the demands of an Austinian-inspired analytical jurisprudence if its positivists ambitions were abandoned. In insisting that law's social facts had inescapable moral components, Dworkin located his jurisprudential contribution between the broader sweep of traditional natural lawyers and the narrower focus of legal positivists.[10]

---

9   Hart, *id.* at 207. *See* Herbert Hart, *Positivism and the Separation of Law and Morals*, 71 HARV. L. REV. 593 (1958) and LON FULLER, *Positivism and Fidelity to Law—A Reply to Professor Hart*, 71 HARV. L. REV. 631 (1958). *See also* LON FULLER, THE MORALITY OF LAW (1964). For a modern Fullerian-inspired defence of the union of law and justice, *see* N.E. SIMMONDS, LAW AS A MORAL IDEA (2007).

10   JOHN MACKIE, *The Third Theory of Law* in RONALD DWORKIN AND CONTEMPORARY JURISPRUDENCE (M. Cohen ed. 1983). Of course, Dworkin's contribution has developed considerably over time, even though Dworkin himself insists that it has hardly changed. I will attempt to offer Dworkin's response to Hart and other positivists as

Throughout his extensive and shifting *oeuvre*, Dworkin has remained adamant that Hart's mode of conceptual analysis and the resulting account of law is woefully inadequate. He begins by noting that there is widespread disagreement among officials and scholars about the most basic aspects of legal practice. In particular, judges and lawyers are conflicted over not only what is the correct resolution of any particular conflict, but also over what is the correct method by which to arrive at the correct resolution. For Dworkin, it is this underlying methodological conflict about legal reasoning that forms the *raison d'etre* of jurisprudence. He is interested in the theoretical disagreement over the grounds of law—namely, under what circumstances should "particular propositions of law . . . be taken to be sound or true." Though jurists may disagree over what those propositions are and how they are to be identified, there is widespread agreement about the fact that there are some standards that determine what propositions of law are true and sound. Accordingly, Dworkin wants to provide a theory of law that will tell judges what it is that they are supposed to be doing when resolving competing accounts about what decision to make in any particular case. To do this, Dworkin argues that, although the disagreement appears to be about what the law is, it is really a disagreement about what the law should be. For Dworkin, therefore, jurisprudence concerns "arguments over whether and why propositions of law can be controversial."[11]

From Dworkin's epistemological standpoint, it is clear that Hart's conventional and rules-based account of law is lacking. In particular, Dworkin contends that rules are merely a particularly inflexible variety of legal norms. Other standards and principles of a more pliable and overtly moral provenance comprise a large part of the legal process; their existence cannot be not be ascertained in rote fashion, but demand resort to justificatory arguments. Moreover, no master rule can be devised to identify and control these principles because "they are controversial, their weight is all-important, they are numberless, and they shift and change so fast that the start of the list would be obsolete before we reach the middle."[12] As such, the vital analytical process

---

it presently stands and in its best light. Although Dworkin makes many mischaracterizations of Hart, the most significant of which is the claim that Hart offers a semantic account of law, he still offers a telling critique of Hart's general positivist claims. *See* R. DWORKIN, LAW'S EMPIRE 31–43 (1986). For more extensive engagement with the constructive side of Dworkin's theory, see *infra* ch.6.

11   Dworkin, LAW'S EMPIRE, *supra*, note 10 at 110 and 13.

12   R. DWORKIN, TAKING RIGHTS SERIOUSLY 44 (1978). *See also* M. DETMOLD, THE UNITY OF LAW AND MORALITY: A REFUTATION OF LEGAL POSITIVISM (1984) and D. BEYLEVELD AND R. BROWNSWORD, LAW AS MORAL JUDGMENT (1989).

of fixing the operative precepts of any legal system is inevitably controversial and can only be resolved by reference to moral considerations; legal theory is a branch of normative political theory. Consequently, contrary to the claims of the positivists' separation thesis, Dworkin concluded that issues of legal validity are inexorably linked to matters of moral legitimacy. To operationalize this approach, he develops his sophisticated law-as-integrity account of law and adjudication in which "propositions of law are true if they figure in or follow from the principles of justice, fairness and procedural due process that provide the best constructive interpretation of the community's legal practice."[13] Under Dworkin's approach, therefore, any true and sound account of law is also a political account of the best moral practice that law can be.

Dworkin's anti-positivist stance did not endear him to most analytical jurists. The immediate response was dismissive and negative; much emphasis was placed on Dworkin's insistence upon viewing general jurisprudential issues through the distorting lens of adjudicative practice. However, Dworkin had clearly touched a deep nerve and positivists began to adjust their accounts so as to be able to make a better case for relying upon the separation between law and morality in jurisprudential study. As positivists acknowledged, a moment's glance at constitutional provisions, legislative enactments, and common law rules reveals that they are larded with moral terms and standards—reasonable search and seizure, fair dealing, due care, good faith conduct, etc. For positivists, therefore, the question was how could these obvious occurrences be squared with the analytical demands of the separation thesis. In attempting to close the moral door which Dworkin had thrown open, disagreement among positivists can be plotted along the axis of whether morality can play any role in the conditions for identifying valid law. There have been three significant trends in the continuing efforts to defend the validity and wisdom of the separation thesis:

- *The Softies*—These jurists have rallied around Hart and insisted that, although law and morality must be kept analytically distinct, moral values can still be incorporated and feature in determining matters of legal validity. The essential point is that their inclusion does not require any independent judgment about their moral truth and does not ask jurists to take a stand on their controversial quality. As such, law's identity can be still determined by its source-based pedigree, not its intrinsic moral merit.

- *The Hardies*—These jurists broke with the softer Hartian approach and held that legal norms must be capable of being identified strictly

---

¹³ Dworkin, Law's Empire, *supra*, note 10 at 225.

by their pedigree and with no resort to moral considerations at all; the incorporation of moral standards in any way would undermine the analytical strength of the separation thesis. As such, law's identity must be determined exclusively by reference to factual sources.

- *The Ethicalists*—These jurists abandon any pretense that positivism demands an abdication of normative arguments. Instead, they offer a defense of the separation of law and morality in unabashedly normative terms. As such, they maintain that the benefits of keeping issues of legal validity and moral legitimacy separate are primarily ethical and political.

The test, therefore, for modern positivists is whether they can resist Dworkin's moralist challenge by clarifying how law and morality do and do not interact and, at the same time, hold on to a clear and workable account of the separation thesis. In doing this, positivists have tended to take very different stances. Indeed, there are now greater differences among positivists than there are between some positivists and some moralists.

Soft Landing?

In response to Dworkin's moralist criticisms, the basic thrust of the soft positivists is that there is no difficulty in recognizing moral principles as part of law. In the same way that there is no necessary connection between law and morality in determining *what is law*, there is also no prohibition against the nature of law being contingently tied to moral criteria; it is how they are so incorporated, not whether they are. It is possible for there to be a moral dimension to law's validity as long as there is no necessary resort to morality, such morality is incorporated by another source-based norm, and there is no consideration of whether that moral feature is a good or bad thing. For these positivists, there is no *must* to the connection between law and morality; law and morality can be interdependent if it is in a contingent and conventional way. For the softies, therefore, the incorporation of morality into law is not considered fatal to the positivist cause as long as the convergence of law and morality is by way of law's pedigreed and acknowledged sources. Accordingly, moral considerations can figure in determining what is and is not valid law without impairing the positivist claim that there is no necessary connection between law and morality.

The most coherent statement of this soft or inclusive clarification came from Hart himself. In the posthumously published *Postscript* to his *The Concept of Law* in 1994, he responded directly to the moralist criticisms of Dworkin, his successor to the Oxford Chair of Jurisprudence. Hart took pains to emphasize that being a positivist did not commit him to the analytical position that the truth of legal propositions is always reducible to bare historical facts. He acknowledged that values can be fully implicated in the determination of law's validity: "the existence and content of law can be identified by reference to the social sources of law . . . without reference to morality except where the law thus identified has itself incorporated moral criteria for the identification of law." In particular, Hart sought to make plain that his positivist account was simply a denial of the moralist claim that it was always necessary to involve moral judgments in answering the question, What is law? This meant that he was prepared to concede that the rule of recognition as "a criterion of validity may be in part a moral test" and that its meaning may be controversial, although not "in all or most cases." By way of conclusion, Hart confirmed that his own account of law's nature was meant to be "*descriptive* in that it is morally neutral and has no justificatory aims; it does not seek to justify or commend on moral or other grounds the forms and structures which appear in my account of law."[14]

Various Hartian followers have elaborated on these soft themes and offered further defenses of this inclusive brand of legal positivism. They have settled on a position which seems to recommend that the separation thesis is less about the actual separation of law and morality and more about the separability of law and morality (*i.e.*, the concept of law can be understood separate from morality, but this is not the same as arguing that law and morality must remain separate as historical or social phenomena). As presently characterized, therefore, the soft positivist position is very much a conceptual claim about the theoretical possibility of there being a legal system in which legal validity and moral legitimacy can be treated separately. As part of this watered-down approach, Jules Coleman has defended a position in which he abandons any pretense that analytic jurisprudence can or need be about actual legal systems and confines itself to the thoroughly abstract task of being able to "*imagine* a legal system in which being a principle of morality is not a condition of legality for any norm."[15] Consequently, the response to Dworkin

---

14   Hart, *supra*, note 4 at 269, 253, 251, and 240.

15   *See* J. COLEMAN, THE PRACTICE OF PRINCIPLE: IN DEFENCE OF A PRAGMATIST APPROACH TO LEGAL THEORY (2001). *See also* W. WALUCHOW, INCLUSIVE LEGAL POSITIVISM (1994); KENNETH HIMMA, *Inclusive Legal Positivism* in THE OXFORD HANDBOOK OF JURISPRUDENCE AND LEGAL PHILOSOPHY 1235–36 (Jules Coleman and Scott Shapiro eds. 2002).; and ROBIN BRADLEY KAR, *Hart's Response to Exclusive Legal Positivism*, 95 GEO. L.J. 393 (2007).

has been along the lines of a confession-and-avoidance strategy—morality can be part of law and usually will be, but not in any way that is philosophically necessary to understanding law's essential nature.

There are many problems with this stance. However, two particular and related shortcomings stand out in regard to the soft response to the moralist critique. First, as a corollary of their inclusive view of morality's role in fixing law's identity, soft positivists have been obliged to draw a distinction between the existence of a rule and its meaning. They contend that, as long as there can be agreement about what the rule is, there can be disagreement over what it means or requires in particular circumstances; "some disagreement about a rule's requirements is not incompatible with the rule's conventionality." However, as with Hart's recognition that rules are ambiguous, there has to be some appreciation that there is only so much disagreement that can be tolerated because, as soft positivists concede, "broad disagreement about [what the practice is] is incompatible with the conventionality of the practice."[16] Yet, as Dworkin originally pointed out, it is difficult to contain such disagreement so that controversy does not subvert the central positivist claim that rules can be grasped without resorting to the very moral or political considerations which are out of bounds to the positivist. In short, it is difficult to understand in exactly what sense a rule exists as a fact, if there is insufficient agreement about what the rule generally means or its application entails.

Second and perhaps more important, the refinement of the separation thesis has become so subtle and so qualified that it seems to lost any practical relevance or significance. If the soft positivists are claiming that morality is almost always a stipulative feature of legality in all actual legal systems (as opposed to those that might exist in the conceptual imagination), there is little explanatory or critical force to their claims. By implicit admission, this means that they have almost nothing to offer by way of understanding the workings of law or illuminating anything important about law's essential character as law. This is as far as one can get from Hart's initial and admittedly frail "essay in descriptive sociology:" legal positivism has become a truly abstract and almost speculative posture. The difference between Dworkin's moralist position and that of the soft positivists seems to be so subtle as to be almost non-existent. Indeed, Dworkin has rightly noted that this version of inclusive positivism is "stunningly like my own" and that it is "hard to see any genuine difference."[17] It might be said that, therefore, soft

---

16   Coleman, *id.* at 116 and 153. On Hart and indeterminacy generally, see *supra*, ch.3.

17   RONALD DWORKIN, JUSTICE IN ROBES 188 (2006).

positivists have maintained their conceptual integrity at the expense of practical triviality. In their hands, there is simply nothing that follows from the assertion that "we are all positivists now" other than the banal reminder that, because something is law, does not mean that it is necessarily morally good or bad. Even moralists can accept and even embrace such a claim.

Hard Resistance

If soft positivists maintain that there are no necessary connections between law and morality, it might be thought that hard positivists would insist that there are necessarily no connections between law and morality. But this is not entirely accurate. Hard positivists argue that, although there are many connections between law and morality, law's identity does not depend at all on it meeting any test of moral legitimacy; law is entirely source based in its claims to validity and moral considerations have nothing to offer or any role to play in such inquiries. As such, legal rules are held to be strictly social phenomena that can be identified in an entirely objective and factual way by reference to an uncontested source of authority; there is an analytically unbridgeable chasm between formal pedigree and moral substance. In direct opposition to the soft positivists, therefore, these hardy scholars stand firm against Dworkin's moralist criticisms and give no moral quarter in their defense of analytical jurisprudence as a thoroughly positivist pursuit.

The leading exponent of this uncompromising stance is Joseph Raz. Beginning from a different view of law's conceptual character than Hart, he is uncompromising in demanding that any test of legality must always distinguish law from other modes of authority by exclusive reference to social and non-moral sources. His defence of a strict interpretation of the separation thesis is based upon his concept of authority. Although there may be many reasons for requiring or precluding certain actions, legal rules provide a series of institutional reasons for action that preempt reliance on other dependent and perhaps moral reasons for action. A corollary is that it must possible to identify these directives as being issued by the legal authority without resort to those other reasons or considerations over which a directive purports to take precedence: "The subjects of any authority . . . can benefit by its decisions only if they can establish their existence and content in ways which do not depend on raising the very same issues which the authority is there to settle."[18]

---

[18] JOSEPH RAZ, *Authority, Law and Morality* in ETHICS IN THE PUBLIC DOMAIN: ESSAYS IN THE MORALITY OF LAW AND POLITICS 203 (1994). *See also* J. RAZ, THE AUTHORITY

As such, Raz claims that, if it were not possible to identify the directive, then law's authority would be entirely redundant. In other words, a decision is serviceable only if it can be identified by means other than those normative considerations whose weight and outcome the law's directives are intended to resolve. Accordingly, Raz concludes that it is a necessary fact about legal systems that they claim authority and, therefore, whatever else the law is, it must be capable of possessing authority; this precludes any assumptions or assessments about whether the law or particular legal rules has moral virtue.

Though Raz accepts Dworkin's observation that law consists of moral principles as well as legal rules, he considers this insight to be trite and untroubling. In response, he insists that reliance upon moral principles in adjudication does not make them part of law. Many sources are relied upon by judges in the practical implementation of the law (*e.g.*, the rules of grammar and mathematics), but this does not mean that they are bestowed thereby with legal status.[19] In Raz's view, past judicial opinions will be valid sources of law as long as only the propositions of law contained within them are treated as law's social facts. So, although moral considerations feature in the adjudicative application of legal rules, they do not become law until they are incorporated by a legal decision. Contrary to many false perceptions about positivist theories, law is presented by Raz and other hardies as an organic and shifting body of authoritative directives. In this sense, Raz reaches the controversial conclusion that there is less law than most lawyers and judges think there is.

The appeal of Raz's harder account of law from a positivist perspective is that it claims to draw the sharpest lines between law and morality; there is no equivocation or compromise with Dworkin's moralist criticisms. However, although it sets out its positivist stall in stark and unyielding terms, it is no more convincing for that fact. Three particular deficiencies stand out—it fails to mesh with most participants' views of what law is; it assumes that the existence of a centralized state is a neutral background premise; and it only accounts for some, but not all political schemes of governance, including

---

OF LAW (1979) and THE CONCEPT OF A LEGAL SYSTEM: AN INTRODUCTION TO THE THEORY OF LEGAL SYSTEM (1980). For other hardy works, see ANDREI MARMOR, INTERPRETATION AND LEGAL THEORY (1992); and A. MARMOR, *Legal Positivism: Still Descriptive and Morally Neutral*, 26 OXF. J. OF LEG. STUD. 683 (2006). For the more recent scientific turn in positivist jurisprudence, *see* B. LEITER, NATURALIZING JURISPRUDENCE (2007) and *infra*, ch.5.

[19]   RAZ, *Legal Principles and the Limits of Law*, 81 YALE L.J 823 (1972).

democratic ones. Taken together, these critical flaws render the hardy variant of legal positivism unconvincing.

First, Raz offers his theory of law as an exercise in conceptual analysis. As such, it is supposed to be compatible with and explanatory of the conventional views of citizens and lawyers about what law is and what social practices comprise it; conceptual jurists claim to take the conduct and attitude of legal actors, identify their essential and shared features, and work them up into rational account of law.[20] Of course, the fit need not be complete or replicative of all views; it might well offer unexpected or surprising results, and it might serve to discipline certain mistaken views. Nevertheless, it must still mesh in some non-trivial way with most lawyers' experience of what they view to be law or what they are doing when they engage in law. If the gap between what participants think they are doing and what the jurist reports is too large, then the resulting account of law will appear more stipulative and *a priori* than conceptual and descriptive. And this is exactly what Raz's account becomes: He offers an account of law that not only fails to reflect participants' widely held views, but also flatly contradicts them—that legal argument and judicial reasoning are not law. When this is added to the changing attitudes about what counts as legal argument (*e.g.*, the Learned Hand test in torts[21]), it is hard to claim any analytical credibility for a concept of law that tells most judges and lawyers both individually and collectively that, whatever they are doing, they are not doing law when they go about the prosaic routines of their lawyering or judicial lives.

Second, as with Hart's account of law as a union of primary and secondary rules, Raz assumes that the existence of a state-like entity or centralized authority is an uncontroversial background premise in identifying what counts as law. Yet the notion of a *state* is very much a contingent feature of modern European societies and their colonial empires; it arose under specific circumstances a few centuries ago and is beginning to be reconceptualized in the early years of the twenty-first century. As the development of so-called transnational law suggests, law can exist in much less centralized and bottom-up settings than is recommended by a state-centered model. Raz's whole account of law assumes that law only exists in situations in which states also have been established.[22] However, such an assumption has the effect of placing

---

20   See *supra*, ch.3. *See generally* BENJAMIN ZIPURSKY, *The Model of Social Facts* in HART'S POSTSCRIPT 219 (J. Coleman ed. 2001).

21   *See US v. Carroll Towing*, 159 F.2d 169 (2d Cir. 1947).

22   *See* MARTIN VAN CREVELD, THE RISE AND DECLINE OF THE STATE (1999) and GLOBAL LAW WITHOUT A STATE (Gunther Teubner ed. 1997). It is worth noting that

many tribal or indigenous organizations and arrangements outside the ambit of legal systems. If that is the case, then Raz is simply passing off one contested and contingent understanding of law (*i.e.*, in late second millennium European political groupings) as possessing the essential qualities of law, and denying all modes of regulation in other organizational schemes the label of law. Understood in this way, Raz's hardy approach looks less a conceptual and universalistic project and more like a parochial appreciation of what counts as law in particular societies at particular times.

Furthermore, if the assumption about centralized state-like authority is relaxed, the whole idea that it is possible to treat law's identity as a social fact, so crucial to the positivist project of analytical jurisprudence, begins to run into even more serious difficulties. In those circumstances in which prevailing notions of obligation and bindingness are tied to less top-down situations and fluid social conditions, the effort to fix with any certainty or reliability upon an overarching or enduring *grundnorm* seems to defy success or attainment. For instance, Savigny's historical notion of law is suggestive of an alternative approach. In a more romantic and less analytical vein, he considered that the paradigm of law was not that of a set of formal rules laid down by a sovereign authority, but a series of working norms that arose from and captured the habitual practices of the people or community. This *volksgeist* was organic and shifting as the needs and values of society changed: "law grows as the people grow, develops with the people, and declines when the people lose individuality." As such, law is not considered to be created or validated by the state through legislative enactment or judicial decision, but is crystallized in custom and popular acceptance: Law is nurtured "by internal silently-operating powers, not by the arbitrary will of a lawgiver."[23] There are no foundational, systematic, or rational sources (or, as Raz would have it, social facts) which could completely underwrite legal validity. Although Savigny's Historical School of Jurisprudence degenerated into a rather mystical movement

---

alternative schemes of law have always tended to flourish alongside the more formal state laws. *See* H.W.A. ARTHURS, WITHOUT LAW (1985) and ROBERT ELLICKSON, ORDER WITHOUT LAW: HOW NEIGHBORS SETTLE DISPUTES (1991).

[23] FRIEDRICH VON SAVIGNY, OF THE VOCATION OF OUR AGE FOR LEGISLATION AND JURISPRUDENCE 11 and 30 (A. Hayward trans. 1831). For a good introduction to Savigny's ideas, *see* Hermann Kantorowicz, *Savigny and the Historical School*, 53 LQR 326 (1937). For criticisms of Austin from a historicalist standpoint, *See* HENRY MAINE, THE EARLY HISTORY OF INSTITUTIONS 347–61 (1875). Some of Savigny's claims (*i.e.*, that private law is apolitical) are unsupportable, but this fact does not invalidate the basic thrust of his historicalist insight.

and was utilized by political groups for various and often diabolical purposes, its central theoretical insight remains illuminating and its challenge to the philosophical ambitions of a more scientific and analytical approach is telling. This historicalist alternative leads directly into the third deficiency of Raz's hardy approach to legal positivism.

Finally (and more importantly from a democratic point of view), Raz's concept of law relies upon a general theoretical commitment that undermines his hard account of legal positivism. If he insists upon a sharp separation between law's validity and its moral legitimacy, it will be incumbent upon him to demonstrate that no legal system can or could exist which made law's validity depend entirely and exclusively on its moral legitimacy; the existence of such a legal system would confound the underlying universal structure and claims of Raz's schema by fusing rather than keeping separate law's validity and moral legitimacy. However, that is what many theological systems of law do. For instance, there are numerous legal cultures which are founded on the underlying assumption that what is moral is law by that fact alone and that only God's will can be law; there is no law that is not moral and, therefore, there is no law that can be immoral. Morever, in some societies (*e.g.*, those adhering to the Muslim Shari'a system), civil law applies to all life and is not at all distinguishable from morality or religion; law does not so much overlap with morality and religion as it is coterminous with them.[24] Consequently, contrary to the claims of Raz and other hard positivists, legal validity cannot be described or determined without reference to its content or independently of its moral legitimacy. This important critical insight is not limited to theological cultures, but becomes especially pertinent in regard to legal systems with a strongly democratic mode of governance and social way of life. There might be no need or basis to distinguish between law (whatever that might look like or entail) and other modes of social regulation in a strong democracy. I will develop that insight in the next section.

Closing the Gap

Democracy, of course, comes in many shapes and sizes. Its central thrust is that the preference for ordering power and authority in line with the views and requirements of a society's members. At its strongest, democracy is seen

---

24   *See* Brian Tamanaha, *The Contemporary Relevance of Legal Positivism*, 32 AUST. J. OF LEGAL PHIL. 1 at 14–23 (2007).

to be not only a formal process for tallying people's preferences and distributing political power, but also a substantive vision of what the good life should or could be.[25] Understood as a social as well as political way of life, it encompasses everything that affects the conditions of people's lives: People can tackle all those matters within a framework in which their active participation is the most important feature. All elite power—be it, the monied few, the judicial aristocracy, the political elite, the bureaucratic oligarchy, the corporate nabobs, or whoever—is to be distrusted. This suspicion extends to those philosophers or sages who claim that there are eternal values or objective truths to which a democratic society must conform or by which it can be disciplined; there is simply no basis in a strong democracy to be held hostage to the possibility, however remote, that such eternal values or objective truths exist. Moral authority is a quality to be earned in democratic exchange, not bestowed from elsewhere.

For strong democrats, therefore, moral progress or legitimacy is not to be found by abandoning the political or social sphere. There is simply no need to posit the existence of objective moral facts or truths. Moral backing or justification is not about bringing extant values into abstract line with elusive moral truths, but is itself a social practice that has or requires no external authority to its own democratic development. There are no facts-of-the-matter which are independent of argument and debate within democracy; the grounds of political morality are inside, not outside or regulative of that debate. As such, there is no metaphysical authority that can claim priority over a democratic community of good-willed participants coming together and deciding the most useful thing to do in difficult circumstances: "There's no court of appeal higher than a democratic consensus."[26] Consequently, there is no standard of moral evaluation that is somehow a process separate from a democratic society's own efforts to act justly and fairly. In a strong democracy, there is no privileged method that can get beyond any prevailing justifications about what counts as moral facts or truths and that can claim any theoretical warrant that is outside those situated and contingent modes

---

[25] *See, for example*, B. BARBER, STRONG DEMOCRACY: PARTICIPATORY POLITICS FOR A NEW AGE (1994) and A. HUTCHINSON, THE COMPANIES WE KEEP: CORPORATE GOVERNANCE FOR A DEMOCRATIC SOCIETY ch.4 (2006).

[26] *A Conversation with Richard Rorty*, ATLANTIC UNBOUND, April 23rd 1998. *See also* J. DEWEY, EXPERIENCE AND NATURE 407–08 (2d ed. 1958); HILARY PUTNAM, THE COLLAPSE OF THE FACT/VALUE DICHOTOMY 94–95 (2002); R. RORTY, PHILOSOPHY AND SOCIAL HOPE 266 (1999); and ROBERT WESTBROOK, DEMOCRATIC HOPE: PRAGMATISM AND THE POLITICS OF TRUTH 142–54 (2005).

of justification. There are no conversation-ending or truth-fixing arguments other than those that gain acceptance in democracy's own engaged debate and open inquiry.[27]

In contrast, both positivists and naturalists seem to share the assumption that there is some objective ground or moral facts-of-the-matter in regard to moral disputes. Whereas positivists insist that law and morality are softly separable or hardily separated entities, moralists claim that they are connected in important, if contested ways. However, both accept that there is a way of evaluating law's moral worth by reference to some independent or objective criteria. This runs counter to the epistemological and ontological claims of a commitment to strong democracy. In a strong democracy, it is a point of principle and practice that ends and means are integrated as closely as practically possible. The process by which laws are enacted or by which adjudicative decisions are made is not a matter of indifference for the strong democrat: The society's democratic status and the legitimacy of its governing structures are the only benchmarks against which both the legal system and any particular enactment's moral legitimacy can be measured. The greater the extent and quality of a society's democratic way of life, the greater the legitimacy of its ruling arrangements and substantive provisions. In a fully realized strong democracy, laws are morally illegitimate and without legal validity if they cannot be traced back to a functioning set of institutional arrangements which enable regular and revolving participation among and by citizens.

In a genuine strong democracy, there would be no independent or superior standard of moral legitimacy beyond that derived from the processes and procedures by which laws and legal decisions are made. In particular, there would be no supra-democratic method that could be invoked or appealed to that would have greater moral authority than the society's own routine engagements through its democratic infrastructure and according to its prevailing social ethos. As such, strong democrats place more emphasis on enabling good lives than engaging in the detached search for some elusive Good Life. In a strongly democratic account of governance, therefore, the source of laws and their moral legitimacy will be intimately related, but not completely collapsible into each other; the law's moral legitimacy will overlap and be commensurable with the existence conditions for law. Both the source and substance of law become mutually reinforcing so that validity and

---

[27] RICHARD RORTY, CONSEQUENCES OF PRAGMATISM xxvi (1982). *See also* Rorty, *Texts and Lumps* and *Representation, Social Practice, and Truth* in PHILOSOPHICAL PAPERS, vol. I, 81 and 154 (1991).

legitimacy begin to approximate to each other. In such societies, the extent and depth of democratic commitments will be the measure of law's validity and its moral legitimacy; they are neither separated nor separable as positivists insist.

Of course, that does not mean that each citizen will agree entirely with the worth or merit of every single enactment or decision by the society's democratic institutions. However, it is a strength of democracy that it encourages rather than stifles disagreement and discussion about such matters. Accordingly, those who lose out in any genuinely democratic debate will know that they can participate in and take advantage of continuing opportunities to redebate those same issues in the normal flow of politics; winning and losing will be part and parcel of the democratic compact. In such circumstances, these dissenters might well be prepared to accept and acknowledge the overarching moral legitimacy of the governance and legal system in spite of their disagreement about any particular rule or holding. Once it is appreciated that the body of extant rules and principles "stands *for the time being* in the name of the whole community,"[28] questions of validity and legitimacy will begin to coalesce, if not entirely merge.

If one takes a strongly democratic approach to law, it becomes not only possible, but imperative to move beyond the positivists' bifurcation of law's nature and moral legitimacy. Instead, the task of legal theory becomes to chart the different ways in which the form of law is connected to its democratically determined content. This is because, if the appropriate and indispensable structural conditions for strong democracy are in place and if there is widespread participation, then the substance of the laws generated will be considered morally legitimate largely by that fact alone; their connection to moral value will not be simply "precarious and contingent."[29] As such, legal theorists' attention must shift towards the critical elaboration of those conditions which make legal enactments and decisions more or less democratic and, therefore, more or less morally legitimate. It will then become more apparent that legal validity and moral legitimacy are not separate or separable as positivists claim, but are intimately connected through their democratic derivation. Although the content of laws will vary along with changes in a democratic society's ethos, they will remain morally legitimate as a result of their origin in society's democratic enabling sources and institutional settings. In contrast to the positivist's foundational commitment to the separation

---

[28]   JEREMY WALDRON, LAW AND DISAGREEMENT 102 (2001).

[29]   Leslie Green, *The Functions of Law*, 12 COGITO 117 at 123 (1998).

thesis, there would be a permanently inseparable connection, if not a perfectly collapsible distinction, between the law's formal validity as law and its moral legitimacy in a full and functioning strong democracy.

Consequently, because the hard positivists rest much of their analytical claims upon the maintenance of a strict separation of law and morality, they are unable to accommodate the philosophical and political commitments of a strongly democratic society in which both law's validity and its moral legitimacy are intimately connected. However, the soft positivists might point out that their basic stance is unaffected by such democratic complaints and might actually be strengthened by them. Such Hartian loyalists argue that soft positivism does not deny that there might be perfect symmetry between the legal validity of a system's rules and the moral legitimacy of those rules; validity and legitimacy can be separate, but need not necessarily be so. However, as I have already shown, such a concession seems fatal to any ambitions that they might have to say something important or telling about the nature of law, especially when combined with their insistence on separating the functions and attitudes of officials and citizens.[30] This leaves only the response of the ethical positivists to consider. If the hard and soft varieties of positivism tend to win some of their discrete battles with moralists, but lose the overall war, then the ethical positivists give up the fight entirely.

Ethical Positivism

Both hard and soft positivists see law as social fact whose moral rightness or wrongness has no necessary connection to its status as valid law; the congruence of law with morality is a matter of contingent happenstance, not conceptual necessity. However, there has always been a very different response to Dworkin-style criticisms of the positivist project. Rather than attempt to shore up the traditional understanding of the separation thesis, they have sought to defend its benefits in blatantly normative terms. The main thrust of a variety of interventions is that it is possible to showcase the virtues of legal positivism and its insistence on the separation of law and morality as a full-blown ethical account. They do not shy way from moral arguments, but utilize them to recommend the ethical payoff of treating law's identity and

---

[30] *Supra*, pp. 73–76 and ch.3.

its moral substance as distinct analytical tasks.[31] As such, they tread a thin line between soft positivism and moralism; they concede that some moral values are always present in law, but they resist the claim that law's validity as law is entirely reducible to its moral legitimacy.

The most sustained effort to develop an extended version of this ethical positivism has been made by Tom Campbell. He treats positivism as a normative theory that seeks to formulate those values that will govern the form as opposed to the content of law. Defending an autonomous rule-based schema as a morally defensible embodiment of "a vision of what a good legal system looks like and how it contributes to a just, effective and democratic polity," he maintains that this can be effected in a way that "adjudicators need not have reference to moral (or economic or political or private preference) criteria in their determination of law" and, therefore in their exercise of power. For Campbell, although the overall ethos of a society's governance scheme need not be democratic to maintain its status as a valid legal system, there is no tension between democracy and his account of positivism because "legal positivism is itself a democratic prerequisite and therefore partially constitutive of any acceptably democratic system."[32] Consequently, he offers his ethical positivism as a normative hedge against the propensities of legal officials to act out of self-interests and political prejudice. As such, it is an aspirational model of how the Rule of Law can function as a foundational part of a modern and democratically attuned polity.

These interventions are very encouraging as far as they go. However, the problem is that they do not go far enough. In their efforts to occupy a precarious ledge between positivism and moralism, these ethical positivists still remain trapped within the philosophical confines of analytical jurisprudence. Although ethical positivism represents a clear advance over the increasingly unproductive squabbles between soft and hard positivists, it still seems to place a naive faith in the disciplinary effect that rules can have over judges and officials; the history of constitutional and common law adjudication

---

[31] *See, for example,* NEIL MACCORMICK, *A Moralistic Case for A-moralistic Law,* 20 VALPARAISO L. REV. 1 (1985); JEREMY WALDRON, *Normative (or Ethical) Positivism* in HART'S POSTSCRIPT 410 (J. Coleman ed. 2001); and LIAM MURPHY, *The Political Question of the Concept of Law* in HART'S POSTSCRIPT 371 (J. Coleman ed. 2001). However, MacCormick's recent work suggests a change of tack. *See* NEIL MACCORMICK, RHETORIC AND THE RULE OF LAW 1 (2005).

[32] TOM CAMPBELL, THE LEGAL THEORY OF ETHICAL POSITIVISM 2, 84 and 5 (1996). *See also* TOM CAMPBELL, *The Point of Legal Positivism,* 9 KING'S COLLEGE L.J. 63 (1998) and *Democratic Aspects of Ethical Positivism* in JUDICIAL POWER, DEMOCRACY AND LEGAL POSITIVISM (T. Campbell and J. Goldsworthy eds. 2000).

strongly suggests that such formalistic confidence is unwarranted. As such, the jurisprudential maneuvering of Campbell and other ethical positivists exhausts itself in trying to make the best of a thoroughly bad analytical job.[33] As Campbell recognizes, his ethical positivism will need to be supplemented by a wider political philosophy of democratic justice. Yet, having cracked open the law/morality debate, it is difficult to understand why the ethical positivists would confine their attention only to Fuller-style positivistic values (*e.g.*, clarity and prospectivity) and prioritize them over other possible values. Having revealed the need for normative argument, the least that they must do is to provide a normatively compelling account of the special importance and deep compatibility of such values in a more strenuous democratic account of law and justice.

Of course, it remains useful to be reminded that because something is law, it does not mean that it is necessarily morally good or bad. However, this reminder works best as a matter of practical politics than as an insight of analytical jurisprudence. Indeed, even more than their soft colleagues, the ethical positivists rest their case upon an insight which is banal even by the standards of a jurisprudential intervention that claims to have broken partly free of the analytical mind-set and made its case in openly ethical terms. Nevertheless, although they suffer a failure of critical nerve, the ethical positivists do create an opening through which it becomes possible to develop a more bracing and pervasive critique of the philosophical project of analytical jurisprudence. Having shifted from conceptual analysis to normative argument, the next step is to demonstrate that normative argument itself is taking place within an overtly political context. In contrast to the ethical positivists, my line of pragmatic criticism does not shy away from the claim that both law and legal theory are ideological in the sense of resting on deeply controversial and contested premises. My criticism of positivism's separation thesis is part of a larger commitment to a jurisprudential position which accepts and works with the notion that legal theory arises in political circumstances, is motivated by political concerns, and has political consequences; it is politics and values all the way up and down. As such, my critique goes beyond the analytical tradition of both a positivist and naturalist approach to legal theorizing in its insistence that there are no stable or secure footings on which the jurisprudential debate can be based which are not themselves part of that very debate; there is no escape from the historical and social circumstances of theorizing which an analytical or conceptual jurisprudence seeks to transcend.

---

[33]   *See* A. HUTCHINSON, EVOLUTION AND THE COMMON LAW (2005) and *supra*, ch.3.

However, while I also insist that law is unavoidably about moral values and any effort to understand or apply law is fraught with political concerns, I do not adopt a moralist approach. To be anti-positivist is not to be pro-moralist; the (moralist) enemy of my (positivist) enemy is not necessarily my (democratic) friend. To reveal that positivist accounts of law are based on or dependent on substantive political morality is not the same as suggesting that the law has a necessary commitment to any particular set of substantive moral principles, let alone that they are the best or right ones. Indeed, I maintain that the moralists' claims about the relationship of law and morality are as mistaken and as flawed as those of the positivists, but in a very different way. Although values and morality are inextricably involved in the legal enterprise, I do not accept the naturalist claim that "justice plays a role in fixing what the law is" in all legal systems.[34] Law is about values, but that does not mean that those values are necessarily just or 'meritorious' (as Austin would put it) wherever and whenever law is found. In an important sense, therefore, I remain committed to the moralist position that understanding what law is does implicate and depend on normative considerations, but that such a commitment does not entail an acceptance that what the law is and what the law ought to be are necessarily connected and inseparable across political systems of governance.

Conclusion

When understood less as an analytical truth about law's nature than as part of a normative intervention in jurisprudence, the separation thesis loses much of its philosophical luster and authority. When studied through the sharply focused lens of strong democracy, it is revealed to be built on contested theoretical and normative arguments about the moral character of law and morality itself. There is, of course, some value in holding on to the separation thesis as a political warning, more than as an analytical imperative: any system of law must be alert to the ever-present possibility that its modes of governance and law are open to appropriation by those immoral and opportunistic actors determined to subvert and hijack the law's moral legitimacy for their own self-serving purposes and agendas.[35] This danger is particularly acute for the strong democrat who places considerable confidence in the views and values

---

[34] Dworkin, JUSTICE IN ROBES, *supra*, note 17 at 35. For more extended critique, see *infra* ch.6.

[35] *See* Tamanaha, *supra*, note 24 at 33.

of its citizens when expressed in and through participatory processes and political forums. Nevertheless, the strong democrat will work towards demonstrating how the moral legitimacy of law can better be understood as something that is connected to its status as law than as something opposable to it. This less grandiose agenda for jurisprudential inquiry might make a more telling practical contribution to that pressing democratic task; it might show how law can have authority without being authoritarian. And, of course, such a legal theory would make such claims as a matter of political engagement, not from a position of philosophical detachment.

CHAPTER FIVE

The Province of Jurisprudence Predetermined

*There is no such thing as either philosophical or scientific method {as meaning
'neutral decision procedure'}. There are only local and specific agreements on
procedure within such expert cultures as stellar spectroscopy, modal logic,
admiralty law, possible-world semantics, or Sanskrit philology. There is
no method shared by geologists and particle physicists but not employed
by lawyers and literary critics.*

—Richard Rorty

Since John Austin's initial call to develop "the *science of jurisprudence* (or, simply
and briefly, *jurisprudence*),"[1] legal theorists have tended to recognize that, if
there is a key to jurisprudence, it is not to be found in treating it as a science.
Although most jurists have strived to be rigorous and demanding in their
analytical efforts, they have foregone the outright scientific pretensions of
Austin. However, as the more preferred mode of conceptual analysis has come
under increasing critical attention, the attractions of the scientific method
have been given a new lease on jurisprudential life. The lack of scientific
ambition is considered by some to be the failing of contemporary legal theory,
and there has been a renewed call to scientific arms. Although they look to
a broader and less confining source of inspiration than Euclidean geometry
(as Austin did), they ransack a range of scientific disciplines (*e.g.*, evolutionary biology, social psychology, neuroscience, and psychoanalysis) in order to
put law and its jurisprudential study on more secure and predictable footings. In so doing, the hope is that such scientific interventions will be able to
avoid some of the more normative blind alleys and cul de sacs that jurisprudence has recently encountered. In short, if legal theory is to maintain its

---

[1]   JOHN AUSTIN, THE PROVINCE OF JURISPRUDENCE DETERMINED 77–78 and 126
  (1832: H.L.A. Hart ed. 1955). The most renowned American version of this appeal is
  Langdell's insistence that law is a science. See Langdell, Harvard Celebration Speeches,
  5 *Law Quarterly Review* 124 (1887).

intellectual authority and prestige, it is urged that it must assume the rigors of scientific inquiry.

There has always been a recognizable and respectable branch of empirical legal studies; its contribution was generally confined to modest and focused studies of discrete legal phenomena (*e.g.*, automobile accident recovery, contractual remedies, and police behavior). Although largely neglected by mainstream legal scholarship, this data-based work offered a welcomed counterbalance to the theoretical abstractions of jurisprudential efforts to appreciate law's workings. However, there is now a marked effort to take more seriously this mode of academic inquiry and to celebrate the birth of a New Legal Realism.[2] By extending science's data-rich and causality-dominant methods to law's social practices and adjudicative routines, the hope is that jurisprudence will be able to share in the success and cachet of the natural sciences. Thus, it will deliver some of the secure truths and dependable knowledge that have so far eluded traditional analytical jurisprudence.

In this chapter, I want to challenge this scientific turn towards the tried-and-true methods of natural science as being entirely the wrong direction; a naturalized jurisprudential methodology is less a scientific undertaking and more a scientistic smash-and-grab.[3] Moreover, contrary to the epistemological claims of its supporters, such a scientific rendition of analytical jurisprudence is far from a turn away from morality. The detached and objective merits of the scientific method are themselves embedded in a contingent context of social values and political interests which both animate and channel scientific research. Rather than try to breathe new life into the flagging methodological project of analytical jurisprudence, it is much more productive to abandon the Austinian project entirely. Accordingly, after introducing the main thrust of this naturalistic turn, I will explore its epistemological (*i.e.*, What methods can be used to ground true legal conclusions?) and ontological (*i.e.*, What is involved in saying that law or rules exist?) failings as a possible source of scientific authority for legal studies. Throughout, my

---

[2]   Thomas Miles and Cass Sunstein, *The New Legal Realism*, 75 U. CHI. L. REV. 831 [(2008). *See also* Frank B. Cross, *Political Science and the New Legal Realism: A Case of Unfortunate Interdisciplinary Ignorance*, 92 NW. U. L. REV. 251 (1997) and Howard Erlanger, *et al.*, *Is It Time for a New Legal Realism?*, 2005 WISC. L. REV. 335 at 337 (2005).

[3]   By scientism, I mean "a misunderstanding of the relations between philosophy and the natural sciences which tends to assimilate philosophy to the aims, or at least the manners, of the sciences." See Bernard Williams, *Philosophy as a Humanistic Discipline*, THE THREEPENNY REVIEW (spring 2001). *See also Scientism* in ENCYCLOPAEDIA OF SCIENCE, TECHNOLOGY AND ETHICS (Martin Ryder ed. 3rd ed. 2005).

ambition is to urge jurists and lawyers not to succumb to physics-envy, but rather to get beyond analytical jurisprudence and its scientific pretensions; the humanistic values of conversation and moral engagement still have an important role to play in understanding and evaluating law and adjudication. Of course, such values must be appreciated in their political and social context.

A Naturalistic Turn

As with any influential scholarly trend, the legacy of Legal Realism is far from settled or straightforward. In the 1920s and 1930s, a group of American scholars resisted the prevailing conceptualist mind-set and sought to demonstrate that the appeal of an objective and impartial system of legal thought was illusory. Concentrating on the adjudicative process, they maintained that the power of formal rationality was suspect; precedent could be manipulated to justify any decision at all. However, there was little agreement on why this was the case. Some argued that it was the psychological and idiosyncratic make-up of judges that drove the process, whereas others took a more structured and fact-based explanatory perspective.[4] It is the latter, old sociological approach that has been revived by the new realists who, more than any other jurists, seem committed to providing the 'essay in descriptive sociology' that Hart promised, but failed to deliver. For them, particularly in regard to the exercise of adjudicative responsibilities, the attractions of an empirical method are to be embraced.

The economic analysis of law has been one of the most successful (and controversial) initiatives to build on the New Legal Realist legacy. However, as its predictive and prescriptive capacities have been increasingly found wanting, one response has been not to abandon or cut back on its use, but to redouble the effort to place it on more solid and scientific foundations. Under the general rubric of behavioral economics, the idea is to utilize psychological and sociocultural theories to assess more precisely the influence of law in society. As such, the general trend has been to raid the scientific disciplines and to incorporate their more causally grounded predictive insights into the legal and jurisprudential project. The basic epistemological claim is that the scientific analysis of human behavior can offer a more reliable basis on which

---

⁴ Contrast JEROME FRANK, LAW AND THE MODERN MIND (1930) with Karl Llewellyn, *A Realistic Jurisprudence—The Next Step*, 30 COL. L. REV. 454 (1930) *See generally* NEIL DUXBURY, PATTERNS OF AMERICAN JURISPRUDENCE (1995).

to formulate better and more effective legal rules. In their seminal article of 1998, Jolls, Sunstein, and Thaler contended that such a theoretical innovation will enable legal scholars "to model and predict behavior relevant to law . . . with more accurate assumptions about human behavior, and more accurate predictions and prescriptions about law."[5] This recommended reliance on other scientific inquiries has extended to evolutionary and social psychology as well as neuropsychology.[6] In each case, the underlying ambition is that their harder methodologies will serve to put some empirical backbone into the mushier techniques of traditional legal analysis and ensure that the policy-making practices of law will be "ultimately grounded in empirical analysis rather than mere ideology."[7]

Although there are a growing number of new scholars who are busy working this re-discovered old empirical seam, there are very few who have bothered to clarify and defend the deeper philosophical foundations of such a jurisprudential renaissance. One who has is Brain Leiter. Biting the epistemological bullet, he has made a strong and unequivocal intervention into jurisprudence's methodological debate—Is it possible to participate or intervene in the jurisprudential debate about explanatory theories of law without being implicated in or taking a stand on contested values of a social, moral or political character?[8] At its sharpest, the issue is whether the whole enterprise

---

[5] Christine Jolls, Cass Sunstein and Richard Thaler, *A Behavioral Approach to Law and Economics*, 50 STAN. L. REV. 1471 at 1474 (1998). *See also* Russell Korobkin and Thomas Ulen, *Law and Behavioral Science: Removing the Rationality Assumption from Law and Economics*, 88 CALIF. L. REV. 1051 (2000).

[6] On Evolutionary Psychology, see Neal P. Parekh, *Theorizing Behavioural Law and Economics: A Defense of Evolutionary Analysis and the Law*, 36 U. MICH. J.L. REFORM 212 (2002); Owen D. Jones and Timothy H. Goldsmith, *Law and Behavioral Biology*, 105 COLUM. L. REV. 405–502 (2005) and Todd J. Zywicki, *Evolutionary Psychology* in ENCYCLOPAEDIA OF LAW AND SOCIETY: AMERICAN AND GLOBAL PERSPECTIVES, (David S. Clark ed. 2007). On Neuropsychology, see Stephen J. Morse. *Symposium: The Mind of a Child: The Relationship Between Brain Development, Cognitive Functioning, and Accountability Under the Law; Brain Overclaim Syndrome and Criminal Responsibility: A Diagnostic Note*, 3 OHIO ST. J. CRIM. L. 397 (2006). On Social Psychology, see Mark R. Fondacaro, *Toward an Ecological Jurisprudence Rooted in Concepts of Justice and Empirical Research*, 69 U.M.K.C. L. REV. 179 (2000); Lee Ross and Donna Shestowsky, *Contemporary Psychology's Challenges to Legal Theory and Practice*, 97 Nw. U. L. REV. 1081 (2003); and Claire B. Steinberger, *Persistence and Change in the Life of the Law: Can Therapeutic Jurisprudence Make a Difference?*, 27 LAW AND PSYCHOLOGY REV. 55 (2003).

[7] See Fondacaro, *id.* at 196.

[8] *See generally* Julie Dickson, *Methodology in Jurisprudence: A Critical Survey*, 10 LEGAL THEORY 117 (2004).

of analytical jurisprudence is built on the insecure footings of evaluative sand rather than on the stable foundations of descriptive rock. If it is only the former (as I will insist), then this scientific project is in genuine theoretical peril as any analytical contribution has no greater validity or cogency than the extent to which those values are shared or uncontested among the jurisprudential community. In advocating an empirical scientific turn, Leiter is as concerned with highlighting the nature of law's validity as with defending legal theory's validity. He argues that, if jurisprudence is to fulfill its traditional role and expectations to say something true and valid about law's nature and operation, it must commit itself to a naturalized jurisprudence in which its "methods and answers must be continuous with (perhaps supplanted by) scientific inquiry."[9]

Taking his lead from the ground-breaking work of W.V.O. Quine in sabotaging the important analytic/synthetic distinction that supports conceptual analysis, Leiter insists that there is no non-circular way to fix the notion of analytic truth (*i.e.*, propositions which are true in virtue of their meaning) without resort to or reliance on synthetic truths (*i.e.*, propositions which are true because they are grounded in fact).[10] However, Leiter claims to add a certain *pragmatic* demand to a Quinean-inspired jurisprudential theorizing and offers a more relaxed naturalism. Resisting the traditional need to hit metaphysical bottom, he insists that philosophy is not about establishing justificatory foundations for what we know so that philosophy underpins science, but is about delivering the goods, having cash-value, and going with what works. As such, "the only possible criteria for the acceptance of *epistemic norms* . . . are pragmatic: we must simply accept the epistemic norms that work for us" and that "help[] us cope with experience better than other practices." In short, if we are to acquire reliable knowledge about law, *"causal power is all we have to go on."*[11]

---

⁹ Brian Leiter, Naturalizing Jurisprudence: Essays on American Legal Realism and Naturalism in Legal Philosophy 138 (2007).

¹⁰ Although Quine insisted that science was the best bet for advancing any epistemological or ontological project, he worked to hard to revise its analytical orientation. He argued persuasively that analytic and synthetic propositions are not unrelated, but are actually codependent. In his arresting words, "the lore of our fathers . . . is a pale gray lore, black with fact and white with convention, . . . [but] I have found no substantial reasons for concluding that there are any quite black threads in it, or any white ones." W.O.V. Quine, *Carnap and Logical Truth* in The Ways of Paradox and Other Essays 100 (1966).

¹¹ Leiter, *supra*, note 9 at 273–75, 50, 149, and 275.

Framing his project as the philosophical reclamation of the realist legacy, Leiter accepts that law, as a body of norms, is both rationally and casually indeterminate. Although it contains a host of signposts and maps, law's usual grab bag of argumentative resources (*e.g.*, rules, principles, doctrines, reasoning) can never fully justify nor explain a judge's decision to reach one particular and only one decisional destination; there are simply too many reasons to warrant any dependable causal connection between those reasons and the decision reached. Instead, Leiter maintains that it is the facts of the case that provide a better causal explanation and prediction of judicial decisions than the rules of law; judges are more influenced by prevailing cultural and socio-economic norms than strictly legal ones which function as after-the-fact rationalizations. As such, it is the psychosocial profile of judges individually and collectively (*e.g.*, social background, professional training, ideological disposition) that will do the most work in illuminating the pattern and predictability of decisions over time. Theoretical and armchair speculation about the normative connection and justificatory fit between theory and evidence will be replaced by the rigorous demands of cognitive science as a descriptive exercise in psychological causal-correlation. Instead of "the 'sterile' foundational program of justifying one legal outcome on the basis of the applicable legal reasons," Leiter recommends that jurisprudence commits itself to "a descriptive/explanatory account of what input (that is, what combination of facts and reasons) produces what output (*i.e.*, what judicial decision)."[12]

Consequently, although Austin may have mused only wistfully about bestowing a scientific pedigree on jurisprudence, Leiter has followed through and sought to bring jurisprudence in line with a truly scientific approach to the problems of legal philosophy. He claims that "the only truths are empirical truths, and thus all questions are scientific questions" and that "science . . . predicts the future course of experience with much greater precision and reliability" than available philosophical methods. In doing so, he effectively proposes the dumping of all manner of conceptual shoddiness and moral posturing: "jurisprudence *per se* is *not* naturalized: just the part of jurisprudence concerned with the theory of adjudication."[13] However, this all assumes that Leiter has made his case on behalf of a naturalized jurisprudence or the New Legal Realism. I will, of course, argue that this is not so and that Leiter's intervention is fatally flawed.

Although scientific thinking can add something to the jurisprudential project, it is folly to maintain that it can completely rule the field and become

---

[12] *Id.* at 40.

[13] *Id.* at 144, 148, and 45–46.

the master method for obtaining knowledge about law which will replace all other techniques and vocabularies. Leiter's naturalized turn is less toward science than it is towards scientism: He manages to pull off the considerable feat of appearing to turn a series of soft and loose intuitions about law into a pseudoscientific theory of supposed hard facts. In short, although Leiter would like to be able to report that he stands on solid ground when he engages with law's facts and practices, the epistemological and ontological place where he stands and the facts that he analyzes are much mushier and evaluative than he pretends. In a manner of speaking, when it comes to understanding law, it is relative mushiness (*i.e.*, historical contexts, social values, and political interests) all over the place and all the way down.

A Walk on the Epistemological Side

For Leiter, the naturalized path to true and reliable knowledge about law and society is to be achieved by a thoroughgoing reliance on a scientific methodology. Because "the only truths are empirical truths and thus all questions are scientific questions," it is imperative that jurisprudence's "methods and answers must be continuous with (perhaps supplanted by) scientific inquiry."[14] As a result of this commitment, Leiter divides the world into those matters which are susceptible to the causality-driven demands of scientific inquiry and those which are not. Whereas the former can deliver dependable truths, the latter are dismissed as so much fluff and distraction. As such, Leiter-side jurisprudence is a stark world in which there is some limited set of hard, empirical, causality-measured factual truths about law and a larger mush of softer and less dependable, intuitive, evaluative data and assessments about law. Like other Austin-inspired jurists, Leiter puts his philosophical faith in fact over fancy.

Despite his initial cautions to the contrary, much of Leiter's account and explanation falls back into the pragmatically suspect habit of emphasizing that science has a special privilege in knowledge accumulation and knowledge validation because "science is the paradigm of genuine knowledge," science has a "special status," and there is "no higher tribunal" than science in matters of ascertaining truth. Although Leiter recognizes that "the scientist is indistinguishable from the common man in his sense of evidence, except that the scientist is more careful," this does not prevent him from defending

---

[14] *Id.* at 144 and 138.

the "the best-going criteria of the knowable and real" and searching for a master-vocabulary in order to represent what the world is really like. In particular, as well as talking about settling on "the real cause of the decision," he declares that there is a hard-and-fast distinction between facts and values. In a central, but baffling passage, Leiter states that:

> "[Scientific norms] . . . have worked very well for us humans: they helped depopulate our ontology of leprechauns and gods and ethers, and they are foundational norms in scientific practice, a practice that sends the planes into the sky, keeps the food from spoiling in the refrigerator, and alleviates human suffering through modern medicine. From a philosophical standpoint, what bears special notice is that the epistemic norms of common sense and the epistemic norms of science are simply on a continuum. . . . The pragmatic necessity of successfully predicting the course of experience is central to ordinary life and to the scientific enterprise; but this means, in turn, that the pragmatic rationale for our most basic epistemic norms can be found in universal features of the human situation, for example, the need to explain our experience with an eye to figuring out what will happen next. Science succeeds at this better than any other practice and this is why . . . science is the paradigm of genuine knowledge. . . . Yet the modesty of this type of pragmatism should also now be apparent: for once we accept a framework of epistemic norms, then the criteria for belief acceptance need not be pragmatic, except to the extent that the epistemic norms we accept—on pragmatic grounds—themselves embody pragmatic criteria. But it is completely consistent for the pragmatic philosopher . . . to distinguish sharply between, say, facts and values, precisely because he has accepted, on pragmatic grounds, epistemic norms that invite this distinction."[15]

In this passage, Leiter puts into play the whole methodological debate about the relationship between the descriptive and evaluative dimensions of the theoretical project. In effect, he wants to offer an analytical and non-pragmatic insistence on the sharp separation of facts and values, but one that is based on a pragmatic and non-analytical account of the scientific enterprise. In other words, he argues for adopting a mainstay of analytical philosophy (*i.e.*, separation of facts and values) because it is epistemically warranted on

---

[15] *Id.* at 51, 149, 117, 161, 239, 44, 51–52. *See also* Leiter, Introduction in THE FUTURE OF PHILOSOPHY 4 (B. Leiter ed. 2004).

pragmatic grounds. If this could be achieved, it would be a powerful and revolutionary move. However, in line with a more thoroughgoing pragmatic approach, I want to insist that this is little more than a philosophical sleight of hand; pragmatic arguments offer no epistemic warrants for anything, let alone a sharp fact/value distinction.

Despite his best efforts, Leiter cannot get to firmer or higher analytical ground than the pragmatic foundations of his account and, as any pragmatist knows, pragmatic foundations are no foundations at all; they are no stronger (and no weaker) than the social standards on which they rest. Once the pertinence of the pragmatic insight is accepted, then it is pragmatism all the way down. There is simply no way to go halfway down the pragmatic elevator, get off at some convenient floor, and then declare that it allows access to the way-the-world-really-is and renders the use of a sharp fact/value distinction defensible and definitive. Although Leiter is true to his insistence that "there is no point of cosmic exile from which to leverage our theory of the world,"[16] he nevertheless maintains that there are some this-world staging posts from which to fulfill the analytical promise. In pragmatic contrast, I insist that it is the whole tradition of epistemology that is vulnerable and suspect. Once the continuity between fact and value is recognized, little is to be gained from pursuing the epistemological agenda of analytical jurisprudence. Leiter's is a faux pragmatism that displays the trappings of pragmatism, but few of its distinguishing philosophical commitments.

The analytical strengths and pragmatic weaknesses of Leiter's naturalized approach is evident in his extended and important answer to the key methodological challenge of whether descriptive jurisprudence is possible. In offering an affirmative response, he does not mount a direct defence of the fact/value distinction. Instead, he posits a further distinction within values between moral/epistemic norms. He begins by conceding the critical force of a post-Kuhnian sensibility in which it is no longer sensible or convincing to talk about facts as something that exists entirely outside of the disciplinary matrix or paradigm within which they are apprehended and which they are supposed to validate: There must be a resort to some informing context of theoretical and methodological values, whether implicit or explicit, that allows a necessary degree of filtering, weighting, and evaluation to occur before the existence of facts can be identified and confirmed.[17]

---

[16] *Id.* at 146.

[17] THOMAS KUHN, THE STRUCTURE OF SCIENTIFIC REVOLUTIONS (3rd ed. 1996).

Nevertheless, Leiter labels this the 'Banal Truth'—"evaluations are an indispensable and decisive component in the selection or formation of any concepts for use in description of such aspects of human affairs as law or legal order." It is 'banal' because Leiter does not believe that it follows from such a concession that moral and political values are implicated in the descriptive enterprise of jurisprudence. Although a demonstration that moral values are in play in the jurisprudential enterprise would be fatal for the theoretical project of descriptive jurisprudence, he does not accept that the reliance on values *per se* will do much harm. Indeed, on the contrary, he recommends that an appreciation that evaluative judgements are inevitably involved in factual inquiry will serve better to ensure that the descriptive undertaking remains theoretically honest by being scrupulous about the type of non-moral values of "importance and significance" that are permitted to inform its performance: "descriptive jurisprudence says that epistemic norms, alone, suffice to demarcate legal phenomena for purposes of jurisprudential inquiry."[18] For Leiter, therefore, the descriptive ambitions of jurisprudence can be addressed more adequately and effectively without the fact/value distinction. As such, jurisprudence can be both descriptive and evaluative as long as it is appreciated that there is a defensible distinction between moral and epistemic (non-moral) values.

So what is the distinction between epistemic values and moral values? Can Leiter explain the precise and stable relation between these opposing modalities, but also maintain a convincing way to talk about that relation that is itself precise, stable and, most pertinently, value-free? For Leiter, whereas *epistemic values* are about qualities such as evidentiary adequacy, simplicity, consilience, and the like; *moral values* touch upon issues like how we ought to live, what are our obligations to others, what political institutions are best, and the like. He tells us little explicitly about the philosophical status of this distinction, but there is good reason to believe that it is meant to do the same foundational work as the fact/value distinction that it is intended to replace: It is part and parcel of the same larger philosophical tradition which undergirds the fact/value distinction. If the account of law

---

[18] Leiter, *supra*, note 9 at 167, 167, and 168. Leiter utilizes John Finnis's arguments as leverage. See J. FINNIS, NATURAL LAW AND NATURAL RIGHTS 16 and 17 (1980). Leslie Green also notes that "while descriptions are not value-neutral, they need not be morally fraught either." Leslie Green, *The Concept of Law Revisited*, 94 MICH. L. REV. 1687 at 1714 (1996). Leiter's spat with Dickson is much ado about nothing as they adopt very similar epistemic/moral distinctions. Leiter, *supra*, note 9 at 194–96 and J. DICKSON, EVALUATION AND LEGAL THEORY (2001).

that follows from a reliance on only epistemic values is to claim descriptive status, then it follows that Leiter's epistemic/moral distinction must itself be immune to the charge that it is somehow anchored in and derived from contested social practices of evaluation. Otherwise, it would not be clear in what way reliance on an epistemic/moral distinction would or could stave off the charge that the descriptive enterprise was fatally compromised by moral or political values.

Although Leiter acknowledges the post-Kuhnian sensibility, he does so only to cabin and ignore its more telling implications. The giveaway is that Leiter refers to his major insight about the possibility of a descriptive jurisprudence as a truth, banal or otherwise. Like his more traditional analytical colleagues, he is still in the game of relying upon in what Leiter himself terms *truth-conducive desiderata* in constructing adequate theories of law's essential nature.[19] The acid test of valid knowledge about law remains its capacity to comply with a refined set of theoretical procedures—collectively referred to as empirical-scientific inquiry—whose validity is vouched safe by something beyond or apart from the contested social debates of evaluative choice. In the same analytical move as the fact/value distinction, Leiter sets off and privileges the theoretical solidity of epistemic values against the mushy quality of moral and political values. However, this binary contrast is not as fixed or sharp as he contends; his epistemic values are not as hard and objective as he suggests, and his moral values are not as soft and subjective as he posits.

The analytical ambition to boil down life or law's rich and varied phenomena to a few simple and essential truths is evaluative at its core. The privileging of formal qualities, like coherence, elegance, clarity, and simplicity is done and defended because it will produce a *better* account of law. When Austin talks about determining law's proper and essential characteristics, when Hart works toward clarifying and sharpening our understandings,[20] and when Leiter claims to illuminate "the knowable and real," they are committing themselves to an analytical exercise which is obviously intended to improve the jurisprudential project. The general claim is that by either climbing higher, digging deeper, being more coherent, being more clear, or

---

[19] *Id.* at 34. For a similar effort to defend Hart's resort to values as epistemic, not moral, see JULES COLEMAN, THE PRACTICE OF PRINCIPLE: IN DEFENCE OF A PRAGMATIST APPROACH TO LEGAL THEORY 178–98 (2001). Coleman's notion of what counts as pragmatic is idiosyncratic and very different from mine.

[20] See Austin, *supra*, note 1 at 1–9 and H.L.A. HART, THE CONCEPT OF LAW 1–17 (1963: 2nd ed. 1994).

being more proper, the descriptions and definitions proffered will by virtue of those qualities alone be more compelling and objective. However, although these qualities might well have some appeal and be helpful to the theoretical enterprise, it is unconvincing to pass them off as being entirely separate from more generally moral assessments. They are evaluative criteria whose privileging and merit must be defended, not simply assumed. As such, Leiter's analytical approach's penchant for "theoretical tidiness"[21] ensures that not only are any and all facts already framed within a pre-existing theoretical matrix, but also that such an explanatory paradigm is itself in need of a more general evaluative defence. The privileging of tidiness above other possible commitments—richness, complexity, usefulness, democratic, and moral worth—is as contestable as any other and, as such, must be evaluatively justified. In short, there is nothing merely descriptive about tidiness that isolates or insulates it as an epistemic norm from more obviously moral values. It is an aspirational precept that recommends itself as being worthwhile and meritorious by that fact alone. Tidiness is as much part of the evaluative vocabulary as other moral values.

Understood pragmatically, the measures of justification for both epistemic and moral values are related in that they each rest upon public standards that have been hammered out and found convincing in social communities and professional subcommunities. And again, it is not that there is no difference between epistemic and moral values, but that there is no bright-line and ahistorical boundary which designates them as qualitatively different. The basis for their difference is located in nothing more (and, as importantly, nothing less) than the same kind of contingent social conventions which underpin the fact/value distinction: They stand or fall in line with their capacity to meet extant and related standards of justification and relevance about what counts as "working best."[22] Leiter may have shifted his ground,

---

[21]   RUTH HIGGINS, THE MORAL LIMITS OF LAW 17 (2004). For an extended critique of analytical philosophy, see J. STUHR, PRAGMATISM, POSTMODERNISM, AND THE FUTURE OF PHILOSOPHY 192 (2003).

[22]   See R. RORTY, PHILOSOPHY AND SOCIAL HOPE 51 (1999). See also R. RORTY, PHILOSOPHY AND THE MIRROR OF NATURE 181 (1979) and R. RORTY, OBJECTIVITY, REALISM AND TRUTH 22–24 (1991). In a recent posthumously published essay, Rorty took Leiter to task for "a relapse from the true pragmatist faith into positivistic science-worship." Richard Rorty, Dewey and Posner on Pragmatism and Moral Progress, 74 U. CHI. L. REV. 915 at 918 (2007). In response, Leiter concentrated on Rorty's rather extravagant claim that "pragmatism puts natural science on all fours with politics and art." Rorty, id. at 917. See Brian Leiter, Science and Morality: Pragmatic Reflections on Rorty's 'Pragmatism', 74 U. CHI. L. REV. 929 (2007). While I agree that there are differences

but he remains at much the same philosophical location as his purported analytical foes, like the soft positivists and the moralists; he is still in the reality game and insists on claiming epistemological authority by virtue of telling it the way it is. This is a distinctively unpragmatic thing for a self-proclaimed pragmatist to be doing.

In contrast, the pragmatic approach that I am proposing works towards abandoning the analytical project entirely. It eschews the possibility of a purely descriptive jurisprudence insofar as that entails any kind of epistemological device, be it fact/value or epistemic/moral, that strives to ascend to a higher ahistorical ground from which to deliver truths about legal or other social practices than their historical context. Moreover, it also rejects the notion that it might be possible, from such a metaphysical vantage point, to regulate the ebb and flow of that social and contingent conversation about what is more or less reliable knowledge. There are only those arguments and reasons which have passed social muster in an open, intelligent, and democratic exchange. The epistemic values espoused by Leiter—evidentiary adequacy, simplicity, consilience, and the like—are worth relying on not because they represent a guaranteed set of ahistorically proven and epistemically verified procedures, but because they continue to earn acceptance in the actual philosophical and juristic subcommunities and work best. There are simply good reasons to treat such values as dependable for a certain set of purposes and projects where *good* means that communities of philosophers have, through experience and debate, sufficient confidence in their capacity to produce reliable results. However, this certainly does not mean that they can claim an authority that runs beyond or rules over the social context in which they arise: They are only as authoritative as their present users deem them to be useful for their aims and ambitions. As such, a pragmatic account insists that there is nothing more to truth than that "a sufficiently well-placed speaker who used the words in that way would be fully warranted in counting the statement as true of that situation."[23]

---

between the natural and social sciences, this does not validate Leiter's epistemological claims about scientific methodology as a privileged way for illuminating "the causal structure of the world" and "what the moral, legal, and scientific 'situation really is'". Leiter, *id.* at 930 and 931.

[23] H. Putnam, Representation and Reality 115 (1988). *See also* J. Dewey, Experience and Nature (2d ed. 1958) and Hilary Putnam, The Collapse of the Fact/Value Dichotomy (2002).

The Values of Science

Leiter is not insensitive to the pragmatic claim that values and scientific method are on intimate terms. Yet he views it as an illicit coupling. Although he is concerned that "non-epistemic values or norms, like the political ideology of the inquirer or the political climate in which the inquiry takes place" might infiltrate the scientific inquiry, he is reasonably confident that "the intersubjective agreement in judgment, the publicity of evidence, and standards of proof" will guard against bias, even though this will likely be more successful in physics than in the social sciences. Nevertheless, although "entrenched interests and values . . . [will] distort cognition of the social world and warp scientific inquiry accordingly," it will be the burden and responsibility of the (social) scientist and naturalized jurist to be scrupulous in guarding against such distortion and warping.[24] As such, Leiter maintains that there is no necessary or unavoidable meshing of scientific inquiry and entrenched interest and values; there is some ideal scientific methodology that is capable of being separated from and defended against the encroachments of social values, political interests, and other historical contaminants.

Leiter's attachment to the possibility of some pure and unadulterated empirical predictive way to proceed to scientific and valid knowledge is deeply problematic. It is not only that there is a present failure to keep scientific inquiry and extant values separate, but such inquiry and values are inextricably connected to, even if they do not collapse into, the inquirers' political ideology or their informing political climate. There is simply no way to engage in scientific inquiry that does not inscribe evaluatively as opposed to describe empirically. Leiter's reliance on a fact/value split distinction is intended to privilege science and science-like discourse from discourse about social order and moral worth. However, the values which are supposed to be kept at arm's length are those very contextual circumstances, informing assumptions, and instrumental ambitions that enable scientific inquiry in the first place. In short, epistemology has no privileged or preferential ground from which to demand social authority and professional discipline by dint of its plain and simple truth; there is no outside that can govern the inside by virtue of its separate and bounded superiority (and vice-versa, of course). In Leiter's favored Neurathian imagery, the scientific empirical planks of the

---

[24]   Leiter, *supra*, note 9 at 261, 262, and 262.

lifeboat are already and always held together by values; they are part of the fiber and grain of the available timber.[25]

Although there is a definite, if attenuated, link between refined science and raw interests, it is shifting and varying: knowledge, values, interests, power, and even justice interact and (dis)enable each other in manifold ways. This is not to conflate scientific proof with political interests, but to emphasize their interconnectedness and resist the traditional claim that science's exact knowledge is insulated from society's evaluative orientation.[26] The natural world can never speak for itself, but can only be voiced by historical actors who themselves are never sequestered from or innocent of their own informing social and political context. This is the unrelenting import of the pragmatic claim that science's handiwork and methodological resources are as much an embedded social practice as an Olympian intellectual idea. What counts as good science is, therefore, part of the debate about the preferred agenda of social values and political interests. Although scientists must always be attentive to the subtle pressures and temptations which press upon their work, it is not possible to expunge all social values and ideological commitments from their work. To posit such a possibility is to slip back into an analytical posture in which the availability of a value-free and supra-historical access to physical reality is treated as being obtainable and capable of exerting a disciplinary effect. Pragmatists reject such a characterization of the scientific method because all knowledge and its methods for acquisition must be appreciated in their particular social and political context; power's dynamics and demands are ever present and cannot be bracketed or expunged entirely.

Of course, technology has done so much in modern society. But the inevitable acceptance that 'it works' is not the same as declaring that science has unparalleled access to truth and knowledge, untouched by social forces and political interests. Science and society are so intertwined that one cannot appreciate one without the other; it is not that science is somehow false or

---

[25]   Neurath analogizes the validation of scientific knowledge with the piecemeal reconstruction of a boat while at sea. See W.O.V. QUINE, WORD AND OBJECT 3 (1960).

[26]   There are still useful occasions when it is important to recognize relevant differences between factual inquiries and value judgments. For example, the rejection of the fact/value distinction does not jeopardize or threaten the wisdom of Hume's guillotine. It is solid advice that, without more, it is inadvisable to draw a moral *ought* from an historical *is*. See D. HUME, A TREATISE ON HUMAN NATURE Bk. 3, pt. 1, s. 1 (1739). For more modern reminders of this, see A. EINSTEIN, OUT OF MY LATER YEARS 114 (1950); S.J. GOULD, EIGHT LITTLE PIGGIES: REFLECTIONS IN NATURAL HISTORY 266 (1993); and S. PINKER, HOW THE MIND WORKS 52 (1997).

fabricated, only that it is never apprehendable outside of the social contexts and political interests that foster it. It is not that ideology infects science because there is no science that is severed from and secure against society's concerns and interests. It is the network of professional practices and institutional settings which facilitates the dynamic traffic between laboratories and the public realm. Although scientists and researchers might no longer be as overtly indebted to and in the service of their sponsors and their cultural milieu as of yesteryear, the connection remains marked and inescapable. The simplistic positivistic account of scientific inquiry is belied by historical studies which reveal the social embeddedness of science and its related institutional claim to technical authority.[27]

An obvious example of this science/values complex is the contested relationship between medical science and gender. There is much to support the view that science and superstition are historically interrelated and that the difference between myths and methods is too subtle for distinction; there is always something of the artifactual in all facts.[28] Like all professions (including, of course, law), scientists are trained within a particular social and political

---

[27]   *See, for example,* STEVEN SHAPIN AND SIMON SCHAFFER, LEVIATHAN AND THE AIR-PUMP (1985) and YARON EZRAHI, DESCENT OF ICARUS: SCIENCE AND THE TRANSFORMATION OF CONTEMPORARY DEMOCRACY (1990).

[28]   See Kuhn, *supra*, note 17. For instance, biomedical research has been affected by gender bias (as well age, race, and class bias); the FDA excluded women from clinical drug trials until 1993. The two main justifications for this exclusion were the "complex" hormonal fluctuations that occur during the female menstrual cycle and the potential risks to a fetus if a woman became pregnant during the trial. Of course, it seems obvious that any drug that is not efficacious throughout a woman's menstrual cycle is not safe enough to be put on the market: the risks of *not* knowing the safety and efficacy of drugs on pregnancy is a greater risk of a woman getting pregnant during a drug trial. See Donald Mattison and Anne Zajicek, *Gaps in Knowledge in Treating Pregnant Women*, 3 GENDER MEDICINE 169 (2006). Male drug testing has resulted in male-tailored pharmaceuticals and clinical data cannot be accurately extrapolated to women. Studies demonstrate that adverse drug reactions are more common and more severe in women; there are approximately 2,000 American cases annually of fatal acute liver failure induced by medication use, and three-quarters are women. The gender disparity has been duly noted by regulatory bodies and guidelines have been implemented to achieve gender equality in research, but they are either ignored or inefficient. See Stacie Geller, Marci Goldstein, Molly Carnes, *Adherence to Federal Guidelines for Reporting of Sex and Race/Ethnicity in Clinical Trials*, 15 J. OF WOMEN'S HEALTH 1123 (2006). There is also evidence to suggest that male scientists do better in peer-reviewed research; see Lutz Bornmanna *et al.*, *Gender differences in Grant Peer Review: A Meta-Analysis*, 1 J. OF INFORMETRICS 226–238 (2007). Of course, none of this will comes as news to legal feminists. See *infra*, ch.7.

contextual framework which affects and frames what is done and how it is done. The influence of governments, foundations, corporations, and individuals and their needs influence the research agenda and, subtly and not so subtly, make scientific study as interested as it is disinterested; named chairs, institutes, centers, and facilities can serve the priorities of the donors as much as the endowed scholars.[29]

Of course, the demonstration that science is a profoundly social practice is not a bad thing; it only becomes so if there remains a lingering claim to be speaking in the name of some detached and supra-historical authority. Perhaps the most well-known and pragmatic example of science's sociality is Charles Darwin's framing of his natural-selection theory of evolution. Although Darwin is still considered to have offered the most compelling account of evolution's workings, its own makings and reception cannot usefully be severed from its distinctly Victorian *laissez-faire* origins. He openly drew upon Adam Smith's notion of a sorting mechanism and Thomas Malthus's notion of perpetual struggle not simply as allusive references, but as the intellectual engines of his account of how species originate and develop. Building on those contested political texts, Darwin was able to map and explain the general role of natural selection in evolutionary history.[30] However, although Darwin's theory is firmly situated in and representative of the historical temper of his times, it is not only reducible to them. While the basic idea of natural selection is generally accepted today, the force and domain of that principle are far from settled; debate still rages over to what it applies and whether it possesses an exclusive explanatory function. From a pragmatic viewpoint, it is sufficient to conclude that Darwin's work offers a usable and reliable framework which works and is conducive to further evolutionary studies. Whether it is true in any grander sense seems besides the point. Moreover, to appreciate his theory without an appreciation of its enabling historical and political context is to miss something significant and indispensable about it.

---

[29]   See D. RHODE, IN PURSUIT OF KNOWLEDGE: SCHOLARS, STATUS AND ACADEMIC CULTURE 19–23 (2006) and SHEILA SLAUGHTER and LARRY LESLIE, ACADEMIC CAPITALISM 129–32 (1997).

[30]   See C. DARWIN, THE ORIGIN OF SPECIES (1859). The relevant texts were A. SMITH, THE WEALTH OF NATIONS (1776) and T. MALTHUS, AN ESSAY ON THE PRINCIPLE OF POPULATION (1798). For an historical account of these events, see J. BROWNE, CHARLES DARWIN: VOYAGING (1995) and THE POWER OF PLACE (2002). *See also* A. HUTCHINSON, EVOLUTION AND THE COMMON LAW 30–35 and 91–97 (2005) and S.J. GOULD, THE STRUCTURE OF EVOLUTIONARY THEORY 121–25 (2003).

In portraying scientific method in this way, it is not my intention to play the anti-science postmodernist to Leiter's positivistic true believer. On the contrary, I do not deny that there is a natural world out there to be apprehended and that traditional scientific methods can be useful in solving problems about that natural world. I simply do not accept, as a pragmatist, that it is possible or useful to assume that those predictive empirical techniques give access to some universal truths or are separable from the historical contexts of their deployment. Like most professionals and inquirers, scientists are situated in and affected by their social contexts in seeking to make working sense of the world; findings are provisional, standards are fallible, and absolute objectivity is mythical. Whatever else it is, science is never only *science* and the difference between science and other pursuits is much less stark than is generally conceded: "the negotiations [between working scientists] as to what counts as a proof or what constitutes a good assay are no more or less orderly than any argument between lawyers and politicians."[31] Leiter would do well to remember and resist the temptation to make an epistemological silk purse out of the practical pig's ear of scientific endeavor. Along with Polonius (and other pragmatic-minded observers), he might accept that both madness and method are always part of the human mix.

In an Ontological Bind

The strength of any theoretical contribution is to be found not only in the illuminating power of its central insight, but also in its awareness of that insight's limitations. Even if the force and legitimacy of Leiter's defence of the epistemological superiority of the empirical predictive method in the natural sciences is acknowledged, there is no particular reason why it should be extended to efforts to understand the social world generally and its legal dominions specifically. Leiter has a strong case to make in demonstrating that jurisprudence's "methods and answers must be continuous with (perhaps supplanted by) scientific inquiry" and that a naturalized approach will "effect an explanatory unification of legal phenomena with the other phenomena constituting the natural world *which science has already mastered*."[32] Indeed, there are many strong reasons why such an ambitious move is ill founded

---

[31] B. La Tour and S. Woolgar, Laboratory Life: The Social Construction of Scientific Facts 237 (1979). *See also* Kuhn, *supra*, note 17 and Bruno Latour, We Have Never Been Modern (C. Porter trans. 1993).

[32] Leiter, *supra*, note 9 at 138 and 135 (emphasis added).

and unhelpful; Leiter's introduction of a naturalized methodology into law is less of a scientific undertaking and more of a scientistic smash-and-grab.

Apart from the epistemological shortcomings of naturalized jurisprudence, there are severe ontological difficulties for those who wish to develop a New Legal Realism—what is involved in saying that law exists as an object of scientific study? What are to count as legal phenomena for the purposes of scientific explanation? Leiter is sensitive to this challenge and he concedes that the status of law's social practices as fact is much more contentious than that of objects in the natural world. Although he is not insensitive to whether such scientific methods are capable of "cutting the social world at its causal joints" and how to avoid "intuition-mongering," his efforts to extricate himself by positing a series of "data points in theory-construction" with sufficient factuality and theory-independence are unconvincing.[33]

The difference between inquiries into the social and natural world is not about method *per se*; both possess an hermeneutical dimension and, therefore, cannot offer neutral or value-free access to physical or social reality. However, inquiries into the social world are different because there is a double hermeneutical dimension at work. Not only are the inquisitive practices interpretive and value -infused, but the object to be interpreted is itself not available or present without a similar interpretive commitment. In the natural sciences, there are planets and birds that can be apprehended and will go on doing what they do largely regardless of human inquiry into them; the predictive results of inquiry can be confirmed or invalidated by observation and experiment. In the social sciences, what the social (and legal theorist) concludes and recommends is very likely to change the object of study. As regards social inquiry, therefore, social practices are not fixable or objectifiable without a background matrix of theoretical assumptions about the intentions, motivations, vocabularies, and self-understanding of social actors. As such, there can be no external check on social inquiry other than another set of social practices which comprise the background matrix. Although "physical nature does not organize itself culturally,"[34] social life does; social practices

---

[33] *Id.* at 192, 133, and 4.

[34] Sandra Harding, *After the Neutrality Ideal: Science, Politics, and 'Strong Objectivity,'* 59 SOC. RES. 574 (1992). Sources for my arguments include Hubert Dreyfus, *Why Studies of Human Capacities Modelled on Ideal Natural Science Can Never Achieve Their Goal* in RATIONALITY, RELATIVISM AND THE HUMAN SCIENCES (J. Margolis *et al.* eds 1986) and BEING-IN-THE-WORLD: A COMMENTARY ON HEIDEGGER'S BEING AND TIME (1991); Charles Taylor, *Interpretation and the Social Sciences* in PHILOSOPHY AND THE HUMAN SCIENCES: PHILOSOPHICAL PAPERS, vol. 2, 15–60 (1985) and SOURCES OF

are themselves contingent and unfixable in any useful or dependable way over time. What makes scientific inquiry so successfully predictive in the natural world is the same as what renders its extension to social world so problematic—the relative absence of self-interpreting and self-constituting objects of study which must be accommodated in any satisfactory social inquiry. In non-metaphysical pragmatic style, this is not an *a priori* epistemological privileging of such hermeneutical resources, but an *a posteriori* and historically informed ontological exercise.

Leiter seems clearly trapped within this hermeneutical double-bind. Taking a Razian source-based approach to law, he incorporates so-called folk intuitions (*i.e.,* "informal psychological, political and cultural knowledge about judges and courts" and their "meaningful mental states") as the basic raw material for his scientific endeavor. Even though he concedes that judges are "political actors advancing an ideological agenda," Leiter maintains that it is possible to identify and fix their "unreduced mental states" and "ideological attitudes" as "ineliminable features of the social structure of the social world" and, therefore, as "data points in theory-construction."[35] In Leiter's account of law and adjudication, there is no room for any moral facts or values because they fail to meet the strict causality demands of his scientific method. Consequently, despite his recognition of the ontological problem, Leiter is adamant that these normative folk intuitions are sufficient to enable his favored causal-predictive method to gain purchase, work empirically, and "deliver the goods." By illuminating the predictable pattern of decisions over time, this approach "give[s] us a picture of courts which fits them into a broader naturalistic conception of the world in which deterministic causes rule and in which volitional agency plays little or no explanatory role."[36]

SELF: THE MAKING OF MODERN IDENTITY (1989); NICHOLAS H. SMITH, CHARLES TAYLOR: MEANING, MORALS AND MODERNITY (2002); and KEITH TOPPER, THE DISORDER OF POLITICAL INQUIRY 30–36 and 58–83 (2005).

[35] Leiter, *supra*, note 9 at 55, 188, 191, 4, 190, and 4. Hard positivists, like Raz, look beyond judges' ideological attitudes to "facts regarding the conduct and attitude of certain persons in the community." See Benjamin C. Zipursky, *The Model of Social Facts* in HART'S POSTSCRIPT: ESSAYS ON THE POSTSCRIPT TO THE CONCEPT OF LAW 219 at 225 (Jules Coleman ed. 2001) and *supra*, ch.4.

[36] *Id.* at 273 and 135. Leiter references the work of Jeffrey Segal and Harold Spaeth. An attitude is a "relatively enduring set of interrelated beliefs." See JEFFREY SEGAL and HAROLD SPAETH, THE SUPREME COURT AND THE ATTITUDINAL MODEL 221 (1993). Even they acknowledge that facts, just like the law, are "subjectively perceived" and "not uncommonly." *Id.* at 215. *See also* JEFFREY SEGAL and HAROLD SPAETH, THE SUPREME COURT AND THE ATTITUDINAL MODEL REVISITED (2002).

This effort to pass off the judges' ideological attitudes as adequate 'data-points' and ontological entities from which to animate his naturalized empirical-predictive methodology is unpersuasive; it cannot get to any firmer scientific ground than the mushiness of those inputs. It is hard to imagine—and Leiter gives us no clue—how it would be possible to identify and label such attitudes without some informing account of social behavior. Any such account would perforce be sociological and highly contestable. In dealing with psychosocial inquiries, there simply are no brute facts of the matter. Leiter fails to take seriously the *social* dimension of these social facts. When it comes to social facts, there is no form of pure scientific analysis that passively catalogues without also actively constructing those facts to be catalogued. Accordingly, if judicial attitudes and dispositions are to be the ontological grist for the scientific mill, they must at least be fixable in some reliable and value-neutral way. It would seem that the only way to access that data would be by a hermeneutical reading of the very indeterminate legal materials which Leiter is keen to avoid and which he claims has no causal connection to the judicial decisions actually made.

As if this were not enough, adjudication takes place in a social context which is constantly changing. The historical circumstances within which the dynamic interactions between judicial attitudes and legal materials occur is itself always shifting and changing. Consequently, social setting, historical context, individual disposition, and institutional imperatives are twisted into a thread of historical narrative that can never be fully disentangled or reduced to its component parts without losing its defining character; judicial attitudes cannot be laid bare or exhibited in their pristine untoldness or apolitical thereness as Leiter and other analytical jurists suggest or require. As Nietzsche so succinctly put it, "only that which has no history is definable."[37] And law, as well as legal theory, is inextricably connected to its historical setting.

Even though a strictly scientific empirical causal method did work in social matters (and there is no real evidence that it has any precise or reliable predictive power), scientific inquiry is ill suited to become the primary or exclusive technique through which to understand the social world. It fails to work in the sense that prediction is not the be-and-end-all in human matters; there are other more overtly evaluative considerations which might be more

---

[37]   F. NIETZSCHE, THE GENEALOGY OF MORALS 2:13 (1887). See A.W.B. Simpson, *The Common Law And Legal Theory* in LEGAL THEORY AND COMMON LAW 8 (William Twining ed. 1986) and Roger Cotterrell, *Why Must Legal Ideas by Interpreted Sociologically?*, 25 J. LAW AND SOC. 171 (1998).

important or more central. For instance, in assessing the performance of judges, it might be considered useful to assess the extent to which their justificatory efforts can be squared with the particular political or moral ends to be achieved. This is not at all the same thing as simply predicting what judges will do. Indeed, in a society which is committed to strong democracy, the need to initiate such reason-giving conversations will be paramount.

Moreover, even if we could develop a reasonably successful method of predicting the particular responses of particular judges when presented with particular fact situations, it might still be considered independently important to evaluate the drift and quality of their justificatory reasons. Nor does this normative inquiry depend on there being any strictly determinate connection between the decision made and the legal reasons offered; the good-faith effort to square a decision with a particular set of normative goals might well be the best or only basis for measuring the democratic acceptability of a particular outcome.[38] In the exercise of public power, the *ex post* craft and substantive cut of a judgment might well trump its *ex ante* predictability. After all, if predictability was all we cared about, we might as well replace adjudication with other formulaic devices for decision making (*e.g.*, every third case files wins). Accordingly, it is simply not the case that "causal power is all we have to go on" and that "all questions are scientific questions." Although Leiter might well be right that "the philosophical track-record of all forms of *a priori* analysis, conceptual or intuitive, is not especially encouraging," it is difficult to see how exclusive reliance on the psychosocial branch of empirical science can be any more reassuring.[39]

Conversational Values

It is not that such science-based inquiries and results have no relevance or usefulness; they can contribute significantly to the broader project of developing a more informed understanding of social behavior, but they cannot usurp or replace it. Leiter's proposed naturalized jurisprudence is a case of the methodological tail wagging the social dog. It seems backwards to first posit the existence of only one reliable method (*ie.*, predictive empirical) for social inquiry and then to analyze law exclusively in terms of those facts that lend

---

[38]   For an account of the role of legal reasoning in judicial decision making, see A. Hutchinson, It's All in the Game: A Non-Foundationalist Account of Law and Adjudication (2000).

[39]   Leiter, *supra*, note 9 at 275, 144, and 180.

themselves to such a causality-driven technique. Consequently, it is as important not to ignore the contribution, albeit limited and circumscribed, that empirically based inquiries can make to social studies as it is to unearth the contested values with which such inquiries are infused. Whether we want science to become the master vocabulary of social studies is itself a non-scientific and evaluative decision which will require reference to moral and political debate; the problems of society and law are not simply about prediction and control, but about whether social actors and judges advance particular moral and political purposes, be they reactionary or radical—What do we want to become as a society and as individuals? How do we want to live our lives?

For example, in thinking about the death penalty, there is a revived debate over its continued use. A number of empirical studies have begun to revisit the issue of whether it has a genuine deterrent effect. Although there remains much scientific debate over the methodological validity of these studies, there seems to be a growing recognition that capital punishment might well work as an effective disincentive for potential murderers.[40] Yet, even assuming that such studies are reliable, no amount of empirical research can foreclose the debate one way or the other. There is an irreducible moral and political dimension that affects legal, moral, political, and judicial attitudes. As such, economists and other social scientists have little to tell us as empirical chroniclers about the death penalty's continued use. Although a demonstration that the death penalty has no deterrent effect would be morally significant in curbing its use, there is no particular or free-standing moral significance to the claim that it does have some deterrent effect. There are all manner of punishments and innovations that might be introduced if deterrence were the only or main determinant of its social acceptability: Chopping off limbs, stoning people, and corporal punishment might be usefully retried. However, many will consider that the death penalty, like limb-chopping or stoning, is a morally outrageous practice whatever its deterrent effect. Science only has any place in jurisprudence, if it knows its place. And that place is to supplement other inquiries (*e.g.*, humanistic, sociological, religious, philosophical) rather than supplant them entirely.[41]

---

[40] *See, for example*, Naci Mocan and Kaj Gittings, *Getting Off Death Row: Commuted Sentences and the Deterrent Effect of Capital Punishment*, 46 J. OF LAW & ECON. 453 (2003) and Cass R. Sunstein and Adrian Vermeule, *Is Capital Punishment Morally Required? Acts, Omissions, and Life-Life, Tradeoffs*, 58 STAN. L. REV. 703 (2006).

[41] For extensive critiques of the scientistic tendency in sociology and law, see HARRY COLLINS and ROBERT EVANS, RETHINKING EXPERTISE (2007) and JAMES R.

Leiter's commitment to a naturalized jurisprudence seems to preclude any participation in these value conversations about capital punishment or political morality more generally, let alone the development of a critical theory of social values. His insistence on the centrality and sharpness of the fact/value distinction is so lopsided that it undermines any serious or useful discussion about values and morality. Within his black-and-white universe of naturalized jurisprudence, there are those matters that lend themselves to a casually driven empirical predictive inquiry and that can, therefore, meet the "the best-going criteria of the knowable and real." And then there are the rest—those matters, like values and conversations about them, that do not make "a causal difference to the course of our experience" and, therefore, are of little or no value. Under the tutelage of psychoanalysis and evolutionary psychology, Leiter reduces moral commitments to "the deterministic forces" of innate drives or biological functions. Within such a realist world, talk about values is reduced to little more than the rhetorical reflex of "brute and opposed evaluative attitudes or 'tastes.'"[42] Value conversation is so much hot air.

Yet this is a perplexing and unnecessary stance. Leiter remains still too much in the shadow of the logical positivists and their claims about moral claims being unanalyzable and mere pseudo concepts.[43] In the same way that scientific inquiry is less hard and more valued connected than Leiter contends, so value conversation is less soft and more useful than Leiter suggests. The scientific method need not be deified or demonized and value conversation need not be parodied or privileged. If the pragmatic critique of science as a fact-based and value-free enterprise is accepted, then any superiority that scientific inquiry might claim is less epistemological and methodological, but more historical and sociological. On a pragmatic and non-naturalized account, it is not that there is some available method on offer that can reliably deliver the moral goods. But that is not the same thing as abandoning any prospect of a conversation about values. As Rorty observes, it is not that there is some super-methodological procedure that science possesses, but that "there are only local and specific agreements on procedure within such expert

---

HACKNEY JR., UNDER COVER OF SCIENCE: AMERICAN LEGAL-ECONOMIC THEORY AND THE QUEST FOR OBJECTIVITY (2007).

[42] Leiter, *supra*, note 9 at 239, 240, 210, 208–09, and 254–55. In a similar vein, Richard Posner dismisses moral theory's value to law and recommends that judges should develop "a disposition to ground policy judgments on facts and consequences than on conceptualisms and generalities." See R. POSNER, THE PROBLEMATICS OF MORAL AND LEGAL THEORY 133 (1999) and LAW, PRAGMATISM, AND DEMOCRACY (2003).

[43] A.J. AYERS, LANGUAGE, TRUTH AND LOGIC 107 (1936).

cultures as stellar spectroscopy, modal logic, admiralty law, possible-world semantics, or Sanskrit philology."[44] Accordingly, rather than privilege one procedure above all others and then seek to extend its dominion over all inquiries and subject-matter, a pragmatist levels down and chooses between available methods on the basis of which is the most useful for grappling with the type of problem at hand.

For Leiter, when it comes to value conversation, "once [the demands of logical consistency and factual accuracy] are exhausted, . . . we have left the space of reasons behind."[45] This renders Leiter mute (and presumably everyone else) on most of the contested and important matters in society. For instance, if Leiter takes the position that the invasion of Iraq by the United States is "criminal and immoral,"[46] is this simply the result of some evolutionary instinct, emotional trigger, or psychoanalytical tick? Beyond being logically consistent and factually accurate, would he or could he have anything to say by way of argument about such a view? Presumably, he might put forward a series of justificatory arguments in the hope that he might be able to persuade others of his position. Or, in such a value conversation, he might himself be persuaded that his original assessment was wrong and that he should take a new and, now for him, more defensible view that the war is lawful and moral. None of this seems unreasonable and might better capture people's existential experience of value conversation. There will be no independent or enduring standard by which to determine which view is right in any enduring or final sense; the criteria for evaluation will be forged and accepted within the social bounds of the conversational exchange. Nevertheless, in engaging in value conversations over time and in different settings, people might and often do change their views.

This seems to be close to what goes on in adjudication. Although judges might well decide cases mostly in line with their attitudes (and it would surely be more surprising if they did not), there needs to be an explanation of why judges have the attitudes they do and how they change over time.

---

[44]   Richard Rorty, *A Pragmatist View of Contemporary Analytic Philosophy* in RICHARD RORTY, PHILOSOPHY AS CULTURAL POLITICS: PHILOSOPHICAL PAPERS, vol. 4, 133 at 143 (2007). As Cornell West put it, pragmatism has an "unashamedly moral emphasis and its unequivocally ameliorative impulse." See C. WEST, THE AMERICAN EVASION OF PHILOSOPHY 4 (1989).

[45]   Leiter, *supra*, note 9 at 255.

[46]   Brian Leiter, *The End of Empire: Dworkin and Jurisprudence in the 21st Century* fn.48, 17 (U of Texas Law, Public Law Research Paper No. 70, 2007).

Indeed, mindful that "ideological drift is pervasive" in adjudicative performance,[47] it seems wholly unreasonable to pretend that value conversation, whether in the form of legal argument or some other normative engagement, does not have some impact upon that drift. This is not to suggest that such value conversation is determinative or decisive, let alone that its effects are predictable or fixed in any empirical manner. It is simply to make the reasonable pragmatic contention that value conversation has a role to play and, depending on the circumstances, that role may be larger or smaller. Consequently, although it is imprudent to ignore the role that evolutionary instincts, emotional triggers, or psychoanalytical ticks might play in the formulation and maintenance of people's moral commitments, it is equally to unwise to reject any possible transformative role for value conversation. Although science might well work because it "sends the planes into the sky, keeps the food from spoiling in the refrigerator, and alleviates human suffering through modern medicine,"[48] there is little evidence that it works at all in deciding whether to send war planes into the sky, give partially spoiled food to homeless people, or share modern medicine with those societies that cannot afford it. Eschewing any particular epistemic claims, experience might tell us that scientists have as little to tell us *as scientists* about morality as non-scientists do about scientific inquiry. In developing such value conversations, a more democratic approach has much to recommend it.

Conclusion

In their efforts to recommend a naturalized jurisprudence as a neutral and descriptive account of law's knowable and real facts, Brian Leiter and the New Legal Realists seek to adopt the avuncular posture of a juristic Walter Cronkite. Widely hailed in the 1970s and 1980s as "the most trusted man in America," Cronkite ended his CBS Evening News broadcasts with the his trademark phrase "And that's the way it is." However, even though Cronkite

---

[47] Lee Epstein, Andrew Martin, Kevin Quinn & Jeffrey Segal, *Ideological Drift among Supreme Court Justices: Who, When, and How Important?*, 101 Nw. U. L. Rev. 1483 at 1486 (2007). Mainstream jurists spent decades resisting the conclusion of critical legal scholars that "adjudication is politics." See Hutchinson, GAME, *supra*, note 38. The fact that this insight is now introduced as *scientific* makes the main point about method and values that this whole chapter urges.

[48] Leiter, *supra*, note 9 at 51. *See also* KWAME ANTHONY APPIAH, EXPERIMENTS IN ETHICS (2007).

was a paragon of integrity, he was not without values or prejudices. It was more that he showcased the values and interests that his audience shared and aspired to at that time. He was admired because of his values, not in spite of them. Yet the renewed philosophical plea to acknowledge, "And that's the way it is," is equally unpersuasive as a final achievement of Austin's analytical project for jurisprudence. There are no deep and sustaining truths about law and adjudication that arise in and inform, but are somehow detached from particular historical practices and social interests. If "the first call of a theory of law is that it should fit the facts,"[49] this will require jurists to pay heed to the social forces and political interest that frame and support those facts. Abandoning its pretension to discover scientific truths about law, legal theory might more profitably begin to take seriously the challenge of exploring the social conditions and institutional circumstances which are most conducive to facilitating a thoroughly democratic conversation about important decisions and informing values. Analytical jurisprudence, whether of Leiter's scientistic variety or any other more mundane kind, is an evasion of that task. If science is to have any chance of saving jurisprudence, it must first save itself.

---

[49] See O.W. HOLMES, THE COMMON LAW 167 (1881). *See also* Hart, *supra*, note 20 at 80.

CHAPTER SIX

The Province of Jurisprudence Moralized

To set up as a standard of public morality a notion which can neither be defined nor conceived is to open the door to every kind of tyranny.
—Simone Weil

Analytical jurisprudence has been dominated by legal positivists. Beginning with John Austin's own efforts, a primary objective of many analytical jurists has been to insist upon the philosophical benefits of keeping inquiries about the facts of law's existence separate from assessments of its moral worth. Yet not all those jurists who have taken up analytical jurisprudence's invitation to grasp and appreciate *law* as something to be studied on its own terms have felt the need to subscribe to the positivist cause. Indeed, although their work has remained largely conceptual and analytical in scope and ambition, these jurists have insisted that law's identity as a separate and authoritative mode of social regulation cannot be understood without paying close attention to its moral content and normative purposes—questions of legality and legitimacy are inextricably and necessarily connected.

However, in claiming that law's essential nature and structure has an indispensable moral dimension, they also acknowledge and accept Austin's warning that "the teacher of jurisprudence . . . ought not to attempt to insinuate his opinion of merit and demerit under pretence of assigning causes."[1] Accordingly, the challenge for such moralists is to put forward a convincing account of law's political morality and, at the same time, to demonstrate that such a commitment flows from the law itself, not from the particular leanings of the inquiring jurist. This is a sizeable and pressing task. Although modern moralists' attempts to fulfill the ambitions of analytical jurisprudence are an important improvement on the influential positivist offerings,

---

[1] JOHN AUSTIN, THE PROVINCE OF JURISPRUDENCE DETERMINED 374 (1832: H.L.A. Hart ed. 1955).

they are destined to fail, albeit honorably and helpfully so. By insisting that moral values are an inescapable feature of law's existence, the moralists have rightly rehabilitated values and their critical interrogation into the institutional heart of the jurisprudential enterprise. However, because they remain within the stultifying grip of the analytical tradition, the considerable promise and potential of this worthy initiative have been largely dissipated and lost; moralists manage to reintroduce values into the jurisprudential project, but only to cabin and contain their disruptive impact by treating them as being largely untouched by political pressures and historical exigencies. Most important, from a democratic perspective, moralism tends to flatter the particpatory imperative, but only to deceive it by initially suggesting a way beyond the limitations of positivism, and then allowing its analytical affiliations to prevail.

In order to appraise this moralist strain of analytical jurisprudence, I will concentrate on the sophisticated and controversial work of Ronald Dworkin. After introducing his basic ideas, I will look at how he manages to capture both the best and worst of this anti-positivist approach and its connection to a more democratized rendition of jurisprudence. To paraphrase E.M. Forster, I will offer "two cheers" for Dworkin's version of analytical jurisprudence—one because it puts values at the center of the law's operation, and two because it begins to evaluate those values in terms of their contribution to the democratic project. However, two cheers are quite enough: there is no occasion to give three—the value-based inquiry is encumbered by both its unconvincing analytical epistemology and the fact that its democratic commitment is only half-hearted at best. As such, though Dworkin's ideas can work as a convenient bridge to a more serious democratization of law and legal theory, his work has remained too much part of the very tradition which he seeks to discredit.

A Democratic Two-Step?

Although Dworkin began his scholarly career as a critic of legal positivism, he has gone on to develop a body of constructive work that can be most usefully identified as *liberal legalism*. As well as being an anti-positivist jurist of the first rank, he is also a political and moral theorist of high standing. Over the decades since his initial interventions in the late 1960s,[2] Dworkin has

---

[2] See *supra*, ch.4.

taken up the moralist mantle of Lon Fuller and sought to expand and deepen his efforts to identify a jurisprudence in which "law . . . is deeply and thoroughly political . . . , [b]ut not a matter of personal or partisan politics."[3] In doing so, he has succeeded in putting issues of politics and morality squarely on the scholarly agenda of law and legal scholarship, particularly in the field of constitutional law. In becoming the chief proponent of a moralist jurisprudence, Dworkin has also been the main and most energetic flag-bearer for progressive liberalism in contemporary American society. In his most recent work, he has brought these initiatives together into an integrated theoretical proposal that claims to be the best and most desirable vehicle for advancing a democratic agenda in modern society.

On the jurisprudential front, Dworkin has continued to highlight the philosophical bankruptcy of legal positivism in both its softer and harder guises. He is adamant and unyielding in his insistence that it is not possible to talk about law without also talking about morality; "jurisprudence is an exercise in substantive political morality," and "people who argue about the content of law draw on moral considerations in a way that positivism cannot explain." However, unlike classical natural lawyers, Dworkin maintains that lawyers and judges have a political obligation to remain true to the moral spirit of existing legal norms. They are not free to legislate their own or anyone else's preferences, but are bound by a strict philosophical responsibility to rise above the political fray and make the extant law's social facts the morally best that they can be. To do more (or less) would be to flout lawyers' democratic-based commitments to respect and protect the political rights of citizens. Accordingly, although there have been many twists and turns along the way, Dworkin still holds to the foundational epistemological view that "a proposition of law is true if it flows from principles of personal and political morality that provide the best interpretation of the other propositions generally treated as true in contemporary legal practice."[4] In this way, Dworkin claims to fulfil the analytical mandate by emphasizing and explaining how law and jurisprudence is both a strict philosophical undertaking of conceptual inquiry as well as a contingently engaged exercise in moral evaluation.

On the moral and political front, Dworkin has also been busy in formulating a truly liberal and distinctive account of social justice. At the same time that he has been connecting inquiries about the law as-it-is with those about the law as-it-should-be in legal forums, he has been substantiating and

---

[3] R. DWORKIN, A MATTER OF PRINCIPLE 146 (1985).

[4] R. DWORKIN, JUSTICES IN ROBES 178, 187 and 14 (2006).

defending a progressive vision of public and private morality in the political arena. At the heart of this enterprise is Dworkin's insistence that the commitment to human dignity must be the gold standard against which to arrange and manage collective resources: It demands that society organize itself so that individuals can be recognized as having intrinsic and objective value and be responsible as well as free to follow their own life plans. This, of course, creates certain burdens; people must respect others' entitlements as equal to their own. As such, much of Dworkin's moral theory has been devoted to demonstrating how these general principles can be developed in the context of various controversial issues—abortion, euthanasia, religion, tax reform, terrorism, and the like[5]—and exploring the institutional implications and practical consequences that flow from this attachment to such a liberal account. In his capable and inventive hands, liberalism becomes both a justification and blueprint for how to constitute a just polity in early twenty-first century industrialized societies. This is no mean feat.

True to his general constructivist methodology, Dworkin offers this vision of justice as not merely personal to him, but as based upon some moral facts which are as given and objective as the law's own social facts. For him, some moral positions are "plain wrong, not wrong only because people think it."[6] However, he concludes that these values and principles are already woven into the fabric of American and similarly situated societies and, as importantly, in their legal doctrines and constitutional commitments. Indeed, Dworkin defends both his jurisprudential and moral contributions as being the best combination through which to embody and justify a sustained political commitment to democratic governance. For him, this entails a definite preference for *partnership democracy*, which involves a substantive set of moral commitments; it is to be distinguished from a strictly procedural conception that he labels *majoritarian democracy*. The partnership view of democracy qualifies the relationship between majority rule and democracy in order to ensure that decisions are democratic *only* when the conditions that protect the status and interests of each individual as a full partner are met: "democracy is a substantive, not a merely procedural, ideal."[7] In Dworkin's approach,

---

[5] *See, for example*, R. Dworkin, Life's Dominion (1993); Freedom's Law: The Moral Reading of the American Constitution (1996); Sovereign Virtue (2001); and R. Dworkin, Is Democracy Possible Here?: Principles for a New Political Debate (2006).

[6] Dworkin, *Objectivity and Truth: You'd Better Believe It*, 25 Phil. & Public Affs. 87 at 98 (1996).

[7] Dworkin, Democracy, *supra*, note 5 at 134.

therefore, the true test of democratic merit is less whether it has an appropriate institutional source or procedural pedigree in people's political views, more whether it is compatible and can be made to square with the philosophical demands of Dworkin's own two foundational principles of human dignity—intrinsic value and personal responsibility.

Nevertheless, Dworkin believes that the partnership view of democracy has procedural implications. In adopting reliable procedures for reaching collective decisions, he recommends widespread and roughly equal suffrage. However, the test of any procedural arrangement is whether it is more likely than not to advance substantive equality. Accordingly, Dworkin's understanding of democracy leads to a definite commitment to the institutional protection of certain individual rights; certain aspects of each participant's life must not be susceptible to interference by collective decisions. It follows, therefore, that it is not only appropriate, but also necessary that the courts exits to act as a forum of principle to police this contested boundary by way of a constitutional review between those matters of political morality that are open to collective decision by majoritarian procedural processes and those that are not. If judges do this properly, he maintains, that they will offer a moral reading of the United States (US) Constitution that will "elaborate a coherent constitutional morality."[8]

This moralist stance is not presented as a violation of democratic governance, but as a realization of its very highest ambitions. Of course, it will come as little surprise that this defense of democracy not only fits very well the general structure of the US Constitution, but that the most coherent constitutional morality is the one which Dworkin has been at pains to develop and defend in the moral limb of his work. Consequently, there is a seamless match and mutual reinforcement in his liberal legalism between his jurisprudential stance and his moral position—courts have a central and indispensable role in furthering democracy by protecting people's basic entitlements and rights, as exemplified and contained in those enduring principles of liberal justice which flow directly from the best justification of American law and culture. Of course, that does not mean the United States is a paragon of democratic governance, even to Dworkin. However, he does proceed to make a resounding case for why the general structure and practices of American constitutional politics are so desirable and definitive: Exceptional lapses from democratic grace merely serve to prove the general rule of constitutionalist integrity.

---

[8] Dworkin, FREEDOM'S LAW, *supra*, note 5 at 40. See also Dworkin, DEMOCRACY, *supra*, note 5.

Even from such a bare sketch of Dworkin's ideas, it should be clear that this is an ambitious and audacious set of claims. He presents a full-blown theory of constitutional democracy that is threaded neatly together by philosophical analysis, moral reflection, legal recommendation, historical exposition, and political integrity. This represents a significant and impressive advance over the cloistered efforts of those other more positivistically inclined jurists in the analytical tradition. Nevertheless, for all its sweep and substance, there are a broad range of serious flaws with Dworkin's liberal legalism. I intend to concentrate on those that go towards its appeal and legitimacy as a legal theory of democratic governance.[9] Despite its more expansive moralist methods and ambitions, Dworkin's jurisprudence offers only a waystation on the road to a more thoroughly democratic jurisprudence. Although he wrests control of the jurisprudential initiative from the positivists, he remains too securely within the confines of analytical jurisprudence. Even though Dworkin is correct to insist that "we cannot sensibly claim that a philosophical analysis of a value is conceptual, neutral and disengaged," he is mistaken to assert that "we can sensibly claim it to be normative, engaged and conceptual."[10] No matter how normative and engaged that evaluative analysis may be, it will remain unduly closeted if it remains largely conceptual in scope and ambition. Consequently, a democratic approach to law's values rejects the imperial quality of Dworkin's jurisprudence; it suggests a much more pragmatic and much less magisterial approach to understanding the place of values in law and legal theory, apart of a larger democratic commitment.

Accordingly, in the remainder of this chapter, I will develop and contest some of the major threads in Dworkin's liberal legalism. First, the critical focus will be on the theoretical foundations of his account of law-as-integrity; there is an unbridgeable schism between the descriptive and prescriptive dimensions of his adjudicative proposals as a matter of practice and history that fatally undermines his jurisprudential project by its own lights. Second, the philosophical footings of his jurisprudential and moral writings are frail

---

[9] For my other critiques of Dworkin's body of work, *see* DWELLING ON THE THRESHOLD: CRITICAL ESSAYS ON MODERN LEGAL THOUGHT 57–84 (1988); IT'S ALL IN THE GAME: A NON-FOUNDATIONALIST ACCOUNT OF LAW AND ADJUDICATION 116–36 (2000); and EVOLUTION AND THE COMMON LAW 70–86 (2005). Others argue that the Dworkinian canon can best be understand as a hybrid between positivism and natural law. See John Mackie, *The Third Theory of Law in* RONALD DWORKIN AND CONTEMPORARY JURISPRUDENCE 165 (M. Cohen ed. 1983).

[10] Dworkin, JUSTICE IN ROBES, *supra*, note 4 at 155.

and unpersuasive; his resort to and defense of moral facts is ill suited to the ostensibly democratic ambitions of his work. Last, his account of democracy is crimped and cramped; he proposes a system of democratic governance that is a pale and narrow version of its ample possibilities. Throughout, I will emphasize the extent to which Dworkin's recent claim to be "talking about democracy . . . all along" is misleading in that democracy is for him only a subsidiary and secondary concern, not a primary and governing standard for both philosophical inquiry and political engagement.[11] Indeed, Dworkin's efforts to insert values into jurisprudential endeavor fail on two counts—it is more than democratic in that he attempts to pass off a contested version of morality as factual and obligatory, but less than democratic in that he offers an elite account of morality that is intended to discipline and constrain popular debate. For him, "getting it right" (*i.e.*, doing it his way) is more important and paramount than anything else. And that is the antithesis of a genuine democratic sensibility.

Fast and Loose

Dworkin's account of law and adjudication insists that interpretation is an inescapable and value-laden feature of legal practice. As such, it is sensitive to the claim that judges and jurists might be tempted, under the guise of legal interpretation, to fashion and sculpt the law according to their own preferred political inclinations. After all, as opposed to elected politicians, lawyers have no obvious democratic mandate to legislate their own personal views. Although there will still be ample room for creativity and ingenuity, judges must be seen to apply the law over time, not remake it constantly as their personal political views dictate. Accordingly, although he insists that legal validity and moral legitimacy are intimately connected, Dworkin places great theoretical and strategic weight on the extant legal materials' capacity to constrain judges' discretion and check their own moral convictions in determining what is the best moral justification of the "the brute facts of legal history."[12] In general, Dworkin's law-as-integrity exhortation for judges, to offer the best justification of existing legal materials as a coherent moral structure, seems a reasonable and conventional summary of common law adjudication. Although it is unreasonable to expect that all judges will agree on what counts as best, there will at least be a commonality of purpose that

---

[11]   Dworkin, DEMOCRACY, *supra*, note 5 at 155.

[12]   R. DWORKIN, LAW'S EMPIRE 255 (1986).

will go a long way to squaring the inevitability of judicial discretion with the political demand for institutional legitimacy in a broadly democratic society.

However, this approach draws Dworkin into a dangerous interpretive game on both a philosophical and historical fronts. In order to account for the law's progress and ability to adapt to changing social needs, he is obliged to play fast and loose with the judges' obligation to remain true to the existing legal materials. If his law-as-integrity theory is taken seriously, Dworkin is saddled with an account of adjudication which commits judges to making decisions that will, by necessity, be profoundly conservative. Notwithstanding the fact that legal doctrine is far from determinate and inhabited by a host of competing principles, present judges will be appropriately hampered by the legal past in their present efforts to fashion a different and more just future set of legal norms. As such, Dworkin's account of law and adjudication demands a commitment to the basic structure and fairness of the existing legal system. Although this will not be a problem for many judges and jurists most of the time, it certainly will be a problem for a few most of the time and for many part of the time. If the law is capable of being fixed within the broad bounds of judges' and society's moral convictions, there will be little difficulty in heeding Dworkin's instruction to remain faithful to the letter and spirit of the existing law. However, once the law starts to deviate too much from those settled moral convictions, both the judges' and society's commitments will be put to the test. Are judges to abandon the best justification of existing legal materials to keep the law in tune with changing social mores? Or are judges to adhere to that best justification even though the result will be out of step with or contrary to prevailing social values? This dilemma is particularly acute in matters of constitutional review in which the judicial performance is final and checks further democratic debate.

In Dworkinian terms, when and where the demands of law and morality clash, the dilemma is even starker—Is the judge to opt for doctrinal fidelity or moral justice? A choice either way will have severe consequences for his jurisprudential account in both practice and theory. If the option of formal fidelity is preferred, the judge will be subscribing to a stance that severs the law-as-it-is from the law-as-it-should-be and concedes the merit of the positivists' position that law's validity is something separate from its moral legitimacy. But, if the option of substantive justice is preferred, the judge ignores the necessary institutional constraints of doctrinal integrity and accepts that moral justice trumps legal norms. As such, Dworkin-inspired judges and jurists are left in the uncomfortable position of many traditional natural lawyers; they find themselves being "either a radical revolutionary or an unregenerate reactionary."[13] Neither prospect seems particularly appealing. However, it seems to be Dworkin's self-imposed jurisprudential lot to try and occupy both roles at one and the same time. This is obviously an impossible task.

Dworkin's response to this central predicament is far from convincing and does more to reinforce its debilitating quality than avoid it. He tackles this problem in the context of patently unjust laws. In such circumstances, the central challenge is whether wicked legal systems generate legal rights and whether judges must enforce such rights—Did a judge have to recognize a slave owner's right to the return of their escaped slaves? Did a judge have to confiscate the property of Jews at the request of Aryans? Did a judge have to enforce the segregation laws of an apartheid legal system? Dworkin is sorely and genuinely troubled by these cases, not simply because he finds them intolerable as matters of substantive justice, but because his own attachment to law-as-integrity seems to demand that judges are obliged to answer them affirmatively and, therefore, immorally. Indeed, a good-faith reading of the relevant legal materials in early nineteenth-century America, mid twentieth-century Germany, and late twentieth-century South Africa point to the existence of such oppressive rights and, therefore, to their judicial enforcement in the name of democratic justice. Nevertheless, Dworkin seems undaunted and offers a distinction that is intended to finesse these ignominious outcomes:

> A full political theory of law . . . includes at least two main parts; it speaks to both the grounds of law—circumstances in which particular propositions of law should be taken to be sound or true—and to the force of law—the relative power of any true proposition of law to justify coercion in different sorts of exceptional circumstances. . . . If a judge's own sense of justice condemned [the grounds of law] as deeply immoral . . . , he would have to consider whether he should actually enforce it . . . , or whether he should lie and say that this was not the law after all, or whether he should resign. The principle of integrity in adjudication, therefore, does not necessarily have the last word about how the coercive

---

13   *Introduction* in I. KANT, THE METAPHYSICAL ELEMENTS OF JUSTICE xxix (John Ladd ed.1965). Natural lawyers have played varying roles, sometimes as supporters of the *status quo* and, at other times, as instigators of change, whether conservative or progressive in thrust. *See* BRIAN BIX, *Natural Law Theory: The Modern Tradition* in HANDBOOK OF JURISPRUDENCE AND LEGAL PHILOSOPHY 61 (J. Coleman and S. Shapiro eds. 2002).

power of the state should be used. But it does have the first word, and normally there is nothing to add to what it says.[14]

Accordingly, though judges are normally expected to follow the law, they can ignore the law where and when they consider it to be 'deeply immoral'. Although this might seem to extricate him from a tight jurisprudential corner, it actually undermines the whole basis of Dworkin's account of adjudication: He has bought this jurisprudential victory at much too high a price. Shaved so thin, his controlling idea of 'legal integrity' will be so transparent as to be of little use in future skirmishes. The 'judges's own sense of justice' will be regnant and trump the community's legal consensus. This means that judges are unconstrained by past judicial and legislative decisions if they consider them sufficiently wicked or 'deeply immoral'. Yet, wickedness is a notoriously contested concept; one judge's iniquity can be another's equity. Legal history is redolent with judicial pronouncements that reveal the ephemeral character of such moralistic designations. Moreover, the threshold requirement of 'exceptional circumstances' operates as no check at all and it would be logically impossible to ask 'the principle of integrity' to determine the conditions of its own applicability or exceptions to it. According to Dworkin, the primacy of the judge's conscience is not fatal in circumstances that are not 'exceptional' because 'the principle of integrity' will provide the necessary institutional constraint. However, in 'exceptional circumstances', the judge's 'own sense of justice' will be irresistibly paramount. Accordingly, provided that judges have a sincerely held belief that a showing of wickedness has been made, they are free to 'lie', 'resign', or 'refuse to enforce the law'.

This is a profoundly disturbing conclusion for an analytical jurist like Dworkin who is devoted to justifying the self-sustaining legitimacy and moral force of the legal enterprise. In such circumstances, the touchstone of good judging becomes the strength and sincerity of judges' own moral and political beliefs, not the moral force of the extant law or particular judge's fidelity to it. This means that sometimes the law's morality is clear and binding, but at other times it is clear and elective. However, Dworkin has no genuine proposal as to when and how such decisive determinations are to be made. Indeed, the upshot of Dworkin's moralist position seems to be that, if judges can ignore 'the brute facts of legal history' and push off in a new direction whenever the discrepancy between those facts and their own sense of justice becomes too great, then the appropriate decision is always whatever the judge thinks it should be. Judges will only be obliged to follow the law

---

[14]   Dworkin, LAW'S EMPIRE, *supra*, note 12 at 110–11 and 219.

when it does not offend sufficiently their own moral convictions. This seems to contradict flatly Dworkin's ambition to offer an account of law and adjudication which insists upon a sharp and democratically necessary distinction between the law-as-it-is and the judge's own sense of the law-as-it-should-be. Moreover, it is ironic that, although Dworkin has insisted that the analytical enterprise is inescapably about values, he is committed to a much more conservative account of law and adjudication than his positivists colleagues who can, consistent with their basic separation thesis, give no particular weight to the past and countenance radical and abrupt changes in legal doctrine.[15]

Dworkin's account of law-as-integrity is also found wanting in another important and related sense. Mindful that he has been developing and refining both a legal theory and a moral theory, there exists a very dubious relationship between them. In particular, it strains credulity for him to arrive always at the same conclusion that the best justification of the law-as-it-is is exactly congruent with his own moral account of the law-as-it-should-be. Time after time, Dworkin's assessment of whether any important legal decision about legal rights is defensible or not is measured entirely by its substantive conformity with what he maintains is the best decision by the lights of his own moral theory. This congruence is simply too politically convenient to be theoretically convincing. Whether the subject is abortion or school segregation, the best reading of the US Constitution always turns out to be the one that Dworkin favors as a moral theorist.[16] Accordingly, even though Dworkin maintains that "anyone who accepts law as integrity must accept that the actual political history of his community will sometimes check his other political convictions in his overall interpretive judgment,"[17] *sometimes* never seems to happen when it comes to Dworkin's own critique of law or political convictions. This troubling state of affairs defies any reasonable understanding of constitutional law and adjudication.

In proposing his moral reading of the US Constitution, Dworkin's gamble is not only that judges will be capable of utilizing the appropriate philosophical method, but that they will get it right in the sense of settling upon a 'best justification' of the law's facts that is correct (or, as I have been trying to establish, that most nearly matches his own preferred moral theory of law).

---

[15]   See *supra*, ch.4. It is worth emphasizing that positivists are not at the same as formalists; there is nothing in the hard or soft positivist approach that commits adherents to any particular judicial philosophy.

[16]   See the various analyses that Dworkin offers in FREEDOM'S LAW, *supra*, note 5 and in his regular and topical contributions to the *New York Review of Books*.

[17]   Dworkin, LAW'S EMPIRE, *supra*, note 12 at 255.

This is as much a strategic and historical claim as a philosophical one. Yet even a passing knowledge of the historical record suggests that Dworkin's jurisprudence lacks the minimal legitimacy that any philosophical account must achieve if it is to be a superior rendition of the analytical project. Across time, the courts have taken different and divergent paths. Indeed, the history of American constitutional law evidences the oscillation between sets of liberal and conservative principles as they struggle for temporary dominance. The challenge for Dworkin and other moralists, therefore, is to demonstrate that those decisions that are good (*i.e.*, in line with his preferred moral theory) are more representative of the law's deeper structure and enduring identity and those that are bad (*i.e*, not in line with his preferred moral theory) are simply contingent or erroneous.[18] As I have tried to show, such a demonstration is not convincing, at least as part of the kind of analytical project in which Dworkin engages. A more reasonable and defensible stance is that each theorist seems to alight on those legal decisions that best capture their preferred moral theory and then tries to market them as the best or true interpretation of the constitutional framework. This is further confirmation that not only is law politics, but that legal theory is as well.

If a primary and democratically based obligation of judges is to act with fidelity toward law's brute facts, a tipping point will come at which the accumulation of recent facts might well eclipse and overwhelm a previous body of legal facts. The continuing and unfinished saga over the validity and merit of *Roe v. Wade* is a telling case in point.[19] At such a juncture, Dworkin and others must counsel judges either to ignore the brute facts of recent history and champion a moral reading of the US Constitution that is grounded in something other than those brute facts or go with those newly established brute facts and commit to a different and perhaps less appealing moral reading. Almost everything will depend of the judges' own sense of judicial responsibility and moral conviction as well as the balance made between them. However, Dworkin has no independent or neutral basis on which to

---

18 For an application of this argument to jurisprudential theories generally, *see* P. SCHLAG, THE ENCHANTMENT OF REASON 99 (1998). For a compelling history of American constitutional law, *see* MARK TUSHNET, THE RED, WHITE, AND BLUE: A CRITICAL ANALYSIS OF CONSTITUTIONAL LAW (1988).

19 *Roe v. Wade*, 410 US 113 (1973). For a historical analysis of *Roe's* career, *see* DONALD CRITCHLOW, THE POLITICS OF ABORTION AND BIRTH CONTROL IN HISTORICAL PERSPECTIVE (1996). For a jurisprudential analysis, *see* Hutchinson, EVOLUTION, *supra*, note 9 at 139–63. I return to a democratic assessment of the court's constitutional performances later. See *infra*, ch.8.

recommend either course of action other than his own liberal preferences; the gravitational pull of law's brute facts has already been dismissed as indecisive. Yet, if judges are required to ignore 'the brute facts of legal history' too lightly and too often, then Dworkin's account will be revealed as little more than a traditional natural law theory masquerading as an analytical account: Dworkin will simply be approving of those decisions and doctrines that embody his moral theory and disapproving of those that do not. The constraining demands of 'the brute facts of legal history' will be so slight and pliable as to be of little or no effect; they will be observed as much in their neglect as in their acceptance. Law's integrity according to Dworkin turns out to be more about keeping faith with liberal morality than anything else.

Facts of The Matter

An important strand in Dworkin's defense of his law-as-integrity account of law and adjudication is thoroughly philosophical and unapologetically epistemological. He claims that the moralist claims that he makes are not simply based on personal moral preferences on his part, but are predicated upon moral facts whose status is as fixed and objective as the law's own social facts. For him, some moral positions are "plain wrong, not wrong only because people think it."[20] These are audacious claims and, if proven, will not only go a long way to establishing Dworkin's own philosophical stance, but will deliver a devastating blow to the democratic approach that I have been taking. However, needless to say, it is my contention that Dworkin's epistemological exertions are to little positive effect and actually create even further problems for his accounts of law, morality, and justice.

Like other analytical jurists, Dworkin has some difficulty getting his interpretive project off the ground and for much the same reasons. It seems excessively audacious to assert that "we have no difficulty in identifying collectively the practices that count as legal practices in our own culture" and that they are "treated as given in day-to-day reflection and argument." I have sought to demonstrate that identifying what counts as law is neither given nor easy. If it were, there would be little point to the legal positivist branch of the analytical tradition which continues to expend all its energies on this very issue. Indeed, Dworkin seems to confound himself when he concludes that "law cannot flourish as an interpretive enterprise in any community

---

[20]   Dworkin, *supra*, note 6 at 98.

unless there is enough initial agreement about what practices are legal practices so that lawyers argue about the best interpretation of roughly the same data."[21] Again, if that were so, the legal enterprise as well as legal theory would be in even greater difficulty than is presently the case. However, as if all this was not audacious enough, Dworkin has gone on to make some truly extravagant claims about the philosophical nature and epistemological status of law's energizing moral component. Although these claims have been implicit throughout his substantial jurisprudential oeuvre, he has made them more explicit and also even more immoderate in his more recent writings. Dworkin has become almost temerarious in his efforts to defend his account of law and adjudication.

To ensure that there is no misunderstanding about his jurisprudential ambitions, Dworkin reminds critics and fellow travellers alike that he remains fully committed to the idea that "justice plays a role in fixing what the law is" such that "moral considerations figure among the truth conditions of propositions of law" and "a proposition of law is true if it flows from principles of personal and political morality that provide the best interpretation of the other propositions generally treated as true in contemporary legal practice." Having confirmed his continuing attachment to the analytical tradition, he proceeds to elaborate what he thinks is involved in a distinctly moral and constructive interpretation of law. In direct contrast to other analytical jurists, he has no truck with their almost uniform and universal presupposition that any debate about moral and political values is unavoidably contingent and highly contested. Instead, he insists that it is as moral facts that moral considerations "figure among the basic truth conditions of propositions of law."[22] Accordingly, Dworkin takes a huge step beyond the foundational assumptions of his analytical colleagues in positing that not only is there an indispensable moral dimension to law, but that such a dimension has a solid factual basis. This is truly a grand epistemological claim of the boldest proportions.

In his most recent work, Dworkin develops this theme and announces that "there is an objective standard of success in living." By this (and in line with his earlier work), Dworkin means to insist that there is some objective ground or moral facts-of-the-matter which must necessarily underpin the foundational effort to advance the political and democratic project of law and social justice. In doing so, he offers an uncompromising objectivist account

---

[21]   Dworkin, LAW'S EMPIRE, *supra*, note 12 at 91, 66, and 90. For a general discussion of law's allegedly factual basis, see *supra*, chs.3 and 5.

[22]   Dworkin, JUSTICES IN ROBES, *supra*, note 4 at 35, 5, 14 and 224.

of political morality. Despite his philosophical protestations to the contrary and his democratic gestures to establish shared principles among citizens, he takes social practices (*i.e.*, law, morality, etc.) on face value and subjects them to an analytical and abstract inquiry in order to determine and illuminate their essential features. In confronting directly the epistemological footings of his political and jurisprudential inquiry, he states that "there is objective truth to be had in the realms of ethics and morality . . . because the opposite, skeptical claim [*i.e.*, values are just projections of our deepest emotions] is philosophically indefensible."[23] Although he recognizes that these are controversial statements, he maintains that it is not a philosophical mistake to talk about values as being true or false. For him, values are real in that their existence or character are not reducible to anyone's beliefs or preferences. Indeed, he has gone so far as to state that:

> just as a scientist can aim, as a distinct kind of project, to reveal the very nature of a tiger or of gold by exposing the basic physical structure of these entities, so a political philosopher can aim to reveal the very nature of freedom by exposing its normative source. In each case we can describe the enterprise, if we wish, as conceptual. The physicist helps us to see the essence of water; the philosopher helps us to see the essence of liberty. The difference between these projects . . . is finally one of degree. . . . We cannot sensibly claim that a philosophical analysis of a value is conceptual, neutral and disengaged. But we can sensibly claim it to be normative, engaged and conceptual."[24]

In pursuing this conceptual and essentialist goal, Dworkin maintains that reflective height is the guarantor of moral depth. In resolving difficult and contested issues of political morality, he reminds judges that "the ladder of theoretical ascent is always there, on the cards, even when no one is tempted to take even the first step up it," and that "we cannot pursue that indispensable ambition [of living together as equals] unless we undertake, when necessary, to ascend high enough in our collective deliberations, including our adjudicative deliberations, to test our progress in [ensuring that the principles under which we are governed treat us as equals]."[25] Insofar as he expects judges to make an occasional justificatory ascent in order to ensure that substantive or

---

[23]   Dworkin, DEMOCRACY, *supra*, note 5 at 13 and 46.

[24]   Dworkin, ROBES, *supra*, note 4 at 155. Dworkin will be publishing still another new book in early 2009, entitled *Justice for Hedgehogs*, which will further advance and defend this objectivist moral epistemology.

[25]   *Id.* at 56 and 74.

local justice on any particular issue is not achieved at the price of formal inconsistency with the law's own overarching principles, Dworkin would surely expect at least as much and perhaps more from his philosophical interlocutors. Accordingly, although he frames his initial inquiry in the inclusive terms of searching for common ground and shared principles, he also insinuates that there are some objective facts-of-the-matter which can be found and that, once found, should discipline future debate and disagreement. These exhortations to turn all problems into philosophical ones and demand a particular philosophical resolution of them are of the most dubious provenance. With these broad flourishes, he exposes the contrivance of his gesture to look for shared principles and, instead, dismisses not only anyone who disagrees with that, but also any serious attempt to remain true to a democratic spirit of inquiry and debate. Indeed, there is little room for debate when confronted with facts; they demand only acknowledgment or denial.

First of all, even from within Dworkin's own epistemological framework, it is unclear exactly how scientists can go about revealing, for instance, the very nature of a tiger. The very act of identifying a tiger as a separate and distinguishable object of inquiry can only be done within the constructed and value-informed context of a particular taxonomic structure that has its own purposes and problems. Moreover, it is only at a particular moment in history that it is sensible to talk about *tigers* as they presently exist. Being part of life's evolutionary process, they are constantly mutating and changing: there is nothing fixed about biological entities or that constitutes their very nature which somehow stands outside the environment's contingent forces. Also, there is nothing about a tiger on its own that makes its DNA any more essential than any of its other characteristics. Although all tigers can be distinguished from all other things by reference to a certain range of genetic variations, they can also be so distinguished by reference to a certain range of body masses, fur patterns, geographical habitats, or behavioral traits. There is nothing natural, neutral, or factual that prioritizes one set of distinguishing features over others.[26] Consequently, if these difficulties and choices are at work in regard to tigers (which do have some real-world existence and indicia beyond human imagination), the prospects for revealing the very nature of freedom as a normative construct seem especially elusive.

In contrast, a more rigorous democratic approach can better accommodate such contingent circumstances and normative considerations. In particular, there is no need to accept this very particular and frankly elitist characterization

---

[26] *See generally* Hutchinson, Evolution, *supra*, note 9 at 235–70.

of the philosophical enterprise. It is simply wrong to posit that the only alternative to an objectivist philosophy is a skeptical stance which contends that "our opinions about how to live are not reports of objective fact but just projections of our deepest emotions." This is simply not the case and does scant credit to the American philosophical tradition. Dworkin caricatures the skeptical position, particularly in regard to opinion being "just projections of our deepest emotions." As he concedes, these skeptics still continue to "suppose that there is a better and worse way for them to live and that it is important to live in the better way" and that they believe that "we can make mistakes about what it is to live well, and these mistakes are matters for very great regret."[27] To take that stance is not to subscribe to Dworkin's objectivist view and nor is it a matter of emotional projection. The possibilities are much richer than in Dworkin's limited and monochromatic epistemological world. Indeed, he would do much better and be truer to his democratic aspirations if he simply discarded this philosophical paraphernalia and abandoned this ill-fated venture entirely.

Moral clarity or progress is not about ascending to some higher, more removed, and abstract plane on which rationality can hold sway outside of the disabling influence of interests, commitments, fuzziness, history, culture, and ideology; it is about closing the gap between aspirations and actuality, about making the world a better place. There is simply no need to posit the existence of objective moral facts that can be discovered by seeking some ahistorical detachment or justificatory height. Philosophers like Dworkin cannot seem to accept that justification is not about the abstract or special relation between ideas, but is a social practice that has or requires no external authority to its own contextual development. Indeed, it is far more preferable to abandon the conceit that it is only possible to be theoretical if one escapes the bounds of "cultural and social" context and seeks to transcend "traditions and genres" as Dworkin does.[28] So often, this maneuver simply operates as an elaborate ploy to endow personal preference with the trappings of objective truth.

---

[27]   Dworkin, DEMOCRACY, *supra,* note 5 at 13, 13, 13, and 14. Dworkin's marked tendency to posit stark and unrealistic dichotomies is typical of his overall rhetorical approach. As with his representation of democracy, he skews the whole analysis by obliging critics to make a Hobson's choice between two entirely limited and loaded options. See *infra* pp. 135–37.

[28]   Dworkin, *supra,* note 6 at 133–34. For a more extensive critique of that position, *see* Hutchinson, *Casaubon's Ghosts: The Haunting of Legal Scholarship,* 21 LEGAL STUDIES 66 (2001).

In line with a democratic commitment, it is better to work from the premise that, when it comes to morality, there are no facts-of-the-matter which are independent of argument and debate; the grounds of political morality are within the debate, not outside or regulative of that debate. Echoing John Dewey and other pragmatists, Hilary Putnam is persuasive that "ethical talk needs no metaphysical story to support it . . .; it only needs what ethical talk . . . has always needed: good will, intelligence, and respect for what can be seen as grounds and difficulties from within the ethical stand-point."[29] This ethical talk is by its nature social and contextual. It is social in that it amounts to more than the idiosyncratic or private emotional projections of particular individuals. And it is contextual in that it is always located in social settings, but never entirely overwhelmed by them. Consequently, Dworkin's 'standard of success in living' is neither objective nor subjective as he is wont to suggest. Being collaborative and contextual is entirely complementary to and compatible with a democratic appreciation of politics and political debate.

Ironically, Dworkin locates his own philosophical quest in exactly the place that democratic pragmatists would recommend—in the search for a "common ground to be found between the trenches of . . . hostile political armies." This is a laudable project that is not only important for democracy, but also suggests that it will be achieved in a way that is democratic in form and ambition. The project itself is exactly what skeptics approve of and recommend. It is not about confronting people with objective facts which they have little choice other than to acknowledge. It is about working with the available conversational resources, engaging with others, and seeking to build, not impose, a common set of assumptions and shared values through real argument. Sadly, Dworkin fails to sustain this democratic project and, instead, reverts to objectivist type. Although he protests that "no nation's politics can be run like a philosophy seminar; a democracy must give the final verdict on who leads it to many millions," his jurisprudential account belies that; it is an objectivist lesson in moral fact-finding in which the professor speaks and the citizens listen. This is a far cry from a democratic exercise in which people search for "the common ground that

---

[29]   HILARY PUTNAM, THE COLLAPSE OF THE FACT/VALUE DICHOTOMY 94–95 (2002). *See also* J. DEWEY, EXPERIENCE AND NATURE 407–08 (2d ed. 1958); R. RORTY, PHILOSOPHY AND SOCIAL HOPE 266 (1999); and Hilary Putnam, *A Reconsideration of Deweyan Democracy*, 63 S. CAL. L. REV. 1671 (1990).

makes genuine argument among people of mutual respect possible and healing" as a way of stabilizing and moving forward his political agenda.[30]

Democratic Infusion

Although Dworkin defends his account of law and justice in terms of democracy, his preferred understanding of democracy is thin and attenuated. Indeed, he makes no bones about it when he states that democratic politics are an inferior mode of constitutional politics because it is important to put many matters of political morality outside the reach of popular political debate and disagreement. For him, it is simply axiomatic that "[judicially-enforced] constitutional rights . . . are not compromises of democracy, but rather attempts to guarantee it."[31] Yet this strategy is not only mistaken and unnecessary, but contrives to defeat the whole benefits of democratic governance and demonstrate the extent to which Dworkin fails to take democracy seriously as both a political initiative and a theoretical spur. By way of critique, I want to challenge Dworkin's limiting account of partnership democracy. This is not to embrace his impoverished and caricatured vision of majoritarian democracy, but to move towards a richer and more transformative understanding of democracy as it impacts upon the jurisprudential project.

For all the posturing and protestation in support of democracy and its political significance, there has been a distinct distrust of ordinary citizens' capacity to participate fully, freely, frequently, and actively in their own governance. In the twentieth century, democracy came to be associated almost exclusively with the institutional and competitive struggle for people's votes by those leaders who sought political power. This elective democracy has succeeded in thwarting activist efforts to institutionalize the belief that the governed are not only competent to elect their governors, but also entitled to make political judgments for themselves about all, not only some substantive issues and to make bad decisions (*i.e.*, different from the recommendations of pundits and experts). Dworkin's view of the role and place of democracy in constitutional governance fits snugly in this received tradition.[32]

Both of Dworkin's majoritarian and partnership accounts are satisfied and fulfilled by the election of officials every few years. The only fundamental difference is that his favored partnership account qualifies and limits the

---

[30]   Dworkin, DEMOCRACY, *supra*, note 5 at 6, 6, and 127.

[31]   *Id.* at 146.

[32]   See *supra*, ch.1 and *infra*, ch.8.

nature of the laws and policies that those officials might adopt. Whereas majoritarian democracy is *merely* the election of officials every few years, partnership democracy is the election of *good* officials every few years (*i.e.*, officials that only adopt laws and policies that are compatible with Dworkin's shared principles of human dignity). Participation is not something to be valued in and of itself. This explains why Dworkin emphasizes the importance of introducing changes in the public education system and in election law which will directly strengthen the quality of political argument. Although such innovations will likely enhance the popular political culture and facilitate electoral participation, they are limited in focus and ambition. Dworkin's narrow conceptions of democracy reduce politics and popular participation to a system in which people are expected to select among candidates for office as if they were products marketed and sold to them by the major political parties. Political life begins to mimic commercial enterprise and electoral politics is reduced to a hollow spectacle in which form triumphs over substance.[33] Indeed, the problem is that it is exactly this constricted depiction of political engagement and popular participation that helps to bring about the "appalling" and "divisive" state of contemporary politics that Dworkin so rightly deplores in modern democracies.[34] Consequently, his proposals do as much to perpetuate and entrench the problem as remedy and improve it.

Because Dworkin's conception of popular participation amounts to little more than voting and holding office, there is simply no possibility to take seriously a more active and extensive practice of popular participation. Neither of his democratic conceptions seeks to create institutions that maximize the participation of citizens in the continuing processes by which legal and regulatory policies are debated and enacted. This ought not to come as a surprise because, under Dworkin's vision of those substantive principles of human dignity which should animate democracy, an increase in and deepening of popular participation might actually hurt rather than improve democracy. For instance, according to Dworkin, a system that maximizes the greatest involvement by ordinary citizens in deliberation and decision making in a variety of settings and by a variety of devices might well be less democratic than the United States today if that system produces the wrong decisions. On the other hand, a system that leaves those decisions in the hands of an unelected group of officials might well constitute an exemplary democracy as long as the right decisions are produced. As such, it is clear that both

---

33 *See* A. HUTCHINSON, WAITING FOR CORAF: A CRITIQUE OF LAW AND RIGHTS 198–206 (1995).

34 Dworkin, DEMOCRACY, *supra*, note 5 at 1.

Dworkin's conceptions of democracy potentially deprive the political system of the participation of citizens in the adoption of the rules that govern their lives. Democracy cannot merely require a system that gives "the final verdict on *who leads* it to many millions of people."[35] This is to put popular participation squarely and perversely in the service of oligarchy, not democracy, and to treat voting as having only consequential and *symbolic* value.

Consequently, even if it requires some tradeoffs and compromises to be put into practice in large societies, democracy is a regime of popular self-government which not only allows for, but relies upon participation by citizens in the formulation and enactment of the laws that govern their lives. At its most general, it is the rule of everyone by everyone. However, the fact that those contemporary institutions and arrangements considered democratic allow only limited and occasional participation is not considered a weakness or failing by Dworkin and other faux democrats. Indeed, they are presented as the very kinds of institutions and arrangements that democrats should defend: The perverse position appears to have been reached in which popular participation is dispensable and no longer treated as an essential part of what is considered to be democratic. Under Dworkin's tutelage, democracy is exhausted by a legal system which establishes representative government, protects liberal rights, and enables all citizens to participate in government by electing officials. This is an impoverished and disabling idea of democracy and one which has little place for the emancipatory potential of popular participation.

Sources of Confusion

Like positivists, democrats are especially preoccupied with sources, but in a different way and for different reasons. No matter how fair a legal principle or rule seems to be, a democrat will always be interested in questions about its origin and, therefore, its legitimacy. In particular, the *whos* and *hows* of any established principle or enacted rule will be of compelling interest. A vital and principled dimension of any just law is the fact that it originated in an

---

[35] *Id.* at 48 and 127 (emphasis added). For general critiques of the tendency to marginalize popular participation, see Claude Ake, *Dangerous Liaisons: The Interface of Globalization and Democracy* IN DEMOCRACY'S VICTORY AND CRISIS 282 (Alex Hadenius ed.1997) and Sheldon Wolin, *Fugitive Democracy* in DEMOCRACY AND DIFFERENCE: CONTESTING THE BOUNDARIES OF THE POLITICAL 37 (Seyla Benhabib ed. 1996).

exercise of self-legislation by the governed, not simply imposed or made on their behalf: democracy is about rule *by* the people and not only *for* the people.[36] However, the democratic pedigree of a law is not the only concern of a democrat. Democratic lineage is a necessary, if not always sufficient condition for an initiative's just quality. Both the matter and manner of laws are important. Indeed, it is the procedural mode of their creation that bolsters and underwrites the substantive merit of those laws; matter and manner are intimately related and re-enforcing. Although this attention to sources has considerable salience in the legislative arena, its implications are even more pressing in regard to constitutional or fundamental laws which, by their nature, are often beyond the reach of day-to-day politics. Accordingly, the amenability of such constitutional arrangements and fundamental laws to periodic reconsideration and revision seems an indispensable part of any democratic compact.

For partnership democrats, the equal attention paid to procedural means in relation to substantive ends is unacceptable because they consider that it is the rightness of the decision that trumps all other concerns. Dworkin is firm on this. In his version of a *substantive* conception of democracy, he welcomes and defends the permanent institutionalization of what are taken to be the right abstract principles. The legislative policies adopted by a representative assembly must accept the intrinsic value of human life and respect the capacity of each individual in deciding what counts as a successful life if they are to be considered democratic. This view fuses together substance and procedure because it asks that policies are not only adopted democratically, but that they are just and, therefore, compatible with the shared principles of dignity. However, substance has priority over procedure in Dworkin's political lexicon. If the results of popular participation do not do not chime with his preferred liberal vision of human dignity, they are unacceptable and, in constitutional terms, should be rejected.

Of course, this places tremendous weight on the democratic legitimacy of existing constitutional arrangements. It obliges serious scrutiny to be given to the relation of democracy to the people and their constitution—how did the constitution come into effect (*e.g.*, Is the constitution the result of a

---

36 For further discussion about what it takes for a body of law to be regarded as the law of the people to whom it applies, see Frank Michelman, *Constitutional Authorship* in CONSTITUTIONALISM: PHILOSOPHICAL FOUNDATIONS 76 (Larry Alexander ed. 1998); FRANK MICHELMAN, BRENNAN AND DEMOCRACY (1999); J. WALDRON, LAW AND DISAGREEMENT ch.3 (1999); and Jeremy Waldron, *Can There be a Democratic Jurisprudence?* (unpublished paper, April 2004).

democratic process?) and how can it be altered (*e.g.*, Can the constitution be altered through democratic means?).[37] However, neither of Dworkin's alternative views of democracy addresses the democratic quality of constitutional arrangements or fundamental laws. Whereas the majoritarian view is perfectly compatible with a constitution that is adopted from the top-down and which contains stringent limitations on popular participation even in times of constitutional change, the partnership conception of democracy sets the traditional content of a liberal constitution as its procedural precondition and renders the issue of popular participation in possible constitutional change as simply irrelevant.

By presenting the content of a traditional liberal constitution as the necessary procedural consequence of a commitment to human dignity, Dworkin moves the fundamental rights provisions of the US Constitution outside the reach of democratic politics: "we may better protect equal concern by embedding certain individual rights in a constitution that is to be interpreted by judges rather than by elected representatives, and then providing that the constitution can be amended only by super-majorities." Yet Dworkin is not finished. He goes on to argue that majorities should not be allowed, "whenever they wish, to change the basic constitutional structure that seems best calculated to ensure equal concern." However, the surprising thing is that he does not allow for the possibility of constitutional change at all, at least in formal as opposed to interpretive terms. If a constitution provides for the rights and procedures that make partnership democracy possible (as Dworkin insists the US Constitution largely does), then there is little reason to be concerned at all with how it came into existence or whether it can ever be rewritten. In light of this, Dworkin's protest that "no nation's politics can be run like a philosophy seminar" seems particularly empty at the level of a society's fundamental laws.[38] If the abstract principles of human dignity

---

[37]   One scholar who has explored how constitutions are ordained by "majority-rule popular sovereignty" and whether that can be done (lawfully) again is Akhil Reed Amar. See Akhil Reed Amar, *Popular Sovereignty and Constitutional Amendment* in RESPONDING TO IMPERFECTION: THEORY AND PRACTICE OF CONSTITUTIONAL AMENDMENT 109 (Sanford Levinson ed. 1995). His central argument is that the US Constitution is a populist document that recognizes the *legal* right of the American electorate of altering their constitution in ways not contemplated in its amendment procedure; the procedure contemplated in Article V enumerates only the modes in which *government* (as opposed to the *people*) can change the constitution. See Akhil Reed Amar, *The Consent of the Governed: Constitutional Amendment Outside Article V*, 94 COLUMBIA L. REV. 457 (1994).

[38]   Dworkin, DEMOCRACY, *supra*, note 5 at 144, 144 and 127. In this, Dworkin follows John Rawls who stated that basic liberties must "no longer be regarded as appropriate

ground democracy, it is philosophy, not politics, that has fundamental priority in the constitutional scheme of things. Indeed, the whole point of Dworkin's philosophical enterprise seems to be to insulate the foundational principles of liberal legalism from democratic politics.

This antipathy to popular participation is reflected in existing approaches to constitutional reform. The motivating idea is that change should be infrequent because the stability of a juridical order is a primary value to be protected. However, constitutional democrats do concede that a large part of a liberal constitution's legitimacy rests in the fact that it can be changed through juridical means. Consequently, by way of compromise, liberal constitutions tend to make the process of amendment so arduous that few proposals for change are able to meet its stringent requirements which are often even more demanding than those met when the constitution was originally adopted. Liberal constitutions rarely include mechanisms which increase popular participation during times of important constitutional transformation: Democratic legitimacy is thought satisfied by the involvement and authority of ordinary representatives.[39] This effort to regulate transformative shifts not only makes constitutional change difficult and infrequent, but also works to effect a permanent barrier to popular participation in such crucial political matters. By making all political power subservient to the disciplinary protocols of the constitution and the Rule of Law, it no longer becomes reasonable to speak of important constitutional transformations except after cataclysmic events such as revolutions and *coup d'états*. Even after those events, it is thought that "by making a constitution, the revolutionary forces are digging their own graves."[40]

Such a political system that has entrenched the right abstract principles in what is thought to be a finished constitution and that has frozen in place a particular juridical arrangement sits very uncomfortably with any genuine

---

subjects for political decision by majority or other plurality voting. . .They are part of the public charter of a constitutional regime and not a suitable topic for ongoing debate and legislation." See JOHN RAWLS, POLITICAL LIBERALISM 151 (1993).

[39] *See, for example*, Canada's *Constitutional Act 1982*. *See generally* Steven Holmes and Cass Sunstein, *The Politics of Constitutional Revision in Eastern Europe* in RESPONDING TO IMPERFECTION: THEORY AND PRACTICE OF CONSTITUTIONAL AMENDMENT 277 (Sanford Levinson ed. 1995) and Jon Elster, *Introduction* in CONSTITUTIONALISM AND DEMOCRACY 3 (Jon Elster and Rune Slagstad eds. 1988). This tendency to prioritize stability and orderliness as neutral values is criticized earlier. See *supra*, ch.3.

[40] Ulrich Preuss, *Constitutional Powermaking for the New Polity: Some Deliberations on the Relations between Constituent Power and the Constitution*, 14 CARDOZO L. REV. 635 at 641 (1993).

commitment to democracy. Democracy resists political closure; it fosters, not forecloses political and popular engagement. Although a strongly democratic position is not indifferent to outcomes and is justified on the basis that it will result in a more just society, its critical wager is that the governed will produce more outcomes which are more conducive to society as a whole than those dictated by abstract and partial principles or by elite institutions and agencies. It should be clear, therefore, that my democratic critique is not simply about the conflict between individual rights and popular participation, but about the entrenchment of a juridical arrangement that, by embodying the principles of liberal legalism, is removed from democratic politics. If democracy is *only* about right outcomes, and if those outcomes are already embedded in a constitutional arrangement and removed from popular discussion and debate, the ideals of openness and popular participation with respect to the fundamental laws are rendered almost meaningless. In contrast, a commitment to strong democracy insists that *all* arrangements must be open and fluid at least on regular and mandated occasions.

Though the concern in non-democratic societies to "organize political institutions so that bad or incompetent rulers can be prevented from doing too much damage" is understandable,[41] it is condescending and inappropriate in ostensibly democratic cultures. If ordinary laws and especially fundamental laws do not result from the regular exercise and confirmation of popular participation, then there may be talk of good or bad laws, but not of democracy. In a robust democracy, everything is always up for grabs and present institutional arrangements should always be open to revision and replacement, albeit not incessantly or haphazardly. It is not a case that anything goes, but that anything might go.[42] With democratic governance comes risk, but that is both its exhilarating promise and its ever-present danger. Unfortunately, Dworkin has not only played safe, but ambushed democracy to his own liberal agenda. In a strong democracy, citizens ought to be democrats first and only liberals or any other partisan supporter second.

Conclusion

As the contemporary moralist *nonpareil*, Ronald Dworkin has put the consideration of values squarely back on jurisprudence's agenda. He has offered a

---

[41] KARL POPPER, THE OPEN SOCIETY AND ITS ENEMIES (1965) vol. 1 at 107.

[42] See also Hutchinson, GAME, *supra*, note 9 and ALAN KEENAN, DEMOCRACY IN QUESTION: DEMOCRATIC OPENNESS IN A TIME OF POLITICAL CLOSURE 10 (2003).

significant and bracing challenge to the positivists' domination of analytical jurisprudence. Although this anti-positivist effort is deserving of genuine admiration and support, his own brand of liberal legalism is unconvincing as an alternative approach; it remains much too beholden to the very analytical tradition that he assails in its predominantly positivist guise. Although Dworkin puts values at the heart of the law's identity and connects questions of legality and legitimacy, his own moralist account falls short on two telling counts. First, he fails to appreciate and incorporate the subversive role of politics and power in the formation and maintenance of law's values: Normative discourse takes place on the volatile terrain of engaged politics, not in some privileged philosophical refuge. Second, while he defends his law-as-integrity jurisprudence in terms of its contribution to advancing the democratic project, he relies upon a vision of democratic governance that is far too stilted and cramped in its thrust and ambitions; it is citizens, not juristic consuls, who must occupy the pivotal position in democratic politics. These two shortcomings combine and deal a fatal blow to Dworkin's moralist stance. Accordingly, if we are to provide an affirmative response to Dworkin's monographical question of *Is Democracy Possible Here*, it will only be done by rethinking and re-invigorating the crucial relation between power and democracy. It is to that task that I now turn in the next two chapters.

CHAPTER SEVEN

The Province of Jurisprudence Regenerated

Power is not an institution, and not a structure; neither is it a certain strength we are endowed with; it is the name that one attributes to a complex strategic situation in a particular society.

—Michel Foucault

Although John Austin's own attempts to fashion a convincing account of law's universal nature have long been discarded, there still remains a deep attachment to the wider jurisprudential project that Austin laid out in *The Province of Jurisprudence Determined* (*The Province*). Analytical jurists continue to devote extensive energies to developing a sophisticated set of conceptual tools by which to identify law's abiding character, refining a more persuasive understanding of the precise relation between legal validity and moral legitimacy, and shoring up the methodological foundations of the overall analytical enterprise. It is, of course, my claim that these continuing efforts to make good on this Austinian mission have been misguided and would be better abandoned entirely. However, the one aspect of Austin's work that might be productively pursued further and more critically has been consistently ignored by modern analytical jurists. For all its one-dimensional and coarse peculiarities, Austin's command theory of law hit upon a characteristic of law that warrants and actually demands much greater attention—the role of law as a primary process through which to establish and handle power in society.

In their haste to get beyond the confining and distorting grasp of law as a series of threats and sanctions, analytical jurists have thrown out the baby with the bathwater. If Austin placed too much emphasis on the part that coercion and force played in law's performance and gave insufficient weight to law's more subtle wiles, modern legal theorists have understated the extent to which law functions as an official medium for ordering society and its power relations. Moreover, even on those occasions in which attention is focused on law's reliance on and relation with power, the tendency has been to fall back on a simplistic understanding of power. Accordingly, in this chapter, I will offer a more expansive and nuanced account of power that is more attuned to the complexities of contemporary society. After canvassing the various ways in which Austin's insights have been neglected, I will explore how such a pragmatic account of power recasts the practices and problems of legal theory and law. The fact is that too much jurisprudence feigns to skate on "the frictionless ice of philosophical discourse."[1] In contrast, I insist that it is only against and within a jagged process of power that the workings of law and legal theory can be best appreciated and reworked.

Guns and Poses

Few observers would deny that law's use of and authority to rely on coercion is a notable feature of law as a mode of social control. The history of both law and legal theory testifies to the resilience and wisdom of such a trite insight.[2] However, there is very little consensus on the precise role that coercion plays in law, its relation to other devices to cultivate obligation, and especially its claim to be *the* distinguishing feature of law. There is a world of difference between depending upon the frequent use of brute force to maintain order and the occasional reliance upon punishment as a last resort. Accordingly, although coercion is almost invariably one legal threat utilized by governing institutions in societies, its centrality to the legal process is a matter of considerable dispute. In other words, guns are part of law's disciplinary arsenal, but it is debatable whether they are the paradigm examples of law's authority or simply an exceptional instance of it.

The view that coercion is the decisive feature in identifying law and distinguishing it from other modes of social control, especially morality, is fairly attributed to Austin. He insisted that coercion as a display of power was an irrepressible feature of law's nature and validity. Picking up on an existing English tradition of political theory, he concluded that "laws and other commands are said to proceed from *superiors* and to bind or oblige *inferiors*" and that "the term *superiority* implies *might*: the power of affecting others with evil or pain, and of forcing them, through fear of that evil, to fashion

---

[1] LUDWIG WITTGENSTEIN, PHILOSOPHICAL INVESTIGATIONS I, s.107 (G.E.M. Anscombe trans. 1953).

[2] *See, for example*, JULIUS STONE, THE PROVINCE AND FUNCTION OF LAW: A STUDY IN JURISPRUDENCE (1947).

their conduct."[3] For him, law was a definite and indispensable tool of the ruling sovereign in order to maintain order, reinforce authority, and, where desired, effect change. As such, law was considered to be neither good nor bad in general form or institutional character; it could be used contingently for morally meritorious or demeritorious ends at the sovereign's behest—law was authoritative, but not necessarily authoritarian. Indeed, Austin was himself committed to lobbying the sovereign in his efforts to reform the law's content so that it more adequately advanced society's general welfare along broadly utilitarian lines; this was better achieved by a strong, if monarchical state than by more inefficient, if democratic means. However, despite his scientific claims to the contrary (and the fact that he was led to adopt implausible conclusions that neither constitutional law nor international law was law properly so-called), Austin's jurisprudential stance reflected and confirmed his own political and parochial agenda rather than comprise any detached reportage of law's universal nature.[4]

However, in treating a legal system as a vehicle of subjection by a privileged few over a disenfranchised many through a body of coercive commands, Austin allowed an important facet of law's historical operation to become its one and only hallmark. Although law was very much an authoritative tool wielded by rulers and backed by oft-realized threats of severe punishment, it was and is much more and much less than that. It is much more in that large parts of the legal process function without overt resort to punishment or pain; vast sectors of private law manage to work efficaciously by relying on the consensual participation of citizens and commercial entities. Yet, law is also much less than sanction-backed orders. Coercion and force are only a couple of the resources that law has at its disposal in maintaining order and establishing the authority of some over others. In modern Western societies, law works on a variety of levels and in a variety of ways; it plays a considerable part in sculpting and instantiating the extant social relations which it later and occasionally intervenes in by way of threat or sanction. As such,

---

[3] JOHN AUSTIN, THE PROVINCE OF JURISPRUDENCE DETERMINED 24 (1832: H.L.A. Hart ed. 1955). See T. HOBBES, LEVIATHAN 83 (1651) ("law properly is the word of him that by right hath command over others") and James Boyle, *Thomas Hobbes and The Invented Tradition of Positivism: Reflections on Language, Power, and Essentialism*, 135 U. PA. L. REV. 383 (1987).

[4] See *supra*, ch.2. Austin's 'coercion' theme was adopted by several other leading jurists of the twentieth century as the legal order's distinguishing feature, albeit on different grounds. See H. KELSEN, GENERAL THEORY OF LAW AND STATE 18 (1945) and K. OLIVECRONA, LAW AS FACT 134 (1939).

law is intimately and inextricably bound up with the power relations in society at any given time. By empowering as well as disempowering in regulating and disciplining society, law has a much richer and profound existence than Austin or other similarly minded jurists allow.

Of course, as is now well known, H. L. A. Hart built his own lauded concept of law as a union of primary and secondary rules on the ruins of Austin's law-as-command theory. Indeed, the first one-third of *The Concept of Law* is given over to explaining why "the model of orders backed by threats obscures more of law than it reveals" and exhibits a "general conceptual inadequacy"—criminal statutes are not representative of laws generally and apply to those who enact them; many laws confer public and private powers without reliance on threats; many laws are created without explicit prescription; and the positing of an omnipotent sovereign was not compatible with modern electoral practices and institutions nor could it explain legislative continuity.[5] For Hart, therefore, the state-wielded gun is not the defining symbol of law's claim to authority, but is a minor feature of law's mechanism for enforcing obligation and obedience to law: Much more explanatory mileage could be obtained from appreciating the extent to which citizens cultivated a critical reflective attitude to laws and the legal system generally.

Yet, as much as Hart offered a fuller and more convincing account of law than Austin, he largely abandoned Austin's insistence on the centrality of power. For Hart, coercion is an available, but largely secondary mode of social discipline that is relatively infrequently used to bolster or supplement people's general inclination to obey and follow the legal system's rules. Indeed, he comes close to leaving the impression that coercion is not a particularly important component of law's essential nature at all. Consequently, in his efforts to broaden the concept of law, Hart allowed law's Austinian-backed connection with coercive threats to recede to such an extent that it played only a peripheral and minor role in his concept of law. This is troubling because, whatever the shortcomings of Austin's exclusive focus on coercion, it is little improvement to overcompensate by giving coercion no real role to play in understanding law's operations. Even in matters of civil or constitutional

---

5. H.L.A. HART, THE CONCEPT OF LAW 49 and 77 (2nd ed. 1994). *See generally id.* at 18–78. It is worth noting that Dworkin takes a different tack and proposes that the abstract point of legal practice is to constrain governmental power by setting the conditions under which the exercise of collective force is justified. On such an account, the task of legal theory to explain how and under what conditions law can perform this function well and, therefore, better explain the connection between law and the justification of state coercion. See R. DWORKIN, LAW'S EMPIRE 93 and 110 (1986) and *supra*, ch.6.

discord, the threat of state force is never far from the legal surface. Whether it is disciplining student protesters, aboriginal dissenters, political separatists, labor organizers, environmental warriors, or similar activists, the legal system and its trustees are not slow to marshal its considerable coercive forces to ensure that law and order is maintained.[6]

For all Hart's endeavor, therefore, he managed to do away with Austin's sovereign, but only to substitute it with a rule of recognition so as to better continue the positivist and analytical tradition established by Austin. In offering a *legal* philosophy and one which insisted on the separability of law and political morality, Hart continued the stubborn adherence to an analytical tradition in which politics and morality were not the province of jurisprudence properly so-called. Although jurists worked on matters of morality and politics, they did so on the basis that law and morality/politics were separate, if intimately related fields of study. Accordingly, although contemporary jurists have almost entirely conceded that law is about more than sovereignty and that it "embodies political power and coercion is the hard edge of power,"[7] there has been little effort to push through on that basic insight. Consequently, a more convincing and democratic-oriented account of power will get beyond the role of coercion as law's distinguishing characteristic, but only to repackage it as part of a much broader appreciation of power's disciplinary role in legal control and organization. Whereas Hart gets beyond coercion by ignoring power's political dynamics, I want to put those political dynamics at the heart of the jurisprudential project by demonstrating the diffuse character of power as not only enabling as well as restrictive, but also constitutive of the social relations that it seeks to affect.

A Powerful Take

Although some deny that power is an essentially contested concept and prefer to see it as "an essentially messy concept,"[8] most theorists agree that power is a fundamental category of analysis in political and legal theory and have striven to understand its multifaceted operation. Following Weber's notion that power implies "the probability that one actor within a social relationship

---

[6] *See, for example*, Law, Violence, and the Possibility of Justice (A. Sarat ed. 2001).

[7] Leslie Green, *General Jurisprudence: A 25th Anniversary Essay*, 25 Oxf J. Leg. Studies 565 at 574–75 (2005).

[8] See Brian Barry, *Is it Better to be Powerful or Lucky?*, 28 Pol. Stud. 338 at 349 (1980) and MacDonald, *Is 'Power' Essentially Contested?*, 6 Brit. J. of Pol. Sci. 380 (1976).

will be in a position to carry out his will despite resistance,"[9] both the political right and left have tended to view it as a possession that can be acquired to manipulate others and be measured by a simple causal metric. Within this paradigm, the disagreement was over the ends to which power ought to be used and to suggest a justifiable distribution and exercise of power. But such accounts of power have been relatively crude and decidedly humanistic: they tend to emphasize the agential, negative, intentional, and programmatic aspects of power's operation as an intentional attempt to dominate. Though this explanatory framework does highlight the more obvious and stark effects of power, it also serves to obscure its more subtle and pervasive dimensions.

Few commentators now hold on to an account of power that restricts itself to its overt and wilfull exercise by one person over another. A social world does not exist, if ever it did, in which Austin was able to construe law as "a rule laid down for the guidance of an intelligent being by an intelligent being having power over him" and to distinguish commands from desire by "the power and purpose of the party commanding to inflict an evil or pain in case the desire is disregarded;" this is no longer a viable construct as either an actual historical context or a hypothetical situation.[10] Such a view treats power as a circulating commodity that is traded in a society in which people have real and presocial wants and interests that are established and maintained outside of power's reach. Although there are clear and obvious examples of such instances of 'power over' that must not be ignored or downplayed, it does not come close to capturing the multiple ways in which power exists and operates. A more sophisticated account of power is as systemic and structural as it is individualized and agential; power is less a negotiable currency than a constitutive medium.

Hart's recognition that it was sensible in legal matters to talk about 'power to' as much as 'power over' offers a glimpse of a different conception of power's character and operation in modern society. In establishing rules and regulations (*e.g.*, wills and contracts), which are intended to facilitate efforts to achieve certain socially desirable ends, law functions to empower and enable individuals in their social relations among and with each other. To construe these commonplace and multitudinous legal devices as being analogous to threat-backed commands or nullification as being fully equivalent to sanctions is rightfully condemned by Hart as far-fetched and implausible.[11]

---

9   M. WEBER, A THEORY OF SOCIAL AND ECONOMIC ORGANIZATION 152 (T. Parsons
     ed. 1957).

10   Austin, *supra*, note 3 at 10 and 14.

11   See Hart, *supra*, note 5 at 26–49.

As such, he was correct to point up that, even if *"superiority* signifies *might,"* "the power of affecting others with evil or pain, and of forcing them, through fear of that evil, to fashion their conduct to one's wishes" was not the sole focus of law's claim to authority.[12] However, Hart was mistaken to ignore as much as he did the role that power played in law's privileged status in affecting others and forcing them to fashion their conduct to one's wishes: he remained too attached to a flat and static account of power's personality and performance.

For instance, though Hart clearly appreciated the more nuanced and diverse ways in which systems of rules functioned as channels and frameworks for directing social life, he evinced a distinct tendency to elide some difficult issues about how power functions and legitimates itself through law. He was content to observe rather cursorily that "so long as human beings can gain sufficient cooperation from some to enable them to dominate others, they will use the forms of law as one of their instruments."[13] Consequently, although Hart's union of primary and secondary rules has a definite edge over Austin's law-as-command in offering a better explanation of law's essential nature, he might well have achieved this success at the considerable cost of marginalizing and understating law's role as a power-ful medium through which to establish social relations and effect social policy making. Moreover, in depoliticizing law in this way, Hart and other analytical jurists have managed to ignore the extent and manner to which law contributes to maintaining hierarchical, patriarchal, racist, or other disciplinary and discriminatory regimes.

A more adequate and instructive understanding of power recognizes both power over and power to as important manifestations of power's operation, but seeks to incorporate them into a deeper and constitutive account. Rather than think of power as only a commodity or thing that exists in social relations between people or organiations, it is better to understand it as a medium within which not only the agenda for problem setting is developed, but also the interests, values, and wants of people are cultivated. In this way, power manages to constitute people's sense of their own values and interests as well as influencing the hierarchical ordering of such values and interests: Power works by "shaping [people's] perceptions, cognitions and preferences in such a way that they accept their role in the existing order of things, either because they can see or imagine no alternative to it, or because they see it as natural and

---

12 Austin, *supra*, note 3 at 24.

13 Hart, *supra*, note 5 at 210. *See also* D. WRONG, POWER: ITS FORMS, BASES AND USES (1980) and J.K. GALBRAITH, THE ANATOMY OF POWER (1983).

unchangeable or because they value it as divinely ordained and beneficial."[14] Contrary to Austin and Hart's depiction, power is not something that can be entirely mastered or rendered completely transparent because, being as much structural as it is agential, it insinuates itself into the very institutional devices and settings within which it is utilized and deployed.

Once this more constitutive sense of power is grasped, it becomes easier to appreciate the different ways in which power works and the different levels on which it functions; it is as much disaggregated and fragmented as unified and integrated. As the context changes, power can be seen as both domineering and liberating, productive and regressive, and transformative and paralyzing. Moreover, these effects can be in play often at one and the same time. Not operating along one axis alone, people can experience simultaneously power's presence as both liberating and disciplinary; personal or political relations, like marriage and commerce, involve tradeoffs between 'power over' and 'power to' dimensions. As a culture more than a commodity, power is no longer treated as a simple relational force that operates between people and organizations with fixed and unitary interests, but an environment that affects and alters people's interests differently at different times. As a constitutive component in social networks or political milieus, power formulates as much as affects people's interests whether they work to satisfy their own interests or challenge the interests of others.

This conception of power has been taken to its extreme by Michel Foucault. In a sustained critique, he contended that power is omnipresent in that it is always operating on social subjects and relations and there are no such subjects or relations free from power's contingent performance. In sharp contrast to Austin, he insists that "there exist relations of power which are not purely and simply a projection of the sovereign's great power over the individual, they are rather the concrete, changing soil in which the sovereign's power is grounded, the conditions which make it possible for it to function."[15] Such an approach sees power as operating in a largely prepositional, anonymous,

---

[14] STEVEN LUKES, POWER: A RADICAL VIEW 28 (2nd ed. 2005). As instructive as the revised second edition of his book is, Lukes still tends to believe that a powerless situation is possible and that people can have true interests. See *infra*, pp. 152–54. See PETER MORRISS, POWER: A PHILOSOPHICAL ANALYSIS (2nd ed. 2002).

[15] Michel Foucault, *The History of Sexuality* in POWER/KNOWLEDGE: SELECTED INTERVIEWS AND OTHER WRITINGS 1972–1977 187 (Colin Gordon trans. 1980). For a more extended, if a little dated account of Foucault's work, see my *Working The Seam: Truth, Justice and The Foucault Way* in A. HUTCHINSON, DWELLING ON THE THRESHOLD: CRITICAL ESSAYS ON MODERN LEGAL THOUGHT (1988).

non-subjective, and localized manner by nurturing and sustaining the ever-changing social network within which the agent arises and is able to act intelligibly. As such, power consists of a mobile multiplicity of force relations which, continually disaggregating and coalescing, shape themselves into shifting and incomplete strategic patterns. These matrixes help to create the individuals and organizations who use and are used by power, the needs power feigns to satisfy, and the truth in whose name power claims to speak.

Consequently, any serious effort to understand the operation and effects of power must eschew the development of a grand conceptual or analytical approach; any attempt to isolate or identify the universal ways and patterns in which power works in society fails to grasp the contingent quality of power's workings. Instead, a pragmatic rendering of power will be attuned to its thoroughly disjunctive character and will work towards assembling rich and specific accounts of power's functioning in particular social sites and historical settings. As Foucault himself concluded, "power's condition of possibility . . . as a grid of intelligibility of the social order, must not be sought in . . . a unique source of sovereignty . . . ; it is the moving substrate of force relations, which by virtue of their inequality, constantly engender states of power, but the latter are always local and unstable."[16] From a pragmatic viewpoint, therefore, it would be folly to imagine that it might be possible to locate some transcendent set of laws or regularities which can be relied upon as a comprehensive framework to predict or control power's effects. As with so much else, the best that can be hoped for is that experience and study will allow societies to learn from the past, muddle through as best they can, and become aware of the unexpected and multi-variant aspects of power. In so doing, a pragmatic sensibility and accompanying distrust of abstract generalizations will be a suitable complement to such a political account of constitutive power in social life.

In the remainder of this chapter, my mandate is to trace out the implications of such a powerful approach for a fresh understanding of legal theory and law. In so doing, my pragmatic ambition is to suggest how efforts to position jurisprudential study as somehow outside or above society's extant economies of power and truth are ill fated; they tend to hide rather than illuminate the formative role of power in the constitution of law and legal theory's historical trajectory and political slant. This inquiry will also hopefully serve as an introduction as to why a political commitment to democracy as

---

[16]   M. FOUCAULT, THE HISTORY OF SEXUALITY 92–93 (1979).

the most favored mode of governance is best suited to complement a powerful approach to law and legal theory.

A Knowledge of Power

Albert Einstein was fond of saying that "a foolish faith in authority is the worst enemy of truth."[17] The main gist of this warning is clear and compelling. However, when taken as a statement of philosophical intent, its assumptions about truth are suspect. As long as truth continues to be understood in the objectivist way of analytical philosophers and jurists as a detached and ahistorical standard, a pragmatic and powerful approach suggests that truth itself might also be one of those authorities in which people should not place faith, foolish or otherwise. This will entail moving beyond the traditional Baconian view that power and knowledge are ontologically separate entities: True knowledge can only be validated outside power's corrupting influence. Pragmatists maintain that this foundational assumption is part of the philosophical problem. Indeed, a pragmatist recommends that society will be better off if it abandons entirely its false confidence in the availability of enduring truth and foregoes its extravagant attachment to epistemological authority. Too often, truth turns out to be simply another maneuver, no matter how innocent and well intentioned, to claim special authority for another contestable version of the way-the-world-really-is.

In contrast, a pragmatic powerful approach insists that power and knowledge are mutually constitutive. The inchoate protocols of power are secreted within the interstices of scientific codes of knowledge which, in turn, impinge upon and reconstitute those protocols. As a pragmatic sensibility demands, there is no universal pattern to this relationship between power and knowledge, and there is no overarching theory of this critical relation: It is necessary to resist strenuously the temptations to confer on these relational routines the spurious status of historical laws or imbue them with a transcendental logic of necessity. The best that can be expected or wanted is the development of an analytical grid through which to examine how certain conceptual techniques have been isolated and privileged on particular historical occasions and, in particular, social settings so as to shape people's interests and formulate canons of intelligibility: "power and knowledge directly imply one another . . . there is no power relation without the correlative constitution of

---

17   WALTER ISAACSON, EINSTEIN: HIS LIFE AND UNIVERSE 22 (2007).

a field of knowledge, nor any knowledge that does not presuppose and constitute at the same time power relations."[18] Because these devices are never outside the dynamic realm of political struggle, they are contingent in force and effect. There is a constant temptation, to be resisted, to confer on these routines the spurious status of historical laws or imbue them with a transcendental logic of necessity.

Perhaps the most obvious and pressing illustration of this relationship between power and knowledge is exemplified in the innovative work of some feminists. Traditional approaches to power were very useful at highlighting the historical record of sexist practices and cataloguing the various ways in which male hegemony has utilized its dominant position to perpetuate the continuing oppression of women in society. At its most subtle, this work went beyond the more obvious occasions of sexism and hinted at the sophisticated tools by which men's superiority was maintained and disguised. However, there were very definite limits to such an analysis and its prescriptive recommendations; it treated men exclusively as the intentional agents of oppression, it understood power as a possession that needed to be redistributed along more egalitarian lines, and it measured both oppression and its remedial correction in largely behavioral terms. This situation gave rise to a body of critical feminism which sought to comprehend male hegemony more along the lines of a powerful pragmatic approach.

Although there were considerable differences between theorists, the basic insight was that male power was held in place not only by instrumental social practices, but by commandeering society's epistemological apparatus; modes of knowing and standards of truth were inculcated which served to reinforce existing relations of power. In classic philosophical mode, traditional theory claimed to be offering a transparent and objective representation of a preexisting social reality. However, critical feminists argued that gender was not a biological characteristic, but a social and political concept. They insisted that this male-favoring discourse and its accompanying protocols of truth validation were far from objective and instantiated a particular and contestable vision of gendered reality: "male power extends beneath the representation of reality to its construction: it makes women (as it were) and so verifies (makes true) who women 'are' in its view, simultaneously confirming its way of being and its vision of truth."[19] Such an approach captures how power and

---

18   M. FOUCAULT, DISCIPLINE AND PUNISH: THE BIRTH OF THE PRISON 27 (Alan Sheridan trans. 1977).

19   See CATHARINE MACKINNON, FEMINISM UNMODIFIED: DISCOURSES ON LIFE AND LAW 132 (1987). See also Robin West, *Jurisprudence and Gender*, 55 U. CHI. L. REV. 2 (1988).

knowledge work to reinforce each other; there is no outside by which to get out of or above the inevitably loaded epistemologically enforced protocols of power. By displaying how the very discourse and ways of knowing which people use, both men and women, manages to naturalize and authorize a particular way-the-world-really-is, it is able to incorporate power over and power to into a deeper and more encompassing constitutive account of power.

As I have already commented, the demonstration that legal thought or science and philosophy generally are a profoundly social and, therefore, political practice is not a bad thing; it only becomes so if there remains a lingering claim to be speaking in the name of some detached and supra-historical authority.[20] Although scientific methods are useful in solving problems about that natural world, it is not advisable to treat their predictive-empirical techniques (or other epistemological methodologies generally) as capable of gaining access to some universal truths or being separable from the historical contexts of their deployment; their findings are provisional, standards are fallible, and absolute objectivity is mythical. Consequently, a powerful approach recommends a reworking of Einstein's warning—"A foolish faith in authority is the worst enemy of justice whether that authority is political, ethical or epistemological." Compliance with or greater conformity with some abstract notion of truth is not a mark of progress or improved justice. Pragmatists place the achievement of practical justice in present society ahead of such *recherché* pursuits.

The Power of Law

Significant parts and activities of law continue to exercise power by way of bare command and retain authority by uncritical obedience and ritualized violence. However, a too single-minded focus on this imperative dimension can manage to obscure the more pervasive and subtle disciplinary techniques of power that are promoted and advanced through law: The legal system is much more than a modern Austinian-like "code of organized public violence" or a thinly disguised process of ideological inculcation.[21] Analytical jurisprudence

---

For an instructive working-through of this approach in international law, see Hilary Charlesworth, *The Sex of the State in International Law* in SEXING THE SUBJECT OF LAW 251 (N. Naffine and R.J. Owens eds. 1997).

[20] See *supra*, ch.5 and R. RORTY, ACHIEVING OUR COUNTRY: LEFTIST THOUGH IN TWENTIETH CENTURY AMERICA 28 (1998).

[21] N. POULANTZAS, STATE, POWER, SOCIALISM 77 (1978) and Alan Hunt, *Marxist Theory of Law* in A COMPANION TO PHILOSOPHY OF LAW AND LEGAL THEORY 355–66 (D. Patterson ed. 1999).

tends to neglect the important ways in which law functions as a sizeable part of other more embracing discursive regimes of power. It is part of that complex strategic situation which serves to instantiate and regularize the contingent patterns and routines of power in installing economies of truth. Being neither only an institution or a commodity, power utilizes the legal process to insinuate itself in social practices: It not only exerts a power over and enables a power to, it also lays down the constitutive terms and conditions through which people formulate and renegotiate their daily lives and entitlements. Law is a combination of toolbox, how-to manual, and raw materials. In the same way that all problems come to resemble nails if a hammer is the only tool that you have, then law cabins and curtails the social process within which power operates and transforms itself; it is both confining and facilitative.

In modern Western societies, law has become an example *par excellence* of such a discursive regime. Law is one of the important activities and regimens through which society generates and maintains various collective goods, such as contract, property, family units, and the like. The particular range and quality of collective goods which a society generates and maintains is one of its major distinguishing features: A society would be a different place if it had a different set of legal paraphernalia and collective goods. Insofar as law and legal doctrine give shape and nuance to the social artifacts of government authority, civil rights, and the like, they help to constitute and preserve existing social arrangements. Moreover, by framing the set of pressing problems perceived and to be resolved as well as the preferred range of available solutions to be employed, law permeates the whole social context and its imaginative appreciation. It is not so much that litigation and adjudication are special social activities that do not cause or condition other social activities and planning, but that they also comprise and are constitutive of the extant social conditions: "[it] is not so much that the court is the natural expression of popular justice, but rather that its historical function is to ensnare it, control it and to strangle it, by re-inscribing it within institutions which are typical of a state apparatus."[22] Power shapes the contingent nature of law and society as they themselves influence shifting patterns of power.

Consequently, participation in the legal process as lawyer or litigant, no matter how radical the claim or cause, runs the risk of reinforcing as it challenges

---

[22] Foucault, *supra*, note 15 at 1. *See generally* ALAN HUNT AND GARY WICKHAM, FOUCAULT AND LAW: TOWARDS A NEW SOCIOLOGY OF LAW AS GOVERNANCE (1994) and Roger Cotterrell, *Subverting Orthodoxy, Making Law Central: A View of Sociological Studies*, 29 J. LAW & SOC'Y 632 (2002).

the dominion of the *status quo*. Litigation occurs *within* the limits of existing social structures and arrangements for the enabling, exercising, and constituting of power. As such, law is not an independent variable in social struggles, but a formative influence in shaping the contours and constitution of those struggles. There is no available outside from which to engage in transformative action: All struggle for change is already sited and framed within the very mechanisms and mediums to be resisted and reworked. In this sense, therefore, law and legal processes are important not simply because they affect social practices (which, of course, they do), but also because they form part of power's protocols that combine to sustain an integrated, if incomplete complex strategic situation of political control and social ordering.

Understood in this way, law is always part of society's power structure; there is no neutral position that the legal process occupies in relation to the existing patterns of power. Law favors the *status quo*: It is an integral part of the general apparatus which holds the existing governmental arrangements in place and places a series of obstacles in the way of those who struggle to bring about political change. From a broadly democratic standpoint, it is not so much whether that change is considered to be good or bad in some objective sense which is, as I have been at pragmatic pains to emphasize, a fraught undertaking. It is because the legal process tends to be strongly aligned with the interests of the established order which is better able to access its formidable authority and institutional resources in order to resist change and/or to divert those transformative efforts into debilitating and decelerating channels. Moreover, legal positivists' insistence that law's validity is separable from its moral legitimacy contributes to the law's political authority in the minds of the citizenry when it moves to resist challenges to that authority. The positivist strain of analytical jurisprudence operates as a powerful apologist tool in convincing subjects of the *status quo's* desirability or, at least, its claim to respect and support; it helps to foreclose the imaginative and practical realization of a very different set of governmental arrangements.

For instance, while Joseph Raz is correct to note that "it is of the essence of law to guide behaviour through rules and courts in charge of their application," he is mistaken to assert that the legal process "is morally neutral in being neutral as to the end to which the instrument is put." The legal process is proestablishment in that it works to entrench and solidify the extant content of law and its application and enforcement by the officially designated agencies. Although it may be neutral in a vague and abstract ahistorical sense, it is almost invariably on the side of conservative political forces; law will help to ensure and enhance the orderliness and stability of the legal system and, therefore, its moral mandate. Accordingly, in a "a non-democratic legal system, based on the denial of human rights, on extensive poverty, on racial segregation, sexual inequalities, and racial persecution," the legal process will work to hamper, marginalize, and perhaps outlaw the efforts of those progressive activists committed to overcoming such oppressive regimes.[23] As such, law is far from neutral in its political effects and moral legitimacy; it functions primarily, if not always successfully to preserve the *status quo* and to give an official imprimatur to its political/moral orientation.

A corollary of this is that, through the formal and substantive dimensions of the legal process, power contributes to casting normativity in its own image, so that people are persuaded to do what they *must* do (from power's perspective) because it is also what they *ought* to do (from morality's point of view). Law works to give a formal stamp of approval to society's moral order. However, law is never only about vested interests or power politics; it is also about the rational justification and masking of those interests and power. Any credible explanation of law's operation and performance must be sensitive to the sophisticated ways in which force and rationality combine to reinforce the other. It is important to be clear, therefore, that the legal process is not always and only the crude instrument of the ruling establishment. In order for law to maintain its prestige and legitimacy, it must demonstrate that it is more than a manipulable resource of the governing elite. On occasion, therefore, it must live up to its own logic and rationality by delivering just outcomes which might well run against the immediate agenda of presently vested interests. Consequently, law will play its role in disciplining society in accordance with the prevailing power coalition of political forces, but will not be able to achieve a fully disciplined society. As an historical appreciation of law's episodic operations displays, the rulers (*i.e.*, politicians, judges, officials) "played the games of power according to the rules which suited them, but they could not break those rules or the whole game would be thrown away."[24] Although this official performance will vary from one context to another, it is a feature of law's intimate relation to power that any

---

[23] Joseph Raz, *Rule of Law and Its Virtue* in THE AUTHORITY OF LAW 225–26 and 221 (1979). On the bias of analytical jurisprudence in favor of stability and regularity, see *supra* ch.3.

[24] E.P. THOMPSON, WHIGS AND HUNTERS: THE ORIGINS OF THE BLACK ACT 263 (1976). See also Hanoch Dagan, *The Realist Conception of Law*, 57 U. TOR. L.J. 607 (2007). This is not to suggest that there is a deep logic to social relations or the general connection between law and those social relations at any particular time or place. See Duncan Kennedy, *Form and Substance in Private Law Adjudication*, 89 HARV. L. REV. 1685 (1976) and A. HUTCHINSON, IT'S ALL IN THE GAME: A NON-FOUNDATIONALIST ACCOUNT OF LAW AND ADJUDICATION 216–51 (2000).

attempt to conceive of them as separate and apart is misleading and politically so.

Accordingly, a powerful and pragmatic perspective recommends an understanding of law that goes beyond its traditional depiction as an instrument or commodity. Although Hart realized better than Austin the more nuanced and diverse ways in which systems of rules function as channels and frameworks for directing social life, he exhibited a distinct tendency to elide some difficult issues about how power functions and legitimates itself through law. He was content to observe that "so long as human beings can gain sufficient cooperation from some to enable them to dominate others, they will use the forms of law as one of their instruments."[25] Yet this tells only part of the story. Law is not simply an institutional device for domination, but is one of the strategic social practices through which human beings and their interests are constructed and inscribed in a society's political script; social relations do not pre-exist law or arise outside of power's protocols. Moreover, as part of the established order, albeit fluid and unfinalized, law is never neutral. It is skewed in favor of the *status quo* and it helps to secure those vested interests, even though it does so with only limited and occasionally counterproductive success. Analytical jurisprudence ignores such issues and approaches at its and everyone else's peril.

A Post-Analytical Calling

Consistent with the pragmatic critique that I have offered of the analytical project, I now need to offer a more constructive set of proposals for jurisprudential study. It should come as little surprise to learn that I recommend a post-analytical approach which is characterized by its insistence on becoming much more sensitive and alive to the social forces and political interests that frame both law and any effort to theorize about it. Whether dealing with scientific, legal, or jurisprudential practices, it will be important to situate them within a broader dynamic context of social forces and political interests. Ironically, it was John Austin himself who recognized the central role of power in understanding law's operation and authority. Although Austin's explanation was too crudely command-based,[26] he nonetheless recognized

---

[25]   Hart, *supra*, note 5 at 210. Although the moralists at least talk about values, they do so in a clinical and apolitical style. See *supra*, ch.6.

[26]   Austin, *supra*, note 3 at 13 ("Every positive law, or every law simply and strictly so called, is set, directly or circuitously, by a sovereign person or body, to a member or members of the independent political society wherein that person or body is supreme.").

that law was fundamentally about power and the effort to control and discipline people in accordance with a particular vision of right conduct. As such, I recommend that Austin's legacy might best be preserved and galvanized by a post-analytical attention to power's pervasive operation. In particular, this will entail not only contextualizing analytical jurisprudence, but also unveiling the ways and circumstances in which analytical jurists have claimed to position themselves as separate and apart from the social forces and political interests which energize and inform them. Accordingly, it is vital that a post-analytical approach builds on the insight that "conceptual and methodological questions are inescapably political."[27] As such, oppression is problematized, but not done away with.

Like almost all other social practices, the disciplines of philosophy and jurisprudence are not immune from the push-and-pull of various social, economic, institutional, ideological, and cultural currents. Because, under a pragmatic view, objectivity is about compliance with those accepted and agreed-upon standards for justifying knowledge, it will be crucial to ascertain and examine the terms and conditions under which such social agreements have been reached and are maintained. By giving the idea of social practices a more political than philosophical spin, it brings the operation of power into the center of debate. For instance, it allows the crucial concept and practice of consensus (and, therefore, standards of persuasion and justification) to be unpacked, showing that the historical extent to which it has been treated is imposed as much as chosen. Indeed, this is exactly what Hart's rule of recognition tends to illustrate. By placing bureaucratic authority at the heart of law's validity, it contributes to the sense in which political acquiescence rather than civic participation is sufficient to ground and legitimize political power; democratic involvement is considered to be an optional extra, not a *sine qua non* of the maintenance and exercise of law's political and coercive power. Moreover, this further explains why democracy recommends itself as the least worse mode of government process: Democracy does not so much obviate, let alone dispense with power, but rather enables citizens to appreciate, challenge and recalibrate its operation.[28]

Consequently, what has managed to get itself accepted in the relevant community of scholarly study will be attributable to more than (or, perhaps, less than) the raw force of a good idea. In regard to analytical jurisprudence, this suggests that the virtues of factual or epistemic values are neither as apparent nor as insulated from political values as their proponents

---

27 Lukes, *supra*, note 14 at 63
28 For a full development of the connection between power and democracy, see *infra*, ch.8.

would recommend: They are similarly, if not equally connected to the social matrix of forces that gestate and perpetuate them. For instance, one important political consequence of the claim of the New Legal Realists that there is "no higher tribunal than science" in relation to understanding both the natural and social (and, therefore, legal) worlds is that it shifts huge epistemic and political power to the scientific community; that community's members become empowered to establish the standards and protocols for identifying the knowable and real in all domains.[29] This is both a sizeable privilege and a significant responsibility. However, because that power is exercised under the guise of scientific authority, it is largely insulated for more direct and active forms of popular accountability.

In adopting such a power-informed account, a pragmatic jurisprudence must not exempt itself from such inquiries. Indeed, it would be fair to say that the pragmatic tradition has failed to give full significance to the effects of power on social life and political engagement. Any philosophical approach which treats the basis of objectivity as an intersubjective social agreement and insists that there is no ahistorical mandate for knowledge creation must surely pay close attention to the political dynamics of power at work. When so much hinges on the openness and freedom of intellectual debate, it is imperative that the crucial relation between power and reason is fully and critically appreciated. This is particularly so in the realms of law and legal theory in which the issue of "what rules of right are implemented by the relations of power in the production of discourses of truth" is most acute.[30] Nevertheless, a pragmatic approach seems at least as well placed as the more traditional and analytical philosophical tendencies to confront directly, not coyly evade this challenge. Rather than duck the realization that knowledge and objectivity are intimately tied to social practices and political interests, jurisprudence needs to incorporate that unassailable insight into its general stance by ensuring that the circumstances in which particular intersubjective agreements are made are constantly being challenged and reassessed.

In doing so, the pragmatic ambition is not to somehow wrest reason free of power's suffocating grip and exhibit it in its unsullied purity; there is neither reason that is entirely outside power nor an Archimedean point from which the acceptable amount of corrupting power can be gauged so as to

---

[29] See BRIAN LEITER, NATURALIZING JURISPRUDENCE: ESSAYS ON AMERICAN LEGAL REALISM AND NATURALISM IN LEGAL PHILOSOPHY 117 (2007) and generally, *supra*, ch.5.

[30] Foucault, *supra*, note 15 at 119. It is on the role of power and politics that I take issue with Rorty. See *infra*, ch.9.

render consensus sufficiently free and reliable. Instead, the pressing task is to detail how power and reason work together so that society can determine for itself when the play of reason and power is sufficiently balanced and understood in the present circumstances to grant temporary authority to the resulting consensus. The task is most definitely not to purge intellectual inquiry and debate of the political as this would undermine the basic force of the pragmatic critique. Instead, mindful that power can be constitutive and enabling as well as restrictive and distorting, a pragmatic approach can meet power's challenge by utilizing available institutional arrangements and opportunities not only to maximize people's life choices and life-styles, but also to provide a set of communal resources through which the bases for these choices and styles can be debated and criticized. In contrast to traditional and analytical philosophers, pragmatists look to extend and proliferate the opportunities for participation in microcommunities rather than to narrow and accrete decision-making power to a small elite in the name of expertise and truth.

Accordingly, when analytical jurists repeat Hart's oft-cited claim that "description may still be description, even when what is described is an evaluation,"[31] they seem to beg or finesse many of the important questions about what counts as *description*. Even the New Legal Realists, like Leiter, who are more rigorous than their conceptualist colleagues, still rely too heavily on an unconvincing depiction of a sharp and fixed contrast between description and evaluation; this is symptomatic of the lingering and definitive analytical attachment to such binary modalities. A close examination of both distinctions must draw attention to the extent to which epistemological practices (*i.e.*, What determines what is it to have true knowledge of law?) and political practices (*i.e.*, What political interests and values are promoted by law and legal theory?) are as related and dependent as much as they are separate and apart. The pragmatically oriented account of power that I have adumbrated is best placed to achieve that ambition.

Tasks To Be Done

What is the role of the legal theorist in this post-analytical project? What distinctive contributions, if any, can the jurist make to advance the post-analytical project? There are, of course, many different answers to these questions;

---

[31] Hart, *supra*, note 5 at 244.

it would be wrong-headed for democrats, of all people, to insist that there is only one true way to make a jurisprudential contribution to this central task. However, there are some particular tasks that seem well suited to those with a democratic approach to legal theorizing:

- *Abandon Legal Theory*—In a manner of speaking, legal theory should become shallow, if deeply and rigorously so. Although pragmatic minded jurists will continue to theorize about law, they will forsake any metaphysical ambition to say something transcendental and true about the-way-the-legal-world-really-is for all time and for all societies. Having rid itself of its longstanding obsession with all matters epistemological, jurisprudence can eschew the misguided search for the last philosophy and work towards cultivating different ways of thinking about law and life. As William James put it, we need a "philosophy of maybes" that strives to be suggestive, not certain, provisional, not final, and only provincial, not universal.[32]

- *Get Hands Dirty*—Having abandoned legal theory, jurists need, as it were, to get out of their armchairs and into the street. They will take seriously the idea that any search for meaning and understanding can only be gained by immersing themselves in the messy social practices and gritty lived experiences of people. In turning away from philosophy and towards sociology, this will not entail a leap from one epistemology to another in a familiar scientistic or positivistic manner; there will be no back-door readmission of the analytical tendency. Instead, being done with a pragmatic sensibility, it will be a hands-on struggle of social engagement, not a scientific journey of discovery. The goal will be to develop a contextual and rich appreciation of law's contingent practices and political possibilities.

- *Go Genealogical*—Relatively unburdened by the props and paraphernalia of traditional legal epistemology, democratic jurists can begin to explore and unpack the combination of historical accidents and contingent circumstances that gave rise to and sustain the reliance on such metaphysical baggage. For instance, by locating the historical determinants of the fact/value or epistemic/moral distinctions relied on by analytical jurisprudence, the social tasks that they perform, the conceptual tools that they valorize, and the political interests that they continue to serve, it will help to demystify legal theory and show how

---

[32] WILLIAM JAMES, THE WILL TO BELIEVE 59 (1897).

there is no legal theory that operates as a detached and apolitical pursuit of legal truths.[33]

- *Focus on Power*—Resisting the temptation to make sweeping and grand explanations in the manner of analytical jurisprudence, democrats can offer a fuller and more bracing account of how power operates through law. Rather than simply look at how law works as a coercive (*i.e.*, power over) and enabling (*i.e.*, power to) force, it will be helpful to illustrate how law functions as a constitutive network in which social relations and political values are nurtured and legitimated. By taking a thoroughly pragmatic understanding of how power and reason work together, a democratic jurisprudence can begin to show how individual decisions not only tend to benefit entrenched interests, but manage to construct and utilize a general mode of legal reasoning which legitimizes those decisions as natural vulnerable and just.[34]

- *Embrace the Political*—Again, having given up on their lengthy romance with a metaphysical phantom, jurists will be eager to experiment with a post-analytical practice of legal theory which reverses the relation between philosophy and politics. Rather than seek to subject politics to the limiting discipline of philosophy, democrats will work towards putting the jurisprudential enterprise in the service of a more emancipatory politics. In this way, sensitive to its contingent context, jurisprudence will give institutional priority to the needs and wishes of ordinary citizens, suitably tempered in the vigorous give-and-take of political debate, over the received opinions of putative experts, like philosophers and jurists, who claim to speak in the privileged accent of scientific reason and analytic truth. Theory is not an end in itself, but a means to improving the conditions of people.

- *Be Useful*—It follows from its embrace of the political that the success of any democratic approach to legal theory is to be judged by its capacity to contribute to the practical realization of those political objectives that citizens have decided are important to themselves. Being out of the business of delivering fixed ends and privileged means

---

[33]   See J. Stuhr, Pragmatism, Postmodernism, and the Future of Philosophy 95–133 (2003).

[34]   Of course, this type of critique is nothing new and runs from John Dewey, *Logical Method and Law*, 33 Phil. Rev. 560 (1924) to Robert Gordon, *New Developments in Legal Theory* in The Politics of Law: A Progressive Critique 41 (David Kairys 2nd ed. 1990) and beyond.

for achieving them, democratic jurists will advise on what goals can be achieved through law and how the legal process can be transformed to work more effectively in doing that. Democratic theorists will be useful to society's members in helping them to confront and resolve the pressing legal issues of the day for themselves. In fulfilling that role, judges and lawyers will play a supporting role rather than occupy center stage; they will facilitate, not hijack society's decision-making processes.[35]

- *Act Locally*—As part of their larger commitment to the notion that it is important to measure the strength of a proposal by its usefulness and it democratic origins, jurists will concern themselves with what works best for their own society. This does not mean that they will pay no attention to other societies, especially those less well off than their own, or future generations. But, because knowledge is connected to particular social arrangements and agreements, they are as likely to do as much harm as good in roaming too far afield. Though there are ample reasons to support democratic initiatives elsewhere, legal theorists will have their hands full in closing the gap between present aspirations and existing actuality so that the world can become a locally better and more democratic place.[36]

Conclusion

In an important sense, therefore, I agree with Ronald Dworkin that "we have no choice but to ask [judges and lawyers] to confront issues that, from time to time, are philosophical,"[37] but I reject the analytical understanding of what it means to be philosophical. Instead, I insist that the whole philosophical enterprise must be reworked in line with a more democratic and less analytical sensibility in which the abstract emphasis on truth and objectivity is replaced with a more practical concern for power, usefulness, and substantive values. Rather than persist in pretending that the best way to engage with and understand law's facts is by assuming that they represent some

---

[35] *See, for example*, ROBERTO UNGER, THE SELF AWAKENED: PRAGMATISM UNBOUND (2007).

[36] See R. RORTY, ACHIEVING OUR COUNTRY: LEFTIST THOUGHT IN TWENTIETH CENTURY AMERICA (1998).

[37] R. DWORKIN, JUSTICE IN ROBES 73 (2006).

independent set of historically given data that can be analyzed from some abstract and largely non-historical vantage point, it is more beneficial and convincing to recognize the inevitable connection between philosophy and politics, between knowledge and power, and between facts and values. In so doing, it might be possible to turn legal theory to more useful effect. Of course, a democratic critique cannot claim for itself any special rationality that allows it to purge legal theory's infected reason so as to reveal power in its stark thereness. Because any critique must also partake of that same reason, the challenge is not to get beyond or through power to some pure reason or empirical truths that will stabilize and underwrite the jurisprudential project. Instead, the task is to work the historical space and strive to develop a power-sensitive reason that is conducive to and welcoming of a wider range of democratic interests. Any alternative to analytical jurisprudence must look to engage, not escape those social forces and political interests that combine to establish the legal economies of truth and power. This is the burden and promise of a post-analytical jurisprudence.

CHAPTER EIGHT

The Province of The Judiciary Democratized

*We are here as on a darkling plain/ Swept with confused alarms of struggle
and flight,/Where ignorant armies clash by night.*

—Matthew Arnold

Despite various protestations to the contrary, the role and performance of
courts is very much at the heart of the jurisprudential project. Even those
who eschew the role of values in determining law's identity and those who
decline to offer a full-blown account of the adjudicative craft are obliged to
accept that the judicial branch of government is where jurisprudential theory
meets legal practice: "Adjudicative institutions are, in a sense, the linchpin
of all legal systems."[1] However, for all its energy and expansiveness, the discussion about how judicial officials do and should go about their tasks is
unsatisfactory and, from a democratic standpoint, unsatisfying. At the contemporary heart of this academic debate is the extent to which adjudication
can be understood as being both about values and political choices and compatible with the demands of a democratic society—Can judges deal with
political matters in a way that is not ideological? Is there some method that
judges can rely upon which will relieve them of or, at least, legitimate the
burden of political choice? Does analytical jurisprudence offer any assistance
or guidance to the beleaguered judiciary in an ostensible democracy? These
questions are pressing and the answers proposed by contemporary jurists are
revealing.

It will come as no surprise that I maintain that a commitment to strong
democracy is unsympathetic to, if not dismissive of the plethora of scholarly
attempts to legitimate the work of courts in modern societies. In particular,

---

[1] John Gardner, *The Virtue of Justice and the Character of Law*, [2000] Curr. L. Probs. 1 at
23. *See also* H.L.A. Hart, The Concept of Law (2nd ed. 1994) and J. Raz, The
Authority of Law (1979). *See generally* Hanoch Sheinman, *The Priority of Courts in the
General Theory of Law*, 52 Am. J. Juris. 229 (2007).

this justificatory effort has become rather fraught and desperate in regard to the role of judicial review in constitutional democracies: The stakes are very high because unelected judges are empowered to countermand the plans of elected representatives. However, no amount of scholarly ingenuity can manage to square two incompatible practices: judicial review and popular soveriegnty. Indeed, judicial review, as presently conceived, is anathema to the strong democrat; it is an elite practice that might, at best, occasionally be democratic in being for the people, but it can never be by the people (or else it would cease to be *judicial* review). As such, it is mistaken to believe that liberal constitutionalism can do anything more than incorporate a weak version of democracy and, as importantly, stymie the development of a stronger practice of democracy. Democracy ought not to be seen as a *form* of government embodied in a constitution because democracy always escapes constitutionalization. Instead, democracy should be advanced as a *substantive* manifestation of popular participation.

Accordingly, in this chapter, my ambition is to shed some light on this 'darkling plain' in which adjudication is defended as not merely an acceptable feature of democracy, but also as an indispensable component in a flourishing democratic society. Offering a less 'ignorant' perspective on the democratic 'struggle', I begin by putting a little more flesh on the bones of the democratic skeleton. Next, I will explore critically the central dynamic that is at work in efforts to justify judicial review in constitutional democracies. By reference both to situated theoretical arguments and historical evidence, the chapter proposes a 'hard-core' case against judicial review and suggests how strong democracy might take up the resulting institutional slack. Throughout the chapter, it will be emphasized how democracy is better understood as being not a ground or foundation for politics, but a dynamic process through which politics is experienced and evaluated; the institutional forms and social practices of democracy must themselves be open to debate and revision in line with the experience of society's participating members. Eschewing the search for final or fixed ends, democracy is not an end in itself, but a process for formulating and pursuing the different ends of different societies. It neither expects nor demands a numbing conformity or consistency between equally vibrant democratic communities.

Strong Democracy

Democracy is one of the most relied upon, but least explored terms in the jurisprudential lexicon. Indeed, its malleable and contested nature is a large part of its enduring political appeal. At the heart of the democratic ideal is the understanding that people should rule over themselves. The smaller the gap between the rulers and the ruled and between the powerful and the powerless, the better and more democratic that society will be. In closing the gap, any sensible democratic theory must pay attention to both the formal and substantive elements of democracy. Although it will be essential to ensure that there exist appropriate venues and processes through which people can participate in government and hold it accountable, it will also be equally important to look at the substantive conditions in which people live so that their participation can be relatively equal and robust. As such, electoral participation is not a full or true indication of a society's democratic health. At its starkest, it would be difficult to suggest that a country which extended the vote to all citizens was deserving of democratic accolades if the largest part of the population lived in miserable conditions, with a short life expectancy, and with little education or employment prospects. This would be more a travesty than a realization of the democratic ideal.

Any society that claims to be democratic will be disposed to take measures to facilitate closing the gap between its governing elites and its governed majority. Although there is no need or warrant for absolute equality (as this would stifle individual initiative and require constant governmental supervision and readjustment), a commitment to democracy suggests that everyone, not only some and certainly not only a few, should share in the good and bad fortune of that society. To be genuine democratic participants, people must be emancipated from bondage of all kinds, economic, social, and cultural. If the extent of participation by lowly citizens in those power centers which affect their lives is the measure of democratic progress, the inimitable Aristotle remains pertinent in his judgment that "the real difference between democracy and oligarchy is poverty and wealth. The rich are few and the poor are many . . . where the poor rule, that is democracy."[2] Equality of opportunity demands more than the dismantling of formal barriers to participation, it also requires continuing substantive and affirmative measures to

---

[2] ARISTOTLE, POLITICS 1279b40–1280b5 (B. Jowett trans. 1943). A maldistribution of substantive resources and opportunities would be less troubling if the most recent trends were towards reducing or modifying it. However, over the past decade or so, the American trend has been in the opposite direction—the extent of inequality in wealth and income is getting worse and the gap between the haves and the have-nots is increasing. *See, for example,* KEVIN PHILLIPS, WEALTH AND DEMOCRACY: A POLITICAL HISTORY OF THE AMERICAN RICH (2002). By any sort of democratic standard, this decline (as opposed to the absolute level of inequality) is profoundly troubling.

actualize those opportunities and possibilities. Consequently, democracy's commitment to equality must be as substantive as it is procedural.

Democracy is better thought of as a social way of life in which everything that affects the conditions of people's lives is potentially encompassed; democracy is a value and process which can inform all aspects of social life. Viewed this way, democracy is the commitment *par excellence* to the idea that almost all choices and actions have political roots and political consequences: people can tackle those politics within a framework within which their active participation is more important than (or, at least, as important as) that of elected representatives and appointed elites of political sages. In particular, democracy need not be construed as simply a set of processes and practices tagged on to a particular political ideology, whether it be liberalism, conservatism, socialism, or whatever. Indeed, democracy is a mode of life, an ethos, a way of day-to-day living within which the best of such ideologies and political commitments can be harnessed and their excesses jettisoned. In that sense, the robust brogue of democratic politics insists that the liberal, libertarian, or socialist is only one kind of democrat and that the democrat is not only one kind of liberal, libertarian, or socialist.

Accordingly, this strong approach to democracy is very strategic and political; it is not conceptual or philosophical. Rather than talk in absolute terms about the overall democratic quality of society, it is preferable to concentrate on those measures which are proposed to be taken to make a society more democratic. From this standpoint, democracy is not a black-and-white idea or practice; a society is not either democratic or undemocratic. It is a matter of shading and degree. While it will be necessary to make tradeoffs *within* a democratic society (*i.e.*, as between distribution and production, and freedom and equality), it is unnecessary and ill advised to make tradeoffs *with* democracy. To think in such terms is to misunderstand democracy. Consequently, rather than think about democracy as one particular thing or evaluate a state of affairs as being democratic or not, it is better to ask whether taking a particular step is likely to advance democracy; this will be a contextual and contingent assessment. As such, the type of democratic commitment that I defend is pragmatic and contingent rather than idealistic or absolutist. The primary consideration in any effort to effect change will always be—What present measures will best increase the greater participation and control which people have over those institutions and practices which most affect their lives today?[3]

---

[3] This account of *strong democracy* draws on my previous work. See particularly A. HUTCHINSON, THE COMPANIES WE KEEP: CORPORATE GOVERNANCE FOR A DEMOCRATIC SOCIETY (2006).

Although it is better that more are involved more of the time than less involved less of the time, it seems counterproductive to deny a reform proposal or strategy the term democratic because it does not involve everyone all the time; it is a democratic mistake to let the best be the enemy of the good.

That being the case, it is possible to highlight several strategic and pragmatic commitments against which any particular proposal or reform to advance the democratic project can be assessed. These are what I will call the five basic precepts of democratic advancement. Taken together, they confirm the emancipatory and transformative potential that lies within democracy:

- *More extensive participation is better than less extensive*—Because democracy is as concerned with the pedigree of power as its effects, any state of affairs which multiplies and broadens the number of locations, whether public or private, in which participation is possible is more likely to advance democracy than not.
- *More participation is better than less participation*—Because involvement is a benefit in itself and can beget a taste for even further involvement, any state of affairs which increases the degree of direct as well as indirect or substantive as well as formal participation is more likely to advance democracy than not.
- *More equal participation is better than less equal participation*—Because people experience a sense of genuine participation only if their involvement is effective and counts, any state of affairs which tends to ensure that no one has more power than any one else is more likely to advance democracy than not.
- *More responsibility is better than less responsibility*—Because people cannot be expected to be involved all the time in all locations in all circumstances, any state of affairs which renders those with temporary power more accountable to others is more likely to advance democracy than not.
- *More transparency is better than less transparency*—Because people must be informed if their participation is to be meaningful and telling, any state of affairs which increases the amount of knowledge to which people have access is more likely to advance democracy than not.

Democracy does not have all the answers to life's challenges. Indeed, democratic theory embraces the idea that there are no once-and-for-all right answers and nurtures a practice which seeks to accommodate differences of opinion rather than do away with them. To date, democracy has too often been viewed as more the icing on the political cake than part of the cake itself. Indeed, the constant pressure to constrain and cabin democracy is plain evidence of a fearful acknowledgment of democracy's potential to subvert the *status quo* and, in particular, to threaten the power of various entrenched elites. By ensuring that democracy's broad mandate (*i.e.*, including social and economic as well as political matters) and deep mandate (*i.e.*, requiring regular sustained acts of participation) are both respected, it will better ensure that the citizenry become full participants in the political process and that they are better able to "reinvigorate the argumentative dimension of [] politics."[4] To do this demands that there are greater efforts to pluralize and circulate the sites and situations in which democracy is at work: It is not possible to have "democracy with a Big D in the system as a whole if you do not have real democracy with a small d at the level where people live, work, and raise families in their local communities."[5] By being flexible and pragmatic, democrats can accept that compromise as well as conviction are important qualities. However, those five precepts outlined can help bridge the existing divide between democracy's past and future, between its commitment and achievement, and between its vision and reality. In particular, they can better inform the project of democratic renewal in the constitutional context.

Viewed in this more ample light, the efforts of weak democrats, like Ronald Dworkin, might well be stymieing efforts to develop and substantiate a more progressive and energized democracy than is likely to exist in the near future. In contrast, I place confidence in the belief that, if provided with better and more extensive institutional opportunities to participate in their own governance, people will cultivate a greater appetite and aptitude for political engagement. The critical gamble is that, if domination breeds largely subservients, then democracy will beget mainly democrats. In short, I hold that the best way to 'reinvigorate the argumentative dimension of politics' is to introduce more democracy, not less. Indeed, democracy will only be possible if there is a willingness to move beyond its presently anemic and weak form and engineer changes that bring it closer to its more full-bloodied potential. Unfortunately, present jurisprudential scholarship exhibits only a weak commitment to democracy as part of a stronger commitment to constitutionalism, more generally, and judicial review, more particularly. Consequently, after examining the tepid enthusiasm for democracy and the continuing

---

[4] RONALD DWORKIN, IS DEMOCRACY POSSIBLE HERE? PRINCIPLES FOR A NEW POLITICAL DEBATE 8 (2006).

[5] GAR ALPEROVITZ, AMERICA BEYOND CAPITALISM: RECLAIMING OUR WEALTH, OUR LIBERTY, AND OUR DEMOCRACY 43 (2005).

defense of judicial review, I will sketch a more affirmative case for increased popular participation.

Constitutionalism and Democracy

Constitutionalism preceded democracy. The main elements of most societies' constitutional orders were firmly in place before all persons were treated as citizens and before the franchise was extended to all those citizens. For instance, in the United States, although the fundamental constitutional compact was in place by 1791, the final extension of the franchise did not take place until over 170 years later in 1964. Yet, even today, the percentage of voting-age population who actually vote in federal elections remains alarmingly low. In the 1950s and 1960s, a high of somewhere around 65 percent of eligible voters participated in presidential elections. Currently, the number has fallen to a low of between 50 and 55 percent. Midterm elections draw no more than between 35 and 40 percent. However, despite the historical priority of constitutionalism and continuing low electoral participation, the growth of democracy as both an idea and practice has raised pressing concerns for political and legal theorists. In particular, though the structures and details of constitutional orders have developed and changed over time, the challenge of increased popular participation has obliged a reexamination of the appropriate and legitimate relationship between constitutionalism and democracy.[6] This relationship is clearly contested and complicated—is it most deeply and best understood as complementary or contradictory? Does the one reinforce and strengthen the other, or is one the negation of the other? Can there be a mode of constitutional democracy which is both coherent and reliable in effecting social justice?

The central notion of constitutionalism is that, although government is established to serve popular interests, government must be constrained in its powers if it is to retain authority in exercising those powers. As such, constitutions not only organize and distribute power, but they place limits upon its exercise. In its predominantly liberal incarnation, there is a strong belief that there must be procedural and substantive limits placed on what policies the citizens can require or expect their political institutions to pursue. Indeed, these constraints on contingent democratic demands can be seen as

---

[6] *See generally* John Wallach, *American Constitutionalism and Democratic Virtue*, 15 RATIO JURIS 220 (2002).

the foundational and enabling conditions for an enduring and virtuous democratic polity. In this vision, democracy is not the main process by which political justice is constituted or achieved, but is merely instrumental to the preservation and expression of that goal. There is, of course, much debate among constitutionalists about the nature and extent of these limitations. Some of the most common arrangements relied upon to achieve such a balance of power and accountability include the familiar notions of separation of powers, adherence to the rule of law, constitutional supremacy, and, of course, the protection of fundamental rights through judicial review. As John Rawls, the leading modern liberal constitutionalist put it, "in a constitutional regime with judicial review, public reason is the reason of its supreme court."[7]

These basic features of modern constitutionalism have much to recommend them and have become accepted as the *sine qua non* of good governance. However, this is not the whole story. Constitutionalism is also characterized by an obsession with permanence, a resistance to constitutional change, and a suspicion of constituent assemblies. Underlying many constitutionalist theories is the idea that, once the constitution contains the right abstract principles and the correct balance of institutional safeguards, it is a good and finished constitution. There is room for fine-tuning in the details of its operation and implementation as circumstances change, but there is no need or warrant for further changes of a substantial or structural kind. Indeed, the claim is that to alter the constitutional arrangements in significant ways is to look for political trouble, play with the stability of the governance system, and risk the precious ideal of the Rule of Law.[8] Moreover, the rise of democracy and the spread popular entitlement has heightened those fears.

Of course, what it means to promote democracy and incorporate its demands into a society's scheme of government is highly contested. At the heart of that dispute is the role of popular participation. The dominant view in both theory and practice has been that a commitment to democracy does not have to entail a decisive or central role for popular participation; it is a necessary feature of

---

[7] JOHN RAWLS, POLITICAL LIBERALISM 231 (1993). *See also* B. ACKERMAN, WE THE PEOPLE, vols. 1 and 2 (1991 and 1998). For a more general appreciation of constitutionalism, see Richard Bellamy and Dario Castiglione, *Constitutionalism and Democracy: Political Theory and the American Constitution*, 27 BRITISH J. OF POL. SCI. 595 (1997); Stephen M. Griffin, *Constitutionalism in the United States: From Theory to Politics*, 10 OXFORD J. LEG. STUDIES 200 (1990); and Michel Rosenfeld, *Modern Constitutionalism as Interplay Between Identity and Diversity* in CONSTITUTIONALISM, IDENTITY, DIFFERENCE, AND LEGITIMACY (Michael Rosenfeld ed. 1994).

[8] *See, for example*, MARK TUSHNET, TAKING THE CONSTITUTION AWAY FROM THE COURTS (1999).

any democratic society, but it is not its final or superior mode of authority. Indeed, popular participation has been relegated to a distinctly second-best position in modern systems of so-called democratic governance. In particular, it is objected that the proposed limits on popular power are not and cannot be self-executing and must be determined by some institutional device, usually some form of judicial review. The fear is that, if popular participation is left unregulated and uninhibited, it will result in acts and policies that are antithetical to social justice more broadly conceived; the majoritarian trampling of minority rights is the most commonly noted complaint.

These concerns about popular participation are not trivial or entirely unproven. However, they are by no means inevitable or unavoidable; they are insufficient on their own to undermine the case for a robust commitment to a strong form of democracy which places popular participation at its dynamic heart. In contrast to weak democrats, the strong democrat insists that there is no philosophical authority or analytical method for illuminating truths that is somehow a separate process from a democratic society's own efforts to act justly and fairly and can underwrite those efforts. Accordingly, because there is no neutral or privileged way to trump popular participation as a process through which to debate and formulate what policies to pursue, the justification for the need to place traditional restraints on popular authority are unconvincing. Moreover, popular participation is not (or need not be) as unprincipled, arbitrary, or self-serving as many constitutionalists suggest. At its more uncompromising, therefore, the democratic critique of constitutionalism is that it operates more as a cover for elite control and facilitates a tyranny of the few over the many. In a strong democracy, political legitimacy is more appropriately secured by obtaining direct consent from active citizens, not subsequently validated by abstract reason from philosophical mentors.[9] In short, strong democracy and constitutionalism (or weak democracy) have very different attitudes and approaches to the wisdom and reliability of popular politics.

In line with this insight, the primary tension in legal and political theory should not be between constitutionalism and democracy *per se*, but between different accounts of constitutionalism in terms of their willingness to place more or less confidence in popular politics in the pursuit of a democratic system of governance. In short, in a constitutional democracy and in contested matters of political morality, the central question is whether the prosaic or primary location of authority and legitimacy is to be found in an entrenched

---

[9] Michael Walzer, *Philosophy and Democracy*, 9 POL. THEORY 379 (1981). Of course, this does not mean that any participation on any terms will be authorized and valid. See *infra*, ch.9.

constitutional order or in the regular participation of citizens. Under the tutelage of the analytical tradition, legal theorists have tended to view this question as primarily philosophical in scope and substance. However, I am recommending that the largely neglected historical, political, and strategic aspects of this inquiry demand much greater attention. Indeed, despite the frequently trumpeted value and importance of democracy in modern politics, its institutional imperatives and normative significance have been treated as decidedly inferior in the constitutional scheme of things: The chronological precedence of constitutionalism has been endowed with continuing conceptual priority by modern commentators and officials.

Indeed, modern legal and political theory displays a discernible uneasiness toward the thrust and influence of a democratic commitment that is both *for* the people and *by* the people. Democrats stand for most of what constitutionalists fear. Unlike constitutionalists, they do not contend that the purpose of constitutional democracy is to protect democracy from itself.[10] Indeed, many constitutionalists only manage to pass themselves off as democrats because they shave the idea of democracy so thin that they transform constitutionalism into the democratic *telos*. In contrast, strong democrats maintain that rule by the people recommends at least two general and indispensable commitments on the constitutional front—(1) an institutional *openness* in which even the most fundamental principles are open for discussion and are always susceptible of being reformulated or replaced and (2) an empowerment of people so that they come together in *political equality* and settle on the laws that will regulate the institutions and practices under which they live. In order for these rules to be the people's own, it must be today's people who rule, not past generations: the constitutionalist idea of precommitment cannot be brought to a final reconciliation with democracy. If people are to rule themselves and not be ruled by others, no matter how benign or beneficial their objectives, it is imperative that strong constitutionalists make way for strong democrats. A reassessment of judicial review is the most obvious place to begin that pivotal task.

Beyond Liberal Legalism

The democratic status of judges has always been suspect. The fragility of their legitimacy arises not so much from their exercise of power, but more

---

10   See STEPHEN HOLMES, PASSIONS AND CONSTRAINT: ON THE THEORY OF LIBERAL DEMOCRACY (1995).

from the nagging doubts about the warrant under which they wield such authority. Lawyers must claim to speak and act in a voice other than their own; they must justify themselves by reference to an authority beyond themselves—law. Of course, no self-respecting modern lawyer or legal theorist pretends that law is "a brooding omnipresence in the sky" that lends itself to formulaic application or provides robotic predictability.[11] It is now trite learning that legitimacy cannot be grounded in law as a sealed system of normative directives. We can never simply 'follow the rules' because the questions of which rule, what it means, and what following it entails remains irresolvably contestable. Accordingly, it is now generally conceded that law is as much a constructive activity as a given thing and that adjudication involves an inescapable dimension of political choice; legal interpretation is not a pseudoscientific practice, but an engaged exercise in value choices. The mainstream jurist must demonstrate that, even if legal doctrine does not compel definite results, it places sufficient constraints on judges to save them (and the citizens they are supposed to serve) from themselves or, at least, to justify the civic trust placed in them. The democratic challenge is to hit upon a way to act decisively as well as legitimately.

The Canadian situation is typical. In the last few decades, with the advent of the *Charter of Rights and Freedoms*, judges and jurists began to question the continuing reliance upon the old standby of liberal legalism—sharp public/private distinction, neutral interpretation, and objective balancing—as a method for legitimizing their decisions and reconciling the courts' role with democracy. This approach was failing to placate either liberal or more radical critics who complained that judicial review was not fulfilling its functions as effectively or as democratically as it might. Not only were the courts' efforts at preserving a sharp distinction between legal analysis and political judgment becoming more transparent and unconvincing, but the substantive political values which animated their decisions were being revealed as increasingly outdated and unresponsive to contemporary sensibilities. Indeed, liberal legalism was unable to command a sustained consensus even among the judges.[12] As part of their role as judicial helpmates, jurists have offered a number of proposals to move forward on the constitutional front. There are two main trends that have been explored in Canada and elsewhere—pragmatic

---

[11]   *Southern Pacific Co. v. Jensen*, 244 U.S. 205 at 222 per Holmes J. (1917).

[12]   For a full and unimpeachable account of these developments, see ANDREW PETTER, TWENTY YEARS OF CHARTER JUSTIFICATION: FROM LIBERAL LEGALISM TO DUBIOUS DIALOGUE (2009). *See also* ALLAN HUTCHINSON, WAITING FOR CORAF: A CRITIQUE OF LAW AND RIGHTS (1995).

reasoning and democratic dialogue. Ironically, these very efforts to bolster democratic legitimacy have managed to reveal even more starkly how thoroughly undemocratic is the judges' involvement in constitutional review. Most significantly, these interventions fail to take seriously that it is the *who* of adjudication as much as the *what* of adjudicative activity that matters most in a society that seeks to be strongly democratic.

The first response has involved a much greater candor and willingness to treat legal reasoning as being a substantially pragmatic enterprise. By this, it is meant that judges ought to worry less about abstract legitimacy and more about practical usefulness. In doing this, they do not abandon the idea of legal reasoning having some distinctive character and they do not treat it as being entirely unprincipled; they view it as being a more modest engagement which is about social consequences, not conceptual properties. The best that can be hoped for, according to these pragmatic enthusiasts, is to view law as a gradual accretion of conventional wisdom that, in the form of rules and principles, gives determinate guidance to judges: There is no single algorithm for decision making, only a potpourri of tried-and-tested techniques. Moreover, being anti-dogmatic, practical, instrumentalist, non-theoretical, problem-solving, and grounded, a pragmatic account of adjudicative practice treats adjudication as more a practiced craft than a drill in systematic reasoning; it is akin to riding a bike, not solving a mathematical equation.[13]

This pragmatic approach undoubtedly improves upon more traditional understandings of legal reasoning. However, they still want to claim that, while not a science, legal reasoning is a lot less contingent and a little more final than other normative vocabularies. Moreover, in its reliance on facts and consequences, they still maintain that, although neither deductive nor analogical, law remains propositional and instrumental in resolving disputes. Rather than accept law as one more way of coping, legal pragmatists cannot resist the temptation to press practical reasoning into service in the analytical workhouse and make it into more of a method than the experiential make-do that it is. Although championed as a practical and socially situated endeavor, judicial performance remains centered on textual, doctrinal, and argumentational matters; little attention is paid to the actual social context in which disputes arise or the political consequences of judicial decisions. Consequently, for all its pragmatic posturing, this response to the failure of

---

[13] *See, for example*, MICHAEL SULLIVAN, LEGAL PRAGMATISM: COMMUNITY, RIGHTS, AND DEMOCRACY (2007) and RICHARD POSNER, HOW JUDGES THINK (2008). It is important to emphasise that 'legal pragmatism' is related to and influenced by philosophical pragmatism, but not derivative of it. See *infra*, ch.9.

more legalistic and analytical approaches to judicial decision making still manages to portray democratic politics as being "subject to the jurisdiction of a philosophical tribunal."[14]

The second trend has been a turn to dialogue theory as an alternative justification for judicial review. Accepting that some reliance upon contested political commitments is not only inevitable, but also desirable in constitutional adjudication, the primary concern of jurists has been less with politicization itself and more with "the degree to which judges are free to read their own preferences into law."[15] The problem has been reframed so that the issue is the sources of values to which judges turn and the extent to which they rely on them rather than whether judges rely on political preferences at all. Cautioning that judges are not free to go wherever their personal political preferences direct them, the dialogic approach still claims to insist upon the existence of a workable distinction between legitimate legal analysis and illegitimate political decision making. It is argued that this crucial differentiation is much fuzzier, that the domain of law is much more expansive, and that the boundary between law and politics is much less breached than traditionalists maintained. However, these dialogists do concede that there is a point at which the judges can be said to be no longer doing law; they will have wandered off into other parts of the constitutional and political domain. In some important sense, law is to exist separately from its judicial spokesperson such that law places some non-trivial constraints on what judges can do and say. Although legal principles are more open and sensitive to political context, law is not only reduced to the contingent political preferences of the judiciary.

The general thrust of the dialogue theory is that courts and legislatures will engage in an institutional conversation about the Charter and its requirements on particular and pressing issues of the day: The courts and the legislators

---

14   RICHARD RORTY, CONTINGENCY, IRONY, AND SOLIDARITY 196–97 (1989). Rorty chastizes Dworkin for his misguided efforts to ground law as an enterprise of general principles rather than as one of "convention and anecdote." Rorty, *Postmodernist Bourgeois Liberalism* in HERMENEUTICS AND PRAXIS 215 (R. Hollinger ed. 1985).

15   KENT ROACH, THE SUPREME COURT ON TRIAL: JUDICIAL ACTIVISM OR DEMOCRATIC DIALOGUE 106 (2001). See also Peter Hogg, Allison Bushell Thornton, and Wade Wright, *Charter Dialogue Revisited—Or 'Much Ado About Metaphors'*, 45 OSGOODE HALL L.J. 1 (2007). In the United States, see Frank Michelman, *Law's Republic*, 97 YALE L.J. 1493 (1988). In the United Kingdom, see Thomas Poole, *Dogmatic Liberalism? T R S Allan and The Common Law Constitution*, 65 Mod. L. REV. 463 (2002) and Richard Clayton, *Judicial Deference and 'Democratic Dialogue': The Legitimacy of Judicial Intervention under the Human Rights Act'* [2004] PUB. LAW 33.

have complementary roles that enable legislation to be carefully tailored to meet the government's political agenda and to respect Charter values as well. Judicial advocates of a dialogic approach insist that "judicial review on Charter grounds brings a certain measure of vitality to the democratic process, in that it fosters both dynamic interaction and accountability amongst the various branches." Of course, in establishing a *dialogic balance* and "retaining a forum for dialogue" between the different branches of government, the courts are urged to tread a thin, but vital line between deferential subservience and robust activism.[16] Nevertheless, done with institutional sensitivity and pragmatic responsibility, the courts and legislatures can be dialogic partners in an institutional conversation to advance shared democratic goals. The problem is, of course, that, under the cover of dialogue and accommodation, the judges might be simply indulging in an overtly political performance; it might be that they have simply given up the ghost rather than exorcised the wraith of judicial activism.

Accordingly, with its apparent rejection of judicial objectivity, lack of normative content and vague invocations of democracy, the most recent juristic approaches to judicial review actually serve to undermine further the project of justifying constitutional adjudication's democratic legitimacy. Although both dialogic theory and pragmatic reasoning (often combined and mutually reinforced) are intended to calm fears that the courts are undisciplined and unlimited in their powers, it manages to reinforce the perception that courts are not only at the center of the crucial process through which political discourse and values are shaped and sustained, but also that courts get to determine the role and contribution of the other branches of government. The "degree to which judges are free to read their own preferences into law" seems to be reducible to the rather oxymoronic conclusion that they will be as "free to read their own preferences into the law" as "their own preferences" allow. There is a huge gap between the rhetoric of democratic dialogue and the reality of judicial performance. Presenting judicial review as part and parcel of a democratic dialogue merely underlines the extent to which democracy has become a pathetic caricature of itself. An elite and stilted conversation

---

[16]   *Bell Express Vu Limited Partnership v R.*, [2002] 2 SCR 559 at paras. 65–66 per Iacobucci J. See also *Vriend v Alberta*, [1998] 1 SCR 493 and *Corbiere v Canada (Minister of Indian and Northern Affairs)* [1999] 2 SCR 203. In Canada, this effort to ground "democratic dialogue" is facilitated by the fact that legislatures possess the final word on Charter matters by virtue of their (almost never-used) s.33 override power and that courts can engage in a more overt balancing of political values under the s.1 "reasonable limits" provision.

between the judicial and legislative or executive branches of government is an entirely impoverished performance of democracy; it is an empty echo of what should be a more resounding hubbub.

An Historical Peek

For all their juristic ingenuity, these efforts at presenting a post-analytical approach to adjudicative practices and questions of democratic legitimacy run leave too much untouched and run very high risks. In a sense, success would be their worst enemy. If the judicial form changes, but the substance of decision making remains the same, a bad job will be made to look good without altering its thorough badness. Admittedly, a transformation in argumentative style might produce greater candor, but it has no necessary implications for the results reached. Moreover, such a move might obstruct any real progress by reducing the political pressure on other institutions more qualified and suited to effecting such substantive change. There is a naïve faith that the stylistic *what* is more important than the political *who*. Judges largely tend to decide as they presently do in large part because of their normative instincts and political assumptions. The intellectual act of making these more visible and self-conscious will not by itself change the decisions reached. Although the unveiling of these assumptions might spur greater reflection and motivate an occasional change of heart, most judges will validate and ratify their informing visions; they decide as they do because of, not in spite of, their instincts and assumptions. As such, the law will remain "a body of practices observed and ideas received over time by a caste of lawyers" with all that this entails.[17] Little suggests that the adoption of the legal pragmatists' or the dialogists' proposals will usher in a more democratic era in which people, rather than their judicial proconsuls, will make crucial decisions about society's governance and, thereby, their own lives.

Setting aside any theoretical concerns and arguments for the moment, the historical record of courts is far from encouraging in terms of the actual outcomes reached. Whatever principled or analytical arguments jurists may successfully make about the need to contain popular participation in the name of liberal constitutionalism (and, as I have argued, these are not successful),

---

17   A.W.B. Simpson, *The Common Law and Legal Theory* in LEGAL THEORY AND COMMON LAW 20 (W. Twining ed. 1986). It is surely axiomatic that, as a privileged class, lawyers can hardly claim to be representative of society's diverse mix.

there are still "the brute facts of legal history" to consider.[18] Such an historical accounting is far from kind or reassuring to the constitutionalist cause, be it of a reactionary or radical stripe. Even a cursory glimpse at the historical sweep of constitutional law strongly suggests that the political performance of the courts has been mixed at best. And there is certainly no historical mandate for a continuing democratic faith in the capacity of courts to deliver the goods.

For instance, the American roads from *Dred Scott* to *Brown* (and perhaps back towards *Plessy*) and from *Lochner* to *Lincoln Federal* (and, again, perhaps back towards *Lochner*) are chastening ones.[19] Whether a liberal or conservative, any political enthusiast who takes seriously the historical record ought to have second thoughts about the wisdom of relying on the courts to deliver the democratic goods. In particular, the *Bush v. Gore* fiasco is strong evidence of why even weak democrats should be at least wary, if not dismissive, of the United States (US) Supreme Court's capacity and willingness to advance any constitutionalist vision of progressive politics over the long haul.[20] But it is a mistake to approach *Bush v. Gore* as an unfortunate aberration from an historical progressive script or a conservative exception that confirms the rule that judicial review is the best way of advancing and protecting democracy. In fact, during the last few years, the Supreme Court has struck down important progressive legislative policies and resisted like-minded interventions on individual rights. For example, the Court in *Lopez*, invalidated a federal criminal prohibition on the possession of guns in local school zones; in *Morrison*, invalidated the civil damages section of the federal Violence Against

---

[18] RONALD DWORKIN, LAW'S EMPIRE 255 (1986).

[19] See *Dred Scott v. Sanford*, 60 US 393 (1857); *Plessy v. Ferguson*, 163 US 537 (1896); and *Brown v. Board of Education*, 347 US 483 (1954). *Plessy* has experienced something of a renaissance in the form of the rebellion against affirmative action: any resort to race-based categories is treated as invalid. There are echoes of Brown J.'s dissent in *Plessy* in Thomas J.'s judgment in *Adarand Constructors Inc. v. Pena*, 512 US 200 (1995). *See also* G. LOURY, INDIVIDUALISM BEFORE MULTICULTURALISM (1996). As regards *Lochner v. New York*, 198 US 45 (1905) and *Lincoln Federal Labor Union v. Northwestern Iron and Metal Co.*, 335 US 525 (1949), the decisions in *Nollan v. California Coastal Commission*, 483 US 825 (1987) and *Dolan v. City of Tigard*, 114 S.Ct. 2309 (1994) seem to embody a *Lochner*-style approach. See Note, *Resurrecting Economic Rights: The Doctrine of Economic Due Process Reconsidered*, 103 Harv. L. REV. 1363 (1989) and Cohen, *Lochner in Cyberspace: the New Economic Orthodoxy of 'Rights Management'*, 97 Mich. L. REV. 462 (1999). For further discussions of these continuing historical episodes, see A. HUTCHINSON, EVOLUTION AND THE COMMON LAW ch.5 (2006).

[20] See *Bush v. Gore*, 531 US 598 (2000).

Women Act, ruling that acts such as date rape were not economic activities that substantially affected interstate commerce; and in *Padilla*, declined, on jurisdictional grounds, to rule on whether Padilla could be held indefinitely in military custody as an enemy combatant without being charged.[21]

Accordingly, even if a strong-constitutionalist/weak-democratic stance were to be adopted and endorsed, there are few historical or strategic reasons to prefer decisively a strong system of judicial review over a system of legislative supremacy. The risks of injustice or, as more analytically inclined jurists would put it, wrong and illiberal outcomes seem to be always present. On the historical record, there is strong support for a regular to-and-fro between progressive and conservative phases, even though the specifics of such shifts are unpredictable. There is simply no reliable way to make a historical projection about whether the courts over the next couple of decades will be more or less like the Warren or Rehnquist court. Whether it should or should not be that way as a matter of constitutional rightness is almost beside the strategic point. Indeed, it might be that defending a moral and correct reading of the constitution will be throwing good theoretical money after historical bad. Of course, strong-constitutionalists/weak-democrats, like Dworkin, might well insist that it is the burden of constitutionalist "seers and prophets" to struggle against historical recalcitrance and persuade judges and jurists of the error of their prosaic ways.[22] But this will be a political claim which itself must be anchored in firmer historical ground than the soft sands of prophetic platitude and wishful thinking.

In referring to the historical record of judicial review, there is another large problem with the strong-constitutionalist/weak-democrat approach and proposals. In lamenting the parlous contemporary condition of democratic politics and prescribing a strong corrective of moral reflection, these jurists fail to consider or comprehend that the very preference to place the courts at the democratic heart of the constitutional compact is very much part of the problem, not the solution. A continuing and heavy reliance on a judicially enforced constitution might be such a disabling disadvantage that it has contributed to the very degradation of democratic politics that it is supposed to ennoble. Unlike appointed and life-tenured judges, elected officials do not operate behind a dubious curtain of impartiality and objectivity;

---

21   See *United States v. Lopez*, 514 U.S. 549 (1995); *United States v. Morrison*, 529 U.S. 598 (2000); and *Rumsfeld v. Padilla*, 542 U.S. 426 (2004). See also *Padilla v. Hanft*, 126 S. Ct. 1649 (2006), where the Supreme Court denied Padilla's petition on certiorari after he was charged with crimes and released from military custody.

22   Dworkin, *supra*, note 18 at 407.

they can be removed through the ordinary electoral process. If the most important issues of political controversy are routinely out of reach of popular politics, it should come as no surprise that this will work to promote democratic disaffection by sapping people's political energies and atrophying their participatory instinct. Ironically, this apparent lack of interest in politics by modern citizens is utilized to justify and preserve nonparticipatory institutions. However, the willingness to situate courts as a primary venue for democratic engagement perpetuates the idea that social justice comes from a judicial act of *noblesse oblige* rather than a popular product forged in the public mill of political debate. Unless the presently disaffected can become part of their own future empowerment, there can be no confidence that apathy and indifference will not persist. Indeed, the continuing efforts to galvanize support for constitutional checks on popular participation by way of judicial review increase the odds that the degradation of democratic politics will become further entrenched.

Finally, an historical awareness suggests a very different appreciation of the relation between constitutional arrangements and prevailing political sensibilities. Constitutions do not speak or act for themselves: Their contingent operation and shifting meaning are closely, if complicatedly, connected to broader political forces and democratic dynamics. A constitution will not hold back an overwhelming political impetus; it is only a bulwark against injustice, apprehended or real, if there is a democratic will to interpret or rely on it to do so. Similarly, constitutional decisions that take a firm stand against injustice do not occur or stick unless there is a popular openness to such interventions. Legal efficacy depends on political viability. The ebb and flow of court decisions do not happen in spite of democratic leanings, but, at least in part, because of them. Any juridical order which is not underpinned by a democratic culture, no matter how liberal its constitution and no matter how stringent its procedures for constitutional change, is always at risk of falling victim to popular disruption and even rejection.[23] Conversely, a juridical order which is more consistent with the idea of democratic openness and has a culture of political equality is also at risk, albeit a lesser risk. No constitutional arrangements are acceptable if they can only survive by keeping democratic politics in an institutional straitjacket. As such, the

---

[23] The events of 1989 in Europe are an example of how "even powerful and long-enduring organizations of state coercion and ideological hegemony fall before radical dissent." Neil MacCormick, *Constitutionalism and Democracy* in THEORIES AND CONCEPTS OF POLITICS: AN INTRODUCTION 144 (Richard Bellamy ed. 1993). *See also* JEREMY WALDRON, LAW AND DISAGREEMENT 310 (1999).

strong-constitutionalist/weak-democratic position overestimates the instrumental impact of constitutions, even as it touts their symbolic significance.

A Hard-Core Case

In their recent exchange, Jeremy Waldron and Richard Fallon join philosophical issue over whether judicial review is a desirable or defensible institution in a democratic society. In his enthusiastic case against judicial review, Waldron insists that, although the outcome-related arguments are inconclusive, the process-related arguments are overwhelmingly on his side— "rights-based judicial review is inappropriate for reasonably democratic societies whose main problem is not that their legislative institutions are dysfunctional but that their members disagree about rights."[24] In response, Fallon puts forward a tentative defence of judicial review on the basis that there are both outcome-related and process-related arguments to warrant a *multiple veto-points approach* to retaining some form of judicial review: "a constitutional democracy with a well-designed system of judicial review would produce a morally better pattern of outcomes than a political democracy without judicial review."[25] Though both these views are illuminating and helpful, I want to suggest a more hard-core case against judicial review in democratic societies. In particular, I want to challenge Waldron's assessment that the outcome-related arguments are inconclusive and Fallon's resistance to that fact.

To do this, I will take a more strongly democratic approach and question Waldron (and Fallon's) views about there being available and reliable epistemological grounds for reaching correct decisions on rights disputes. Once this dubious assumption is abandoned or substantially relaxed, all outcome-related arguments are seen to be undergirded by process-related arguments which strongly support the case against judicial review. However, although I maintain that judicial review has no legitimacy in a democratic polity, I do think that Fallon's talk of multiple veto-points is still valuable. Though a multiplicity of deliberative institutions can play a useful role in a democratic polity, there is no reason at all why judicial review, as presently constituted,

---

[24] Jeremy Waldron, *The Core of the Case Against Judicial Review*, 115 YALE L.J. 1346 at 1406 (2006).

[25] Richard Fallon, *The Core of An Uneasy Case For Judicial Review*, 121 HARV. L. REV. 1693 at 1715 (2008).

should be one of them. Accordingly, an unrelenting commitment to democracy offers a more hard-core and convincing case against judicial review.

Along with Dworkin and others, Waldron and Fallon seem to insist that there is some objective ground or moral facts-of-the-matter in regard to rights disputes. In making their respective cases, Waldron and Fallon both make a similar philosophical claim that, even though there is widespread disagreement about the precise definition and scope of rights, it is possible "to get at the truth about rights" and that "questions involving rights have correct answers."[26] Because rights disputes are so fundamental in placing possible checks on the activities of legislatures, they maintain that is "important that we get them right" and that there is a "relatively, even if not perfectly epistemologically reliable way" to discover "moral truths" and "right answer[s] to questions involving rights."[27] These are not merely claims about the legal indeterminacy around rights disputes, but about the existence of moral truths and the identity of rights as objective moral entities. As such, Waldron and Fallon's stances are foundational and metaethical claims of a grand epistemological kind. However, if outcome-related arguments are to have any purchase at all, Waldron and Fallon are obliged to rely on some objectivist position—if there were no relatively fixed benchmark, however elusive and contested, against which to measure outcomes, then there would be no way to compare the respective merits of different devices for resolving the outcomes of rights disputes.

As foundational as these epistemological claims are to Waldron and Fallon's stances, they are highly controversial. This is especially the case in those societies in which its members are or would be committed to a strong mode of democracy. When measured against an evaluative standard by which democracy is treated as being not only a qualified mode of political governance, but also a thoroughgoing ideal by which to organize social life generally, Waldron and Fallon are revealed to be only half-hearted democrats. Though Fallon is explicitly guarded in his commitment to democracy by treating democratic institutions as only one part of a complete political package, Waldron rests much of his intervention on his supposedly unconditional embrace of "a culture of democracy, valuing responsible deliberation and political equality."[28] The stance of Waldron and Fallon leans towards a constrained democratic understanding in which the formal political process for

---

[26]   Waldron, *supra*, note 24 at 1375 and Fallon, *supra*, note 25 at 1702.

[27]   Waldron, *supra*, note 24 at 1373 and Fallon, *supra*, note 25 at 1703.

[28]   Fallon, *supra*, note 25 at 1725 and Waldron, *supra*, note 24 at 1361. *See also* Waldron, *supra*, note 23.

tallying people's preferences and distributing political power is front and center. In contrast, although strong democrats are concerned about the substantive quality of people's lives, they place more emphasis on enabling good lives than engaging in the detached search for some elusive Good Life; democracy encompasses everything that affects the conditions of people's lives and considers active participation its most important feature.

In regard to the debate over Waldron and Fallon, strong democracy's antipathy to elitism extends to those philosophers, sages, or experts who claim that there is some set of objective values or truths to which a democratic society must conform or by which it can be disciplined. Because they insist that there is no one set of rights entitlements or practical realization of them that will always be morally superior, strong democrats believe that it is for people to determine for themselves what is best for them. Yet, even though Waldron and Fallon emphasize that disagreements over these moral truths might be "for practical political purposes, irresolvable,"[29] there is simply no basis in a strong democracy to be held hostage to the possibility, however remote, that such truths exist or that experts, like judges and jurists, might have some special access to them. Moral authority is a quality to be earned in democratic exchange, not bestowed from elsewhere; there is no independent or superior standard of moral legitimacy than that derived from the processes and procedures by which laws and legal decisions are made. In particular, there is no supra-democratic method that can be invoked or appealed to that will have greater moral authority other than the society's own routine engagements through its democratic infrastructure and according to its prevailing social ethos. There are no conversation-ending or truth-fixing arguments about moral claims other than those that gain acceptance in engaged debate and open inquiry. In allowing for the epistemological possibility that getting it right is somehow a separate process from a democratic society's own efforts to act justly and fairly, Waldron and Fallon are betraying the democratic spirit of inquiry, debate, and action.

By refusing to compromise their non-foundational and pragmatic convictions, strong democrats resist the claim that there are epistemologically-reliable ways to discover 'moral truths' about rights. Indeed, locating knowledge and truth within a communal set of practices and engagements, they evince an implacable opposition to epistemological methodology generally. In this sense, therefore, the strong democrat does not fall foul of Waldron's charge of

---

[29] Waldron, *supra*, note 24 at 1368.

"moral relativism" or Fallon's caution about "rights-skeptics."[30] Because strong democrats eschew all claims to abstract or disengaged truth, they do not hold a relativistic account of truth—all views on all topic are as good or valid as any other—by insisting that the best moral values are those that pass muster under the prevailing democratic procedures and protocols of justification. Strong democrats can make and promote enthusiastically normative arguments, but they simply cannot defend them as somehow eternal or transcendental. Moreover, for much the same reasons, strong democrats do not adopt a skeptical approach to rights; they simply maintain that there are no epistemological or political bases for rights that are above or outside the existing democratic practices that give rise to them. Political and moral rights exist and are justified to the extent that a vibrant democracy holds faith with them.

Accordingly, the reliance by Waldron and Fallon on the existence of moral truths is both a necessary feature of their arguments and a thoroughly flawed one from a strongly democratic perspective. If there are no relatively epistemologically reliable means for ascertaining what rights are or how they apply, any argument about the outcome-related reasons for supporting judicial review founder. It makes no sense to talk about "a morally better pattern of outcomes" or "wrong answers" as separate from the democratic processes which gave rise to them.[31] The lack of any neutral, reliable, or uncontested epistemic procedure by which to resolve disagreements means that there is no way to compare the effectiveness of different institutions in terms of their capacity for determining better or worse substantive outcomes. Indeed, without such a method, the only way to compare and contrast different institutions for resolving rights disputes is by their process-related qualities and participatory strengths. As both Waldron and Fallon tend to agree, this makes the case against judicial review even stronger.

Politics and Processes

Behind the controversy around the democratic legitimacy of judicial review, there lurks a much more compelling issue. The present debate tends to be polarized as a straight democratic choice between rule by a judicial elite or

---

[30]   Waldron, *supra*, note 24 at 1368 and Fallon, *supra*, note 25 at 1703.

[31]   Fallon, *supra*, note 25 at 1715 and Waldron, *supra*, note 24 at 1373. For further discussion of the supporting philosophical arguments for this democratic stance, see *supra* chs.1 and 5.

rule by a governmental elite. As judicial review involves unelected judges invalidating the actions of elected legislators or executives, all judicial review is anti-majoritarian and, therefore, presumptively undemocratic; no theory can reconcile judicial review with majority rule. Because there is no way to bring such a project to a satisfactory conclusion, continuing attempts to do so merely exacerbate the problem of democratic legitimacy and erode the very confidence that the legal establishment is trying to maintain.[32] A better response would be to acknowledge that adjudication in a society of diverse and conflicting politics is an inevitably ideological undertaking. Once this is done, courts will not necessarily become antagonistic or surplus to democratic requirements.

However, the real and neglected issue is not the judiciary's lack of democratic legitimacy and its politicization, but the institutional failure of the executive and legislative branches of government to meet fully their democratic responsibilities and mandate. If governments and legislatures were more truly responsive to popular concerns and more open to popular participation, the question of what judges do would be less pressing and more incidental. Consequently, if there is a crisis in democracy, it is that it is used more as a rhetorical cloak for elitist governmental practice than a measure and guide for popular politics; it is present governmental arrangements generally, not only judicial review, that fails to satisfy or even aspire to the demands of strong democracy. However, though there is no compelling argument as to why democracies should rely on judicial review, it does not follow that all power and authority should be left in the hands of omnipotent legislatures; there is absolutely no warrant to frame the debate as a zero-sum choice between legislatures and courts, as presently constituted. In short, there is a strong and easy case to be made for the creation of multiple possible veto points in ensuring the fulfilment of important democratic ambitions about the protection of people's rights and political entitlements.[33]

Because moral worth in strong democracies is established (but not determined or fixed) through those accepted and agreed-upon standards for justifying knowledge, it will be crucial to ascertain and examine the terms and

---

[32] The crude Bickelian countermajoritarian challenge to the courts' democratic legitimacy has dominated debate and framed the issue in terms that are entirely unhelpful. See ALEXANDER BICKEL, THE LEAST DANGEROUS BRANCH: THE SUPREME COURT AT THE BAR OF POLITICS 14–18 (2nd ed. 1986). For a more sophisticated approach, see EDWIN CHEMERINSKY, INTERPRETING THE CONSTITUTION 11–12 (1988) and *Foreword: The Vanishing Constitution*, 103 HARV. L. REV. 43 (1989).

[33] Fallon, *supra*, note 25 at 1705.

conditions under which such social agreements are reached and enforced. Being experimental and open as well as suspicious of any general claims to truth-validating methods, democracy is sensitive to the inevitable presence of power and its disruptive and self-serving potential.[34] Existing values and settled interests have no democratic valence on their own. Though critics and activists must work with the justificatory tools of their society, they are not condemned to work within its past decisions or remain beholden to its present orientations: The past consensus is only a starting point and the present accord is only a temporary respite from continuing debate and engagement. As such, extant democratic arrangements must themselves not only allow, but also facilitate critical engagement. Justificatory standards endure only as long as they retain the confidence and support of the community as the best and most useful benchmarks available; they thrive and wither in the good-faith debate between intelligent interlocutors about what counts as working best.

As such, legal theorists' attention must shift towards the critical elaboration of those process-related conditions that make legal enactments and decisions more or less democratic. It will then become more apparent that outcomes and processes are not separate or separable as Waldron and Fallon assume, but are intimately connected through their democratic status: democratically passed laws are legitimate not because of their slippery conformity with elusive moral truths, but because they satisfy process-related democratic criteria. In strong democracy, it is a point of principle and practice that ends and means are integrated as closely as practically possible: The status and legitimacy of the initiating procedures is the benchmark against which both the legal system and any particular enactment's legitimacy can be measured. The greater the extent and quality of participation in the legislative and adjudicative process, the greater the legitimacy of their substantive pronouncements.

In fulfilling this critical responsibility, democratic institutions and instincts can assist by ensuring that people are emancipated as far practicable from bondage of all kinds (*i.e.*, economic, social, cultural and, especially in this context, intellectual oppression) and that participation is as wide and unconstrained as possible. The task is most definitely not to purge intellectual inquiry and debate of politics as those traditional jurists who defend a continuing and central reliance on judicial review recommend. Instead, mindful that power can also be constitutive and enabling as well as restrictive

---

[34] See *supra*, ch.7.

and distorting, a democratic approach can meet power's challenge by organizing democratic arrangements so as not only to maximize people's life-choices and life-styles, but also to provide a set of communal resources through which the bases for these choices and styles can be debated and criticized. It is the strength of strong democracy that it can provide a process for debating and deciding upon political means and ends in a contingent way that claims no objective or analytical privilege. This might entail a commitment to devolve and diffuse power as much as practicably possible by fostering multi-veto points.

In line with this commitment, strong democrats will look to extend and proliferate the opportunities for participation in microcommunities rather than narrow and accrete decision-making power to small and centralized elites in the name of expertise and truth. This institutional transformation involves two important initiatives in regard to existing arrangements. First, it will be important to reinvigorate democratically those bodies and organs (*e.g.*, legislatures, municipalities, state agencies) which presently claim to be the decisive seat of democratic government. Rather than function as remote entities that have a tenuous claim to democratic legitimacy through occasional elections, they might begin to be less entrenched in their connections and more responsive in their deliberations and decisions; local government would replace federal government at the heart of democratic involvement. For instance, in American terms, *congress* might begin to approximate more closely to its original meaning as "a gathering of people" and, in Anglo-Canadian terms, *parliament* might more closely resemble its roots in "a place for debate;" representation and participation could be less structured and more popular in action and ambition.[35]

Second, it will be important to ensure that, if there is to be a spread of second-, third- or even fourth-look bodies that contribute to the formulation and implementation of policy making, such institutions will themselves be more participatory and directly accountable to popular views. Of course, judicial review does not meet such standards; appointed (and even elected) judges tend to operate in the same calcified and elitist ways as the elected legislatures that they are supposed to check. Accordingly, it will be necessary to engage citizens directly in more imaginative and participatory ways in such deliberative and policy-making bodies, including special tenure protections

---

[35] For an important effort to re-think the agenda of democratic deliberation and to re-design American institutions accordingly, see Michael Dorf and Charles Sabel, *A Constitution of Democratic Experimentalism*, 98 COLUM. L. REV. 267 (1998) and A CONSTITUTION OF DEMOCRATIC EXPERIMENTALISM (Forthcoming 2009).

and non-legal personnel. Moreover, as part of such a shift, it might be possible, in a Jeffersonian fashion, to develop practices whereby every decade or so all fundamental laws and institutional arrangements could lapse and periodic assemblies convened so that each generation had the "right to choose for itself the form of government it believes most promotive of its own happiness."[36] In this way, citizens might claim the constitution and its amendment-by-review as their own and take responsibility for the deep structure of their political society.

Even with a vastly increased scheme of popular participation, conflict and disagreement will still occur. It is hopelessly naive to pretend that any system of governance, including and especially strong democracy, will be based on complete and lasting consensus; the appeal of strong democracy is that it will foster, not inhibit a pluralist culture of political engagement and this will inevitably generate contention.[37] Under such circumstances, the role of these multiple possible veto points will not be to replicate courts and mimic the judicial (and juristic) pre-occupation with establishing neutral and non-political bases for legitimating their actions. Instead, it might be accepted that, once there is a genuine and widespread practice of strong democracy, all bodies and agencies will be involved in the same game, namely delivering substantive answers to concrete problems. In doing so, while no one institution will have a lock on political judgment about what is the best thing to do, all institutions' decisions will be evaluated in terms of the value choices that they make and the contribution that their decisions make to advancing substantive democracy in the here-and-now. Accordingly, the appropriate inquiry in a strong democracy is not to ask whether particular policy-making bodies have acted politically and, therefore, improperly, but whether the political choices that they have made serve that society's democratic agenda. Because this democratic assessment is a substantive and political undertaking, not formal and analytical, it will always be a contested and contestable issue.

---

[36] THOMAS JEFFERSON, WRITINGS 1402 (Merrill Peterson ed. 1984) at 1402. Mark Tushnet has been developing a rich and provocative body of work on how best to develop non-judicial forums for constitutional decision-making. *See, for example,* TAKING AWAY, *supra,* note 8 and *Non-Judicial Review,* 40 HARV. L. ON LEGIS. 453 (2003). See also Keith Ewing, *A Theory of Democratic Adjudication: Towards a Representative, Accountable and Independent Judiciary,* 38 ALTA. L. REV. 208 (2000) and Hutchinson, *Judges and Politics: An Essay from Canada,* 24 LEGAL STUDIES 275 (2004).

[37] See Waldron, LAW AND DISAGREEMENT, *supra,* note 23.

To revamp the whole system of legislative and executive processes in line with greater and more extensive popular participation will require a monumental effort. Moreover, any changes that are proposed—proportional representation, recall legislation, accountability audits, genuine ministerial responsibility, referenda, etc.—must themselves be legitimate products of the very democratic process that is to be enhanced. There are no easy solutions to the present undemocratic trends. In this sense, the debate around judicial review is something of a distraction. Improvement in society's democratic status will not come from increased interventions by judges in governmental policies. Indeed, judicial supervision is a short-term crutch that might actually harm a limping polity in the medium- and long-term march towards a fuller and stronger democracy. The replacement of one elite rule (executive or legislative) by another (judicial) can only be considered positive under a warped sense of democracy. So, if there is a desire to reign in the judges, there must also be a commitment to ensuring that elected politicians and officials are living up to their own demanding democratic responsibilities. At present, they are palpably not doing so. But simply construing the democratic challenge as being one about whether the judges stay out of or stray onto the political terrain is to misrepresent the problem and, therefore, to hamper any genuine solutions. The twin foundations of democracy—popular participation and political accountability—are going the way of the polar icecaps. Drastic and democratic action is needed.

When Hercules Met Alexis

Many strong-constitutionalists/weak-democrats would conceive Lycurgus as the reluctant embodiment of their theoretical and practical ambitions.[38] According to Greek legend, Lycurgus was the founding father of the Spartan constitution. Before visiting the Delphic oracle, he called an assembly of the people and made everyone, including the kings and senators, promise not to tinker with the constitution until he returned. When the oracle told him that the constitution was well written, Lycurgus starved himself to death; he also had his ashes scattered in the ocean so that it could never be claimed that he had returned in any form. The Spartans kept their promise and the constitution remained unaltered for 500 years. However, despite his championing

---

[38] *See, for example*, Dennis Thompson, *Democracy in Time: Popular Sovereignty and Temporal Representation*, 12 CONSTELLATIONS 251 (2005).

by present-day constitutionalists, debate still rages as to whether Lycurgus had made the ultimate and heroic sacrifice for his Spartan compatriots or whether he had in fact sacrificed them to his own vanity. In many ways, this cautionary legend captures the institutional quandary of those contemporary jurists and theorists who struggle to choose between the competing pushes and pulls of constitutionalism and democracy.

It should not come as a surprise to legal scholars to learn that Lycurgus was a direct and eleventh-generation descendant of the fabled Hercules (which was the Roman name for the greatest hero of Greek mythology, Heracles). Of course, apart from his fabled exploits in fighting monsters and performing physical feats of strength, Hercules is also Dworkin's "imaginary judge of superhuman intellectual power and patience."[39] As such, he is one of jurisprudence's mythic titans who is intended to offer an idealized version of what moralist-instructed judges might seek to emulate, even if they are destined always to fall short of his transcendent example. Yet such epic personae are antithetical to any ideal or practice of engaged democracy; they give the distinct impression that truth and justice are not achievable by ordinary people, that it takes extraordinary abilities to create and interpret constitutions, and that debate and deliberation are superfluous to a fully-realized civic society. Progress is considered to be more a gift from the gods than anything else. In short, the invocation of Lycurgian and Herculean qualities in guiding contemporary politics works to trivialize and discourage popular participation in democratic governance.

Because too much jurisprudential scholarship already seems to be populated by such superheroes and their antics, I am reluctant to add another to their ranks. Democracy certainly does not need another hero in the Herculean or Lycurgian tradition. Indeed, there needs to be a wholesale revision in the thinking about what leadership demands in a political tradition, which is informed and inspired by democracy. The traditional and largely demagogic notion of political leaders is anathema to a democratic sensibility; it conveys images of unquestioned authority, complaint obedience, testosteronic endeavor and hierarchical superiority. In place of this cult of leadership, in which society's fate seems to be tied almost exclusively to the identity and qualities of its leaders, it is important to develop a more appropriate and lower key notion of leadership. However, if democracy were to have a prototypical

---

[39] Dworkin, Law's Empire, *supra*, note 18 at 239 and R. Dworkin, Justice in Robes 55–56 and 67–68 (2006).

leader, it might be the eponymous 'Alexis' who can stand in for the ordinary citizen of the truly democratic polity.

Alexis is a modest and gregarious person. She or he recognizses that, if she or he is a leader, she or he is a reluctant one at that. Although possessing similar energies and dynamism as more traditional leaders, she or he channels them into more popular pursuits. She or he is a good listener and seeks to engage with rather than mold fellow citizen's views. However, Alexis is sufficiently sensitive to context to be that she or he is aware that "the surface of [] society is covered with a layer of democratic paint, but from time to time one can see the old aristocratic colours breaking through."[40] Eschewing the elite accents of the society's power-centeres, she or he travels widely and keeps company with a wide range of people from diverse backgrounds. Most important, Alexis appreciates that democratic leaders are enablers, not enforcers. She or he acts on the idea that democratic leaders are not ones who impose their own personal vision to attain a shallow and fearful consensus. Rather, they help to facilitate the community's efforts at building and implementing its own democratic culture. As such, Alexis knows that "it takes time to arouse minds from apathy and lethargy, to get them to thinking for themselves, to share in making plans, and to take part in their execution."[41] Moreover, more humble than hubristic, Alexis is willing to stand aside and let the people take the credit for their own achievements; she or he recognizes that there is no one right way and that what prevails today might well be rejected tomorrow. She or he is truly a person of the people.

Conclusion

Ironically, at the very time that the theoretical basis for judicial review is coming under serious and sustained challenge, there has been a huge expansion in the introduction and use of judicial review around the world.[42] Nevertheless, this should not discourage democrats, but should galvanize them to redouble their efforts at revealing the flawed and fragile theoretical foundations on which the case for judicial review presently rests. Even its

---

[40] ALEXIS DE TOCQUEVILLE, DEMOCRACY IN AMERICA, vol. 1, part 1, ch.2 (Henry Commager ed. 1946).

[41] J. DEWEY AND J. TUFTS, ETHICS 385 (rev. ed. 1936). *See also*, ADEL SAFTY, LEADERSHIP AND DEMOCRACY (2004).

[42] RAN HIRSCHL, TOWARDS JURISTOCRACY: THE ORIGINS AND CONSEQUENCES OF THE NEW CONSTITUTIONALISM (2004).

supporters, like Fallon and Dworkin, recognize that the case for judicial review is not as obvious or as easy as is often assumed. If ostensible democratic societies are to persist with judicial review, then a variety of steps can be taken—reduced judicial powers, specialized constitutional courts, responsive appointment procedures, legislative overrides, greater judicial accountability, periodic constituent assembles, etc.—to de-sacralize and defrost the constitutional order. However, the preferred course is to work toward the abandonment of judicial review as a pivotal institution in democratic societies. Aristocratic rule is no less palatable because judges and jurists are the new "princes . . . and prophets."[43] And it is certainly no more acceptable when such elites wrap themselves in the trappings of democracy. In a society that takes democracy seriously, there is no privileged place for judicial proconsuls or their scholarly cohorts—citizens can govern best when they govern themselves. Though there has never been a golden age for democracy, what now passes for democracy has no sustained or substantive role for the voices of ordinary citizens—'ignorant armies', 'confused alarms', and 'a darkling plain' indeed.

---

[43] Dworkin, *supra*, note 18 at 407.

CHAPTER NINE

The Experimental Province of Democracy Determined

Let democratic politics be what sets the goals of philosophy, rather than philosophy setting the goals of politics.

—Richard Rorty

My challenge in this book has been as much to the analytical tradition of philosophy generally as it has been to its dominant position in jurisprudence. As exemplified by the larger project outlined in John Austin's *The Province of Jurisprudence Determined (The Province)* and refined by later generations of jurists, the problems of analytical jurisprudence—abstract conceptualism, theoretical universality, ahistorical essentialism, etc.—are very much part of the traditional philosophical methodology which privileges epistemological and ontological inquiries above others. Instead, I have suggested that there needs to be a shift away from the self-regarding agenda of analytical philosophy to the more practical concerns of democratic politics. Rather than exhaust itself in ever-more mannered analyses of what counts as the enduring nature of law, jurisprudence should take a broader and more useful approach to legal theory that emphasises a preference for the practical over the theoretical, the contingent over the certain, the experimental over the essential, the historicist over the enduring, the political over the philosophical, the instrumental over the intrinsic, the hermeneutical over the methodological, the evaluative over the descriptive, and the improvisational over the scripted. By reorienting the focus of jurisprudential study in this way, it might be possible for legal theory to reclaim its relevance and worth to both lawyers and citizens. Insofar as philosophy has a continuing role in democracy, it must earn its critical keep as part of, not apart from politics.

In this final chapter, therefore, I will pull together the main threads of my argument and seek to defend this proposed revitalization of legal theory as an adjunct location of democratic politics more generally. After tackling the contested relationship between philosophical pragmatism and political democracy, I will defend strong democracy as an institutional complement to the experimentalist bent of pragmatic theorizing. Then, in a slight change of perspective, I will round out my defense of the political province of democratic legal theory by brief reference to the literary insights of George Eliot's *Middlemarch*. Throughout, the goal will be to suggest a different role and set of responsibilities for legal theorists. Abandoning the hubris of much analytical jurisprudence, the legal theorist might adopt a more humble posture that attempts to serve, not master the needs of a democratic polity as determined by its members after a full and engaged exchange of views. So transformed, jurisprudence can become better placed to fulfill its supportive mission as an important, if modest resource in the expanded repertoire of democratic politics.

Democracy and Pragmatism

The basic thrust of my reliance on democracy is that it is the form and practice of government and social organization that best allows people to gain the most control over their own lives. In particular, at its most unconstrained and participatory, it permits all and not only some of the people to have a continuing say in as many aspects of their life as is practically possible. Of course, there will be issues of institutional scale in any shift to a strongly democratic society: There will need to be a much greater devolution and localization of power if a truly participatory system of governance is to take hold. For instance, it is estimated that, out of fifth-century Athens' total population of about 250,000, there were some 30,000 adult males of Athenian birth who attained full citizenship and, at any one time, about 5,000 might regularly participate in legislative and other deliberative matters.[1] Nevertheless, strong democracy clearly favors more centripetal initiatives over centrifugal tendencies. In taking seriously the notion that there should be both government *by* the people as well as government *for* the people, democracy offers itself as an extensive process through which people can not only participate in

---

[1] Of course, the implementation of social and institutional schemes by which such exuberant goals might be reached will demand an immense amount of effort and imagination. However, this is well beyond the mandate of this book. For an opening gambit, see ALLAN HUTCHINSON, THE COMPANIES WE KEEP: CORPORATE GOVERNANCE FOR A DEMOCRATIC SOCIETY (2006).

governance, but also be active in the (re)formulation of substantive visions about what good lives might comprise.

As regards legal theory and philosophy more generally, a thoroughgoing commitment to strong democracy suggests a range of recommendations. Most importantly, it accepts that, if people are to participate fully in the governance and ordering of their own lives, they must be emancipated from the many different and insidious modes of elitism that threaten such a personal and pubic ambition. As well as breaking the influential grip that wealth and heritage have upon society's decision-making processes, this means that people must be disabused of the tendency to confer undue authority on all kinds of experts and self-styled sages, no matter how well intentioned or benign they might be. In particular, citizens must be encouraged to grasp that there is no philosophical or jurisprudential claque of scholars who know something about knowing that can claim priority over a democratic community of good-willed and active participants. In a vibrant democracy, it will not simply be a rote matter of counting people's preferences, but about facilitating debate and engagement so that the resulting consensus has a distinctly qualitative as well as a quantitative dimension. Indeed, unlike what some contemporary philosophers maintain, democracy does not rely "for its legitimacy, on its ability to deliver sound decisions."[2] Democracy attains its legitimacy by ensuring that decision making results from as wide and as frequent participation as possible; decisions will be 'sound' by that fact alone and not by their approximation to some independent and/or external metewand as proposed by philosophers, jurists, or similar experts. Insofar as such theorists have any lingering role or authority, it will have to be earned by the local usefulness of their rhetorical interventions in continuing democratic conversations, not asserted as authoritative conversation stoppers.

Although I have placed strong democracy front and center in my critical account of analytical jurisprudence, there is a strictly philosophical tendency which assumes a similar deflationary posture towards inquiries into truth, knowledge, and meaning. This largely American-based tradition of pragmatism is commonly associated with the writings of John Dewey as well as William James and Charles Pierce. In more recent decades, Richard Rorty and Hilary Putnam have been its most vocal and consistent advocates in the philosophy community and Richard Posner has been its most important flag-bearer on

---

[2] J. Raz, The Ethics in Public Domain: Essays in the Morality of Law and Politics 117 (1994).

the jurisprudential front.[3] As with most philosophical tendencies, it has taken a variety of different shapes and shades. However, most pragmatic philosophers share an anti-idealist and fallibilist notion of truth and knowledge that has little time for the claims and methods of traditional epistemology. Pragmatists tend to insist that truth, knowledge, meaning and even (scientific) inquiry itself are not validated by their correspondence to some ahistorical or asocial standard of verification, but by their usefulness and practicality in society. Even those beliefs that can claim to be the most long-standing and/or broadly accepted in society may turn out to be unreliable and revisable over time. As such, pragmatists and strong democrats seem united in their rejection of traditional analytical concerns and in their embrace of a more socially engaged way of proceeding.

That having been said, there is active resistance by some avowed pragmatists towards the idea that an attachment to a pragmatic philosophical stance has any political consequences at all, let alone democratic ones. For instance, Richard Posner is adamant that "pragmatic dispositions—[experimental openness, contextual sensitivity, instrumental application, etc.]—have no political salience."[4] He insists that any claims to establish links between philosophical pragmatism and political democracy (and any other favored political scheme) are unconvincing and without merit. This almost quietist and complacent approach is most puzzlingly championed by Richard Rorty. Although he often wrote with force and enthusiasm about democracy's emancipatory potential, he advanced a decidedly liberal, if progressively so, vision of social justice. In what turned out to be his final published lecture, he concluded on a rather poignant note that:

> I agree with Posner when he says that "the bridge [Dewey] tried to build between epistemic and political democracy is too flimsy to carry heavy traffic.".... One can agree wholeheartedly with Dewey about the nature of truth, knowledge, and inquiry, and nevertheless agree with Posner that what he calls 'our present system of elective aristocracy' is the best we can do.[5]

---

[3] For a general introduction, see CORNELL WEST, THE AMERICAN EVASION OF PHILOSOPHY: A GENEALOGY OF PRAGMATISM (1989) and THE REVIVAL OF PRAGMATISM: NEW ESSAYS ON SOCIAL THOUGHT, LAW, AND CULTURE (Morris Dickstein ed. 1999).

[4] RICHARD POSNER, THE PROBLEMS OF JURISPRUDENCE 465 (1990). One critic opines that "no pragmatist has worked harder to break the link between pragmatism and deliberative democracy than Richard Posner." ROBERT WESTBROOK, DEMOCRATIC HOPE: PRAGMATISM AND THE POLITICS OF TRUTH 197 (2005).

[5] Richard Rorty, *Dewey and Posner on Pragmatism and Moral Progress*, 74 U. CHI. L. REV. 915 at 918 (2007) (quoting RICHARD POSNER, LAW, PRAGMATISM, AND DEMOCRACY

If Rorty, Posner and other like-minded pragmatists are interpreted to be making an historical argument about whether existing democratic institutions are up to the pragmatic job, there is some merit to their observations—existing democratic arrangements need to be substantially extended and deepened if they are to have any chance of bridging the epistemic and political divide and carrying the 'heavy traffic' of social living. However, these quietists are clearly not making such a modest claim. They are rejecting the capacity of democracy *tout court* to serve such a bridging feat. This seems to be a self-defeating claim because, if pragmatism has no political consequences at all, then it is difficult to see why democracy would be any more or less suited to the task than any other mode of governmental organization or social ordering. Nevertheless, there are more important weaknesses in this quietist stance.

The denial that pragmatism has any political consequences is tantamount to stating that there is no connection between philosophy and politics. Yet this distinction seems to rely on the very kind of dichotomous thinking—theory/practice, fact/value, epistemic/moral, etc.—that a pragmatic approach seems dedicated to resist. A bifurcated stance only makes sense *if* it is still considered that philosophy is something separate from history and politics and that it is possible to adopt or pursue a philosophical stance that is not implicated in the social conditions in which it arises and to which it is addressed. But this is a very large and unexpected *if*. The insistence that philosophy can be appreciated as an independent and removed discipline that can interrogate and deliver judgments about extant political conditions from above or outside them smacks of exactly the kind of privileged theorizing that characterizes the analytical tradition itself. Indeed, this kind of philosophical posturing seems to represent the very kind of philosophical practice from which a pragmatic approach is intended to distinguish itself. It suggests the somewhat oxymoronic position that one can be pragmatic without also being engaged and situated. This is a faux pragmatism that adopts several pragmatic gestures and props, but remains very much part of the analytical

---

113 (2003)). Rorty conceded that he was a "quietist" and that "with respect to almost any kind of pure theorising, there are no practical consequences." RICHARD RORTY and PASCAL ENGEL, WHAT'S THE USE OF TRUTH? 33 and 52 (2007). For accounts of how democracy has been considered both uniquely consistent with pragmatism as well as being inconsistent with it, see Matthew Festenstein, *Inquiry and Democracy in Contemporary Pragmatism* in PRAGMATISM AND EUROPEAN SOCIAL THEORY (P. Baert and Bryan Turner eds 2007) and James Kloppenberg, *Pragmatism: An Old Name for Some New Ways of Thinking*, 83 J. OF AM. HIST 100 (1996).

tradition in maintaining that philosophical analysis can be performed in a relatively detached, ahistorical, and apolitical manner.

Once the inevitable link between philosophy and politics is acknowledged, a disengaged and agnostic view of the connection between pragmatism and political arrangements is no longer sustainable. There is no one particular discourse, be it fact, theory, etc., that can claim any special or more compelling access to knowledge or meaning than an opposing discourse on values, practice, etc. In contrast, I insist that philosophical inquiry is a mode of political practice; there is no place from which to be philosophical and there is no way to act philosophically without already being part of some contested political terrain. As Derrida notes, "philosophical activity does not *require* a political practice; it is, in any case, a political practice."[6] That being so, there is no position of political innocence or indifference; all philosophizing is implicated in the contingent circumstances of its occurrence. In other words, philosophy implies and is already embedded in the extant protocols of interpretive practice. As such, the central issue is less whether a pragmatic stance has any political consequences (it does have) and more what concatenation of interests are served by any philosophical posture in particular historical circumstances and in particular social settings. It is entirely idealistic and analytical to insist that knowledge and meaning can be constituted or appreciated outside of power's matrixes. Consequently, although philosophical theorising has no necessary or fixed practical consequences, it will always have some political effects and these will depend on the historical circumstance and social practices in play.

A Political Experiment

Though a pragmatic sensibility restricts the kind of arguments that can be utilized to make political proposals, it does not prevent or preclude political proposals from being made or defended. It is simply that there needs to be a certain caution about what is being proposed and how it is defended.[7] I resist

---

[6] JACQUES DERRIDA, POINTS . . ., INTERVIEWS 1974–94 69–70 (P. Kamuf trans. 1995). *See also* J. DERRIDA, LIMITED INC. 146–47 (1989). For a fuller consideration of the power/knowledge connection, see *supra* ch.7.

[7] For other criticisms of pragmatism's unnecessary quietism, see Stephen White, *The Very Idea of A Critical Social Science: A Pragmatist Turn* in THE CAMBRIDGE COMPANION TO CRITICAL THEORY 314 (Fred Rush ed. 2004). For provocative engagements with this aspect of Rorty's work, see R. KUIPERS, SOLIDARITY AND THE STRANGER: THEMES IN THE SOCIAL PHILOSOPHY OF RICHARD RORTY (1997);

the claim that, once we give up on the idea of Truth, it is no longer possible to engage in meaningful conversation about a variety of issues, like freedom or justice. It is not a straightforward Hobson's choice between the truth-asserting claims of analytical philosophy and endless shouting matches. I do not reject the possibility of reasoned argument, but the possibility that it can be rational in the sense of Right or Final. As such, a better argument is not one that chimes more with an externally validated truth, but one that manages to persuade more people through extensive deliberation in line with available argumentative resources. Moreover, the pragmatic account of truth and knowledge, while deflationary and fallibilist, does not undercut the very real ethical demand that people be honest and truthful; its critical concern is with the epistemological, not ethical or sociological claims made on behalf of and in the name of truth.

Nor do I believe that, in a society that accepts the pragmatic insistence on the contingency of everything, a sense of political resignation or quietism is inevitable. Once purged of its metaphysical pretensions and more attuned to its own historicist insights, a pragmatic approach cannot avoid engaging with its political and social context. Having put the history back into philosophy, there is no warrant for a failure of critical nerve by failing to take the next step of putting the politics back into that history. Without an appreciation of the often grubby, materialistic, and collective conditions under which history is made and remade, a pragmatic tendency remains too cloistered and too precious for its own sake. Accordingly, in place of the quietist's lightness of historical being, those pragmatists who are committed to democracy and social change will choose to appreciate the full political weight of their historical belonging; they will appreciate that philosophy is another way of being politically and historically engaged.

That being the case, there is a strong historical practical argument—not a traditional philosophical or analytical argument—to be made along Churchillian lines that "democracy is the worst form of government, except for all those other forms that have been tried from time to time."[8] Although a commitment to democracy is open to a variety of criticisms and cautions, it

---

RORTY AND HIS CRITICS (R. Brandom ed. 2000); G. ELIJAH DANN, AFTER RORTY: THE POSSIBILITIES FOR ETHICS AND RELIGIOUS BELIEF (2006); ALISON KADLEC, DEWEY'S CRITICAL PRAGMATISM (2007); and THE NEW PRAGMATISTS (C. Misak ed. 2007).

[8] It is worth noting that Churchill said this in a House of Commons speech on November 11, 1947. This was not the convenient opinion of a sitting Prime Minister as he had already lost the post-War election and was, therefore, speaking in opposition after he had been democratically ousted.

remains the mode of governance that can lay contemporary claim to being the best presently available institutional complement to the pragmatic critique. This does not mean that it will always be best at all times and in all places or that one particular style of democracy is always superior to all others. After all, both democrats and pragmatists are united in their firm rejection of elitism whether it be in philosophy or society; the strength of a particular idea or decision is not measured by its approximation to some metaphysical and transcendental ideal, but by its acceptance by the widest and most inclusive consensus after the most vigorous of debates about it being the most useful and beneficial way to proceed. Both democratic and pragmatic sensibilities are suspicious of any general claim that there is one best or enduring way to apprehend and respond to a particular set of historical and social circumstances. As such, the emancipatory and anti-elitist tendencies of democracy make it into credible and recommended institutional option for the pragmatic critic to champion at the beginning of the twenty-first century.

There is nothing about this defence of a robustly democratic society which depends on any philosophical claim or epistemological back-up that such a society is more natural, more rational, more coherent, more pure or more anything else than any other society. And it is certainly not that it more closely approximates to some established notion of Truth. On the contrary, it is simply a practical argument that such a society is more useful in a world in which there are no philosophically mandated truths and in which people must be allowed to experiment for themselves with how they might best be organized and live their lives. Democracy's appeal is that it establishes its own foundations and authority by making them the property of the community and by ensuring that they are always open to critical transformation. Because it is deliberative rather than programmatic, strong democracy reinforces and comes closest to actualising a social and institutional practice which keeps faith with the key pragmatic claim that there is no basis in ethics, epistemology, or politics, to rely on any source of authority other than that which arises in and from social practices. Even if critics cannot speak in the name of Reason or Humanity, they need not celebrate the *status quo* or some reformist understanding of it. The justice of any situation might be measured by the extent and depth of people's participation in the formulation and reformulation of the terms and conditions of their own lives. In this way, people might become genuine citizens and resist the expedient temptation to mistake the contingent nostrums of analytical philosophers for enduring truths about social arrangements and the human condition. The *status quo* is owed no greater (or lesser) respect than any other set of institutional ordering; it is a place from which to begin and experiment.

A politically sensitive pragmatic approach does not duck the realization that knowledge and objectivity are tied to ethical practices and political interests. Indeed, it incorporates that unassailable insight into its general stance by ensuring that the circumstances in which particular intersubjective agreements are made constantly being challenged and reassessed. For instance, although pragmatists insist that there is no escape from particular historical and social settings, it does not follow that morality is simply reducible to whatever passes for morality in a given society. A pragmatic commitment does not simply enable democracy to function as a facilitative process by which "what we do around here" is authorized by virtue of that fact alone to "what we should do around here." In any democracy worth its name, there is space and even support for critical engagement: grounded and situated does not mean unreflective and uncritical. Though such reflection and criticism is dependent on the argumentative and intellectual resources of that society (and not some ahistorical or free-floating standards of truth validation), it is possible to generate a successful challenge to entrenched values. Even the prototypical and relatively conservative Dewey was adamant that "the attainment of settled beliefs is a progressive matter; there is no belief so settled as not to be exposed to further inquiry," and that it was necessary to "use [these settled beliefs] as hypotheses to be tested instead of as dogmas to be asserted."[9] Consequently, although pragmatists must work with the justificatory tools of society, they are not condemned to work within its past decisions or to remain wedded to its present orientations: The past consensus is only a starting point and the present accord is only a temporary respite from continuing debate and engagement.

Democracy offers the least constrictive process through which more people can separately and jointly develop and apply their experimental intelligence. It complements a pragmatic approach as it has no set institutional format nor a predetermined formula for success. It places participation at its deliberative heart and privileges communal conversation over all other modes of discourse;

---

[9] JOHN DEWEY: THE LATER WORKS, 1925–53 vol. 12, 16 and vol. 13, 166 (Jo Ann Boydston ed. 1981–1990). This is not the place to highlight the shortcomings of Dewey's detailed vision of democracy. Suffice it to say that he held a very moralistic account of democracy and its possibilities. He seemed almost wilfully naive about the potential for substantive oppression in his rather uniform depiction of democracy as a way of life and, as such, offered a democratic account that is ill-suited to modern pluralist society. Dewey tends to close down, not open up the moral options for citizens. See HILARY PUTNAM, PRAGMATISM: AN OPEN QUESTION (1995) and C. MISAK, TRUTH, POLITICS, MORALITY: PRAGMATISM AND DELIBERATION (2000).

"particpatory democracy finds its egalitarian roots in the fact that experimental intelligence . . . is not the special possession of a particular class of people, and its participatory thrust in the promise that the development of [experimental intelligence] offers for the realization of individual potentialities, the pursuit of individual and collective goals, and the promotion of the general welfare."[10] Moreover, because it favors experimentalism over any kind of perfectionism, it has no preference for any specific substantive moral position or social policy. Provided particular moral recommendations or policy proposals are not set in stone or rendered immune from challenge, strong democracy is committed to facilitating each community of citizens in its continuing efforts to formulate and implement its own ideas and initiatives. Such a strongly democratic practice will not result in a final harmonization of conflicting ends, but will offer an institutional context within which debate and redebate can be beneficially and respectfully pursued. Indeed, it might be that the citizenry will impose limits on free and open discussion in the name of democracy itself as long as those limits are temporary and revisable.

Accordingly, for all Rorty's encouragement to "let democratic politics be what sets the goals of philosophy, rather than philosophy setting the goals of politics," he failed to pursue that admirable ambition. Indeed, he compromised his pragmatic initiative by relegating democratic politics to a supporting role in the service of a liberal vision of social justice in which private re-invention trumps public renovation.[11] However, pursued more rigorously, this pragmatic recommendation to put philosophy in the service of democratic politics is a worthy and compatible goal. After all, the effort to isolate some eternal and phantom Truth and then to organize society in line with its fixed precepts is problematic on so many grounds—it is futile (because no such Truth exists); it is self-serving (because it tends to reproduce the theorist's own preferred commitments); and it is dangerous (because it treats all other pursuits and concerns as being of secondary importance). In contrast, I have tried to hold firm to the idea that an unflagging commitment to strong democracy represents the least worst scheme of governmental organization

---

[10] Eric Macgilvray, Reconstructing Public Reason 117 (2004). *See also* Mark Timmons, Morality Without Foundations: A Defense of Ethical Contextualism (1999).

[11] Take Care of Freedom and Truth Will Take Care of Itself: Interviews With Richard Rorty 47 (Eduardo Mendieta ed. 2006). *See generally* Richard Rorty, Contingency, Irony and Solidarity (1989). For a full-blown, if slightly dated critique of Rorty's liberalism, see Allan Hutchinson, *The Three R's: Reading/ Rorty/Radically*, 103 Harv. L. Rev. 555 (1989).

for managing political and social affairs as engaged exercises in experimental intelligence rather than as settled instantiations of some putative universal order. Theory is not an end in itself, but another practical means for improving the real-world conditions of people. As Roberto Unger puts it, under a pragmatic outlook, democratic experimentalism becomes "both a means and an end, a method and an outcome."[12]

After Casaubon

One particular corollary of a democratic approach is that philosophical method does not recommend itself as the only or best genre of inquiry through which to learn about or appreciate the social possibilities of human living. Indeed, as I have been at pains to establish, certain analytical forms of philosophical study can be positively misleading in their claims to identify certain foundational truths or traits about social life. Accordingly, it seems useful to conclude my jurisprudential project with a different mode of analysis and instruction that might be better suited to the democratic task at hand. From literature's vast resources, George Eliot's *Middlemarch* is a celebrated work that captures many of the central themes of my democratic critique of analytical jurisprudence. Situated at exactly the time that John Austin was writing his own *magnum opus*, *The Province of Jurisprudence Determined*, Eliot's sprawling novel is a sophisticated comedy of manners about English provincial life around the tumultuous years of the Reform Bill in 1832. It was a time when the old English order was forced to confront the precious privilege of its established ways and to come to terms with the bracing challenge of democracy's fledgling forces.

At the thematic heart of *Middlemarch* is the short-lived and ill-fated marriage between the young reformer, Dorothea Brooke, and the aging scholar, Edward Casaubon. In an early exchange between the two, Dorothea enthuses about one of her most cherished projects to alleviate the condition of the poor by building cottages for those who worked on her uncle's estate: "I think we deserve to be beaten out of our beautiful houses with a scourge of small cords—all of us who let tenants live in such sties as we see round us. Life in cottages might be happier than ours, if they were real houses fit for human beings from whom we expect duties and affections." Mr. Casaubon's only response is to declare that he "did not care about building cottages, and

---

12   ROBERTO M. UNGER, THE SELF AWAKENED: PRAGMATISM UNBOUND 207 (2007).

diverted the talk to the extremely narrow accommodation which was to be had in the dwellings of the ancient Egyptians as if to check a too high standard."[13] There is much in this brief exchange (and in Dorothea and Casaubon's unhappy relation generally) that resonates with the contemporary engagement in contemporary jurisprudential debate. Reduced to its basic essentials, the point of disagreement between the reigning philosopher-kings of the legal establishment and their democratic critics is quite simple—Is it to be the actual construction of cottages for the poor or detached ruminations on abstract points of ancient architecture?

Mr. Casaubon is a contender for one of literature's great misanthropic characters. He was "noted in the county as a man of profound learning" and whose "very name carried an impressiveness hardly to be measured without a precise chronology of scholarship." Piously devoted to researching and writing his life's work, *A Key To All Mythologies*, he was fond of telling people "how he had undertaken to show (what indeed had been attempted before, but not with that thoroughness, justice of comparison, and effectiveness of arrangement at which Mr. Casaubon aimed) that all the mythical systems or erratic mythical fragments in the world were corruptions of a tradition originally revealed." Moreover, although occasionally anguished by deep inward doubts, Casaubon was outwardly confident that, "having once mastered the true position and taken a firm footing there, the vast field of mythical constructions [would become] intelligible, nay, luminous with the reflected light of correspondences." In completing this monumental project, he was intent on not pandering to "the facile conjectures of ignorant onlookers" nor gaining "a temporary effect by a mirage of baseless opinion." For Casaubon and other keepers of scholarship's true flame, "it is ever the trial of the scrupulous explorer to be saluted with the impatient scorn of chatterers who attempt only the smallest achievements, being indeed equipped for no other."[14]

Although Casaubon died before completing his pantologic study (but not before he realized its futility), his scholarly mien remains strong in the jurisprudential community. Although often less pretentious or precious, analytical

---

13 GEORGE ELIOT, MIDDLEMARCH: A STUDY OF PROVINCIAL LIFE 26–27 (M. Drabble ed. 1985). Originally published in 1871 by Mary Ann Evans, it is described by Virginia Woolf as "one of the few English novels written for grown-up people." Woolf, *George Eliot* in THE COMMON READER 166–76 (1925).

14 *Id.* at 7, 19 and 184. Casaubon is also the hero of Umberto Eco's FOUCAULT'S PENDULUM (W. Weaver trans. 1989) who is involved in the search for the One True Meaning of Things. Eco insists that his Casaubon is not named after Eliot's clergyman, but after the great philologist Isaac Casaubon. See U. Eco, *The Text and Author* in INTERPRETATION AND OVER-INTERPRETATION 81-82 (S. Collini ed. 1992).

jurists still cling to the belief that it is possible to locate or fashion a conceptual key that will unlock the universal mysteries of law's historical existence. In Casaubonic style, analytical jurists strive to illuminate law's essential nature with the intellectual lightning of jurisprudential insight. It is not so much that they dismiss other types of jurisprudential study, but that they claim that they are of a secondary and derivative character to their own epistemological and ontological focus. The cool detachment of philosophical reflection is thought to be a necessary prelude to the contestability of political or even democratic critique. As Casaubon might put it, "having once mastered the true position and taken a firm footing there, the vast field of [law] became intelligible, nay, luminous with the reflected light of correspondences."[15] Matters of material or substantive justice are treated as distinctly secondary—the actual construction of cottages for the poor or detached ruminations on abstract points of ancient architecture?

Of course, Mr. Casaubon's approach to life and philosophy did not and has not gone unchallenged. The careers of many such critics resemble George Eliot's feisty, but impressionable Dorothea Brooke. Initially infatuated by "the set of [Casaubon's] iron-gray hair and his deep eye-sockets [that] made him resemble the portrait of Locke" and awed by "a modern Augustine whose work would reconcile complete knowledge with devoted piety," she saw Casaubon as "a guide who would take her along the grandest path." Furthermore, the thought that he might consent to be her husband filled her with "a sort of reverential gratitude"—"Here was a man who could understand the higher inward life, with whom there could be some spiritual communion; nay, who could illuminate principle with the widest knowledge: a man whose learning almost amounted to a proof of whatever he believed!" In that first flush of romance, she spent her days content "to imagine how she would devote herself to Mr. Casaubon, and become wise and strong in his strength and wisdom." There is much in Dorothea's condition that resembles the experience of young lawyers and jurists. Though Dorothea came across her devotion through acculturation and inclination, law students are encouraged by institutional training and collective self-interest to cultivate such an awed and respectful posture towards the law and its intellectual, practicing, and judicial elite. Indeed, under the spell of a Casaubonic mind-set, the life of a neophyte lawyers is "the mixed result of a young and noble impulse struggling amidst the conditions of an imperfect social state, in which great feelings will often take the aspect of error, and great faith the aspect of illusion."[16]

---

15   *Id.* at 19.
16   *Id.* at 12, 19, 23, 22, 17 and 765.

Yet Dorothea's selfless besottedness was unrealistic: No one could live up to such callow adulation, let alone the blighted Casaubon. Not surprisingly, Dorothea's admiration soon turned to disillusionment, which quickly hardened to contempt, even though it later mellowed to pity. On her return from an ill-fated Italian honeymoon with Casaubon, she realized that even in her earliest and most scholarly devotions she had been "visited with conscientious questionings whether she were not exalting these poor doings above measure and contemplating them with that self-satisfaction which was the last doom of ignorance and folly." As these questionings received ever more assured answers, she accepted that a life with Casaubon did not lead to "large vistas and wide fresh air," but to "ante-rooms and winding passages which seem to lead nowhither" and that "her blooming full-pulsed youth stood there in moral imprisonment which made itself one with the chill, colourless, narrowed landscape." Once Dorothea's anger and resentment had run their course, she looked upon Casaubon with a genuine mixture of sadness and compassion:

> For my part, I am very sorry for him. It is an uneasy lot at best, to be what we call highly taught and yet not to enjoy: to be present at this great spectacle of life and never to be liberated from a small hungry shivering self—never to be fully possessed by the glory we behold, never to have our consciousness rapturously transformed into the vividness of a thought, the ardour of a passion, the energy of an action, but always to be scholarly and uninspired, ambitious and timid, scrupulous and dim-sighted.[17]

There is much in Dorothea's predicament that can be profitably related to the critics' reaction to contemporary mainstream jurisprudence. Instead of revelling in the full amplitude and unbuttoned possibilities of human existence, analytical jurists bring to it a narrow and smothering perspective. Wanting to bring everything down to a dry and bloodless endeavor, they resemble taxidermists rather than naturalists; they want to capture and display legal wildlife in museums rather than marvel at their living color and glorious vitality. Under their tutelage, jurisprudence is less about rapture and glory and more about rigor and scrupulousness. Although they present their work in grand and confident terms, contemporary jurists are fearful and desperate—they are fearful that, if the world of law and lawyers is not held in check, it will decline into a chaotic and arbitrary exercise, and they are

---

[17] *Id.* at 28, 179, 250 and 255.

desperate because their efforts to establish such a checking device are increasingly less convincing. Rather than celebrate society's diversity and energy, they wish to leash and corral them. Accordingly in its efforts to rescue law and lawyers from themselves, jurisprudence craves greater theoretical authority not only to bolster individual contributions, but also to salvage its own waning prestige. This characteristic Casaubonic mix of conceit and timidity is held together by an attachment to the idea that there are certain conceptual truths about the legal facts-of-the-matter that can be identified and isolated by rigorous reliance on an uncompromising philosophical analysis.

Yet, on closer inspection, these extravagant claims of analytical jurists are less the imprimaturs of a supra-historical and superior methodology, but more the earnest ways of simply getting by. This is no bad thing. Stripped of their philosophical paraphernalia, these jurisprudential accounts might still have something to offer to law and its task of being substantively just in a world that is constantly shifting and changing. But it is this analytical paraphernalia that must go. The insistence that the theoretical effort to distinguish between law's contingent practices and its essential nature will pay practical dividends must be abandoned. The tendency to abstract theorizing has become a way to remain a spectator rather than a player at Dorothea's "great spectacle of life." Contemporary analytical jurisprudence remains in the scholastic shadow of a Casaubonic need for scientific rigor and abstract detachment as if this was the key to unlock the normative secrets of the universe. Jurists waste valuable energies in this hapless pursuit of some elusive universal and objective truths about the legal and human condition. Elegance, coherence, and simplicity are valued attributes of any theory, but they are hollow and hopeless as ends in themselves; they must be subordinated to a more modest and, therefore, more useful project of inquiry and criticism that can lead to "large vistas and wide fresh air" rather than "ante-rooms and winding passages which seem to lead nowhither."[18]

After Casaubon's demise, Dorothea struggled to come to terms with the meaning of his death for her life. Not helped by Casaubon's vengeful will (which made her inheritance conditional on not marrying Will Ladislaw, a young, if headstrong admirer), it took her a long time to break free of his chilling influence. Moreover, it took even longer for her to confound people's opinion that, despite her reputed cleverness, she had thrown herself "at Mr. Casaubon's feet and kissing his unfashionable shoe-ties as if he were a Protestant Pope." Although she never subscribed to the uncharitable view

---

[18]   *Id.* at 179.

that he was "a cursed white-blooded pedantic coxcomb," she did recognize the false allure of Casaubon's scholarly pretension: "And Dorothea had so often had to check her weariness and impatience over this questionable riddle-guessing, as it revealed itself to her instead of the fellowship in high knowledge which was to make life worthier." Dorothea intuited that intelligible and responsible action was not a gift from the gods or a result of allegiance to *a priori* truths about fixed principles; it was to be achieved in and through a social practice that interrogates standards of action as it formulates them. Moving from the parochial Middlemarch to a cosmopolitan London and marrying the free-spirited Will, she ended her days in "a life filled with beneficent activity." Although she did not engage in grand projects, "the effect of her being on those around her was incalculably diffuse; for the growing good of the world is partly dependent on unhistoric acts; and that things are not so ill with you and me as they might have been, is half owing to the number who lived faithfully a hidden life, and rest in unvisited tombs."[19]

Legal theorists would do well to imitate Dorothea's humility: the self-image of legal theorists as privileged purveyors of special knowledge and as peripatetic traders in universal verities must be abandoned. As practiced in the analytical tradition, jurisprudence ought to have no particular authority or priority over democratic deliberation. In place of Casaubonic conceit, there is a definite need to give a more sympathetic account of Dorothea's complaint and its implications for the practice of legal theorizing. Though most legal theorists are still prepared, through a combination of intellectual naivety, institutional allegiance, and political advantage, to buy into the possible realization of analytical jurisprudence's philosophical project or, at least, to tolerate it as a noble undertaking, a number of pragmatic critics refuse to accept such a pretence. True to the Dorothean spirit of progressive transformation through more humble doings, they realize that traditional philosophical peregrinations not only lead 'nowhither', but that more is to be achieved by practical and unpretentious interventions than by grand and arcane gestures. Indeed, rather than perpetuate popular enthraldom to the cause of philosophical enlightenment, they insist upon the need for there to be critical disenchantment in the name of democratic empowerment. So understood, the pressing question of how people should live or think about law becomes not a methodological puzzle of abstract dimensions, but a substantive challenge of historical proportions. A juristic account or proposal is mistaken not because it is philosophically wrong, but because it is not practically useful.

---

[19] *Id.* at 44, 199, 436 and 766.

So, what is it to be?—Dorothea or Casaubon? The actual construction of cottages for the poor or detached ruminations on abstract points of ancient architecture?

Conclusion

In its rejection of analytical jurisprudence, this book is intended as a jurisprudential call to democratic arms. Because jurisprudence took a wrong turn in 1832 by allying itself with analytical philosophy, this is no longer a reason, if ever it was, for legal theory to be perceived and practiced as such a narrow pursuit that lacks any real usefulness or practicality. Legal theory tends to serve its own scholarly interests more than anything else. Although democracy is in need of much further study and attention, it does at least offer itself as a viable institutional and substantive way of life through which to give people the genuine prospect of achieving some participatory control over their lives and the values that inform them. In particular, it works as a very real standard against which jurisprudence can most usefully measure its own exertions and attainments. In committing themselves to a strongly democratic cause, legal theorists can make a clean break from the sterile philosophical pre-occupations of Austin's *The Province of Jurisprudence Determined* and other such abstract tomes. Instead, they might place jurisprudence in the service of a more vibrant political ambition. Of course, the realization of an unbuttoned democracy most probably will be at bottom a dream. But, like the best of dreams, it might work as a useful awakening to life's fuller and more rewarding possibilities.

> *Not in Utopia, - subterranean fields, -*
> *Or some secreted island, Heaven knows where!*
> *But in the very world, which is the world*
> *Of all of us, - the place where, in the end,*
> *We find our happiness, or not at all.*[20]

---

[20] WILLIAM WORDSWORTH, THE PRELUDE bk. XI, ll. 140-44 (1850).

INDEX